TRADE UNIONS AND
GLOBAL GOVERNANCE

Employment and Work Relations in Context Series

Series Editors

Tony Elger
Centre for Comparative Labour Studies
Department of Sociology
University of Warwick

Peter Fairbrother
Centre for Research on Economic and
Social Transformation
Cardiff School of Social Sciences
Cardiff University

The aim of the *Employment and Work Relations in Context Series* is to address questions relating to the evolving patterns and politics of work, employment, management and industrial relations. There is a concern to trace out the ways in which wider policy-making, especially by national governments and transnational corporations, impinges upon specific workplaces, occupations, labour markets, localities and regions. This invites attention to developments at an international level, marking out patterns of globalization, state policy and practice in the context of globalization and the impact of these processes on labour. A particular feature of the series is the consideration of forms of worker and citizen organization and mobilization. Thus the studies address major analytical and policy issues through case study and comparative research.

Other titles published in the series include:

Changing Prospects for Trade Unionism: Comparisons between Six Countries
Peter Fairbrother and Gerard Griffin

Trade Unions in Renewal: A Comparative Study
Peter Fairbrother and Charlotte Yates

Work and Employment Relations in the High Performance Workplace
Gregor Murray, Jacques Bélanger, Anthony Giles and Paul-André Lapointe

Unionization and Union Leadership: The Road Haulage Industry
Paul Smith

Reshaping the North American Automobile Industry: Restructuring, Corporatism and Union Democracy
John P. Tuman

Globalization, Social Movements and the New Internationalisms
Peter Waterman

Trade Unions and Global Governance

The Debate on a Social Clause

Gerda van Roozendaal

LONDON • NEW YORK

Continuum
The Tower Building, 11 York Road, London, SE1 7NX
370 Lexington Avenue, New York, NY 10017-6503

First published 2002

© Gerda van Roozendaal 2002

All rights reserved. No part of this publication may be reproduced or transmitted in any form or by any means, electronic or mechanical, including photocopying, recording or any information storage or retrieval system, without permission in writing from the publishers.

British Library Cataloguing-in-Publication Data
A catalogue record for this book is available from the British Library.

ISBN 0-8264-5659-6 (hardback)
      0-8264-5660-X (paperback)

Typeset by YHT Ltd
Printed and bound in Great Britain by Biddles Ltd, Guildford and King's Lynn

Contents

	List of Tables	vii
	Acknowledgements	viii
	List of Abbreviations	ix
1	Trade Unions, Labour Standards and Global Governance: An Introduction	1
2	Trade Unions and Global Governance	28
3	Claiming Positions: Debates on Labour Standards	41
4	The Fair Trade Discourse on International Labour Standards: The Case of the United States	71
5	The Neo-liberal Discourse on International Labour Standards: The Case of India	113
6	The OECD Study on Trade and Labour Standards	146
7	Adjusting the ILO to Global Challenges: The Modest Result of the Laborious Debate on the Strengthening of the ILO	173
8	Trade Unions and Global Governance: Summary and Conclusions	202
	Appendix: ILO Core Conventions and Their Rate of Ratification	223
	Bibliography	227
	Index	256

Tables

2.1	Dimensions of influence of secondary and tertiary trade union organizations	30
2.2	Preconditions for the success of trade unions	37
3.1	Socio-economic claims	47
4.1	Interests and impacts: the GSP 1984	101
4.2	Interests and impacts: the NAFTA 1990–4	102
4.3	Interests and impacts: GATT (1986–94) and the Trade Act 1988	103
4.4	Characteristics of collective action	104
6.1	Shifts between drafts and final report	161
6.2	The expression of trade union interests into sensitizing impacts, and the responsible actor	163
6.3	The OECD report and competing views	169
7.1	Discourse coalitions in Phase 1	180
7.2	Positions on applying the CFA procedure	186
7.3	Interests and impacts	194
7.4	Characteristics of collective action	195

Acknowledgements

This book is the result of a PhD project undertaken with a grant from the Amsterdam School for Social Science Research of the University of Amsterdam. The Dutch Organization for Scientific Research enabled me to undertake the necessary travelling to conduct my research. The support of both is highly appreciated.

Too many to mention helped me to improve my chapters by commenting on them or providing ideas to solve all kinds of problems associated with writing a book. In particular I would like to thank, in random order: Joris Kocken, Barbara van Roozendaal, Hetty van Roozendaal, Jos Kocken, Nell Kocken, Gerd Junne, Jelle Visser, Pietje Vervest, Reinhilde König, Marcel van der Linden, Henk Overbeek, Bob Reinalda, E. A. Ramaswamy, the late Arvind Das, Alakh Sharma, S. Goyal, Rohini Hensman, Rene Torenvlied, Biswajit Dhar, Sachin Chaturvedi, Gary Peller, Florence Palpacuer, Marc van der Meer, Jeroen de Kloet, Giselinde Kuipers, Suzanne Kuik, Susanne Rijken, Bas Arts, Sean Chabot, Thomas Stevens, Sikko Visscher, Jan Breman, Maarten Hajer, Paul van der Heijden, Gijsbert van Liemt, Jan Willem Duyvendak, Jos Mooij, Ariana Need, Professor Dr Panchamuki, Duncan Campbell and Richard van der Wurff.

ABBREVIATIONS

ACTPN	Advisory Committee for Trade Policy and Negotiations
ACTU	Australian Council of Trade Unions
AFL-CIO	American Federation of Labor and Congress of Industrial Organizations
AIFLD	American Institute for Free Labor Development
AIOE	All India Organization of Employers
AITUC	All India Trade Union Congress
APRO	Asia and Pacific Regional Organization
ASSOCHAM	Associated Chambers of Commerce and Industry of India
BIAC	Business and Industry Advisory Committee to the OECD
BJP	Bharatiya Janata Party
BMS	Bharatiya Mazdoor Sangh
CBI	Caribbean Basin Initiative
CEC	Centre for Education and Communication
CFA	Convention on Freedom of Association
CFSP	Common Foreign and Security Policy
CII	Confederation of Indian Industry
CIME	Committee on International investment and Multinational Enterprises
CITU	Centre of Indian Trade Unions
CTOs	central trade union organizations
DG	Director-General (of the ILO)
DOC	Department of Commerce
DOL	Department of Labor
ELSA	Employment, Labour and Social Affairs Committee (of the OECD)
EPZs	export processing zones
ESCAP	United Nation's Economic and Social Commission of Asia and the Pacific
ETUC	European Trade Union Confederation
ETUF-TCL	European Trade Union Federation – Textiles, Clothing and Leather
EU	European Union

LIST OF ABBREVIATIONS

FDI	foreign direct investment
FICCI	Federation of Indian Chambers of Commerce and Industry
FLSA	Fair Labor Standards Act
G-7	Group of 7 Industrial Nations
G-77	Group of 133 Developing Countries
GAO	General Accounting Office
GATS	General Agreement on Trade in Services
GATT	General Agreement on Tariffs and Trade
GB	Governing Body (of the ILO)
GDP	gross domestic product
GNP	gross national product
GSP	Generalized System of Preferences
HMS	Hind Mazdoor Sabha
ICFTU	International Confederation of Free Trade Unions
ILC	International Labour Conference (of the ILO)
ILO	International Labour Organization
ILRF	International Labor Rights Fund
IMEC	Industrial Market Economy Countries
IMF	International Monetary Fund
INTUC	Indian National Trade Union Congress
IOE	International Organization of Employers
IPEC	International Programme on the Elimination of Child Labour
IPRs	intellectual property rights
ITO	International Trade Organization
IUF	International Union of Food, Agricultural, Hotel, Restaurant, Catering, Tobacco and Allied Workers' Associations
LAC	Labor Advisory Committee
LILS	Committee on Legal Issues and International Labour Standards
MFA	Multi-Fibre Arrangement
MFN	most favoured nation
MNEs	multinational enterprises
MOL	Ministry of Labour
NAFTA	North American Free Trade Agreement
NAM	Non-Aligned Movement
NEP	New Economic Policy
NGOs	non-governmental organizations
NICs	newly industrializing countries
OATUU	Organization of African Trade Union Unity
OECD	Organization for Economic Co-operation and Development

List of Abbreviations

OPIC	Overseas Private Investment Corporation
PACs	political action committees
SACCS	South Asian Coalition on Child Servitude
SAP	Structural Adjustment Programme
SDL	Working Party on the Social Dimensions of the Liberalization of International Trade
SLC	Standing Labour Committee
SRI	socially responsible investment
TAA	trade adjustment assistance
TC	Trade Committee (of the OECD)
TNCs	transnational corporations
TPRB	Trade Policy Review Body
TPRM	trade policy review mechanism
TRILs	Trade-related International Labour Standards
TRIMs	Trade-related Investment Measures
TRIPs	Trade-related Aspects of Intellectual Property Rights
TUAC	Trade Union Advisory Committee to the OECD
UAW	United Automobile Workers
UN	United Nations
UNCTAD	United Nations Conference on Trade and Development
UNITE	Union of Needletraders, Industrial and Textile Employees
USTR	United States Trade Representative
VERs	voluntary export restraints
WIPO	World Intellectual Property Organization
WTO	World Trade Organization

To Han

1 Trade Unions, Labour Standards and Global Governance: An Introduction

> We renew our commitment to the observance of internationally recognized core labour standards. The International Labour Organization (ILO) is the competent body to set and deal with these standards, and we affirm our support for its work in promoting them. We believe that economic growth and development fostered by increased trade and further trade liberalization contribute to the promotion of these standards. We reject the use of labour standards for protectionist purposes, and agree that the comparative advantage of countries, particularly low-wage developing countries, must in no way be put into question. In this regard, we note that the WTO and ILO Secretariats will continue their existing collaboration. (WTO, 1996a)

The theme of this book concerns the influence of trade unions on the debate that led to the adoption of the World Trade Organization's (WTO) Singapore Declaration, cited above. This text, approved in December 1996 by the member states of the WTO, was the result of an intensive debate, which had started ten years earlier with the attempt of the US government to include core labour standards in the negotiations that launched the beginning of the Uruguay Round of the General Agreement on Tariffs and Trade (GATT, predecessor of the WTO).[1]

What is at stake in this international labour standards debate is whether a regime can be designed to stimulate countries to observe a set of minimum, or core, labour standards. One way to achieve this is to allow member states of the WTO to apply sanctions to those countries that do not comply with these standards. Such a system is called a *social clause*. The notion of core labour standards generally refers to the principles embodied in the following ILO Conventions: No. 87 (on freedom of association and protection of the right to organize); No. 98 (on the right to organize and collective bargaining); No. 100 (on equal remuneration); No. 111 (on discrimination in employment and occupation); No. 138 (on minimum age); No. 29 (on forced labour); No. 105 (on the abolition of forced labour); and No. 182 (on the abolition of the worst forms of child labour) (see the explanation of the content of these Conventions in the Appendix). In short, these Conventions refer to four principles: (a) freedom of association and collective bargaining; (b) child labour; (c) forced labour; and (d) equality.[2]

The final result of the debate linking trade and labour standards was disappointing to the proponents of the inclusion of such a link. The ILO, the United Nations body that traditionally deals with labour issues, was once again on its own in its efforts to ensure the observation of labour standards.

The social clause issue is very controversial. GATT/WTO meetings have been dominated by it, it has been the subject of a considerable body of literature and it has been debated in both national and international contexts. This controversy results from the concern about the future of the international trading system and the increasing competition within this system. Whether one prefers to call it economic 'globalization' or 'internationalization', the fact is that we live in a world in which national economies are increasingly interdependent. This implies that the non-observance of labour standards in one country can have repercussions on other countries in the form of shifting investments and weakening regulation. Moreover, it is widely recognized that the social and economic aspirations of individuals cannot be fulfilled (only) through a liberalized world market. In an integrated world economy, autonomous states are less able – and sometimes less willing – to protect their citizens against world market forces. This induces thinking about alternative international systems to limit economic competition to an extent that citizens – including workers – can enjoy a decent level of protection.

The central argument of this book is that the International Confederation of Free Trade Unions (ICFTU), the world's single largest international trade union organization, has strong views about the problems trade unions encounter as a result of economic internationalization. Consequently, the interest of the ICFTU in tackling these problems by means of international regulation is great. In designing such strategies, however, the ICFTU is hampered by insufficient access to international regulatory bodies, since it has no formal position in most international organizations. In addition, the ICFTU is limited by a lack of common perspectives among its members, as it organizes trade unions the world over. The extent to which these and other factors hamper the ICFTU – and its members – is one of the concerns of this study.

INTRODUCTION

Oppression, Resistance and Competition

Many trade unions face three major problems: oppression of their members, resistance to their activities and increasing global competition that may result in increasing investment and regulatory competition.

First, worldwide, many workers are not able to enjoy basic rights, such as the right to organize or to be free from compulsory labour. The 1999 annual survey of the ICFTU reported that hundreds of trade unionists are killed each year for trade union work-related activities (ICFTU, 2000). Some countries cause constant reason for concern, such as Nigeria, Colombia and Myanmar. In November 2000, an ILO Resolution called both international organizations and ILO member states to reconsider their relationship with Myanmar because of the country's lack of compliance with ILO Convention 29 on forced labour.

Second, and more widespread than oppression, is the daily restriction and rejection of trade unions. The activities of trade unions are often perceived as obstructions to economic growth. The World Development Report (World Bank, 1995) is illustrative in this respect:

> Unions do often act as monopolists, improving wages and working conditions for their members at expense of capital holders, consumers, and nonunion (unorganized) labor. The higher wages unions win for their members either reduce business profits or get passed on to consumers in the form of higher prices. (World Bank, 1995: 81)

Third, trade unions are facing the negative effects of economic globalization. As a result of changes in the global economy, competition is increasing. Global shifts have taken place in the sphere of production of goods and services from the old core (Western Europe and the United States) to parts of East and Southeast Asia (mainly Japan and the newly industrializing countries) (ILO, 1997a: 9–10; Dicken, 1998: 399–406, 426). Although in 1994 the United States, Japan and Germany still accounted for 60 per cent of the total manufacturing output in the world, from the 1950s to the mid-1990s developing countries increased their share in manufacturing output from 5 to 20 per cent. The bulk of this growth was due to newly industrializing countries (NICs). The United States saw a decline of its relative share of world manufacturing output from 40 per cent in 1963 to 27 per cent in 1994. During that same period, Japan's output rose from 5.5 per cent to 21 per cent (Dicken, 1998: 26–30).

Similarly, in the post-war period trade in manufactured products has grown rapidly. Developed countries experienced a rise of their manufacturing exports from 70 per cent of the total export in 1960 to 77 per cent in 1988, while developing economies (mostly the NICs) experienced a rise from 20 to 47 per cent during the same period. Although exports tend to be less concentrated than production, 75 per cent of the merchandise exports are accounted for by the developed countries (excluding the NICs, but including Japan). About 60 per cent of this 75 per cent takes place between the developed countries themselves (Dicken, 1998: 31–5).

A large part of exports of the East and Southeast Asian NICs is destined for the developed markets. Nevertheless, the importance of these markets (excluding Japan) fell from 60 per cent in 1985 to 43 per cent in 1994. Increasingly, the Asian region itself is the destination of export. In other words, Asia is an emerging market for imports. However, this does not mean that the East and Southeast Asian import penetration of developed markets has become less significant. On the contrary, its share in the total of manufacturing imports to developed countries has risen steadily (Dicken, 1998: 31–40).

The service sector provides another field in which internationalization is visible. The service sector, a category covering wholesale and retail activities, and public sector goods such as health, commercial, business and financial services, accounts for a large and increasing share of countries' gross domestic product. In relation to trade, the last three services in particular are increasingly internationalized. In the 1980s, the growth of trade in services exceeded the growth of trade in manufacturing products, especially services in the field of telecommunications, finance, management, advertising, professional and technical services. The two trades – services and goods – are of course closely interlinked (Dicken, 1998: 30–42).

Since the Second World War there has also been an enormous growth of foreign direct investment (FDI). It has been calculated that during the 1980s FDI grew more than four times faster than world GNP (Dicken, 1998: 42). Even though FDI has a geographical bias (the Group of five accounts for 70 per cent of FDI) (Hirst and Thompson, 1996: 196), its mere growth can create opportunities for those countries that can attract it.[3]

Possible Consequences of Global Competition

Many trade unionists, and especially those from economically advanced countries, are fearful of the increased international competition. They worry that capital mobility will stimulate further competition between countries on

INTRODUCTION

the basis of differences in labour standards. As the ICFTU puts it: 'workers' jobs and pay, their conditions and contracts of employment, and trade unions' bargaining strength are increasingly undermined by the pressure of intensified global competition' (ICFTU, 1996d).

Many trade unionists (at least from the North) believe that without a social clause the intensified global competition will result not only in a worldwide lowering of standards, but also in a shift of industrial activities and investments from countries with high standards to countries with low standards, which in turn will lead to unemployment and increased wage inequality in countries with higher standards. This will then affect the level of organization of unions. In addition, trade unionists fear the rise of export processing zones (EPZs) and the increased importance of the informal sector. Finally, they worry that global competition will limit the ability of the state to protect workers.

Unemployment and wage inequality

It is not controversial to argue that unemployment is a major problem affecting many (potential) workers. This is illustrated by the fact that on a global level, of a potential workforce of 2.4 billion, 125 million people are formally unemployed, while no fewer than 750 million people are un- or underemployed. In Organisation for Economic Co-operation and Development (OECD) countries, 6.5 per cent of the total labour force was unemployed in 2000. Europe is experiencing high unemployment rates, while US workers are affected by high wage inequalities. Problems facing workers in other parts of the world are much more diverse, but those that stand out are the increasing informal sector employment, underemployment and high levels of population growth, which, combined with insufficient economic growth, lead to unemployment (De Groep van Lissabon, 1994: 66; Dicken, 1998: 430–49; Global Policy Forum, 1999).

One of the causes of unemployment in developed countries is global restructuring. Because of the intensification of global competition and the possibilities technological development offers, TNCs have subcontracted and relocated parts of their production to developing countries. But besides competition, there are other factors responsible for unemployment increases. The worldwide recession that hit the world from the mid-1970s until the mid-1980s, and another one at the beginning of the 1990s, are two of these factors. Because of these recessions there was a decline in demand for goods and services. Another cause involves the acceleration of technological development. Because of its productivity-enhancing capacities, technological progress tends to be labour reducing rather than employment creating. A last cause concerns the penetration of imports from developing countries, which has – together with the relocation of production – attracted a great deal of discussion (Dicken, 1998: 436–40).

The relative contribution of these factors to unemployment and wage inequality is a hotly debated issue. In spring 1996 in *Foreign Affairs* a discussion was initiated by an article published by Kapstein (1996: 23). In this article, Kapstein argued that trade (i.e. the increased import from Asian countries), in combination with technological innovation, is the most important cause of unemployment and wage inequality. The relationship between trade and technological innovation, he maintained, is that innovation takes place predominantly in those economic sectors threatened by foreign competition (Kapstein, 1996: 23–5). In response to Kapstein, Krugman and Lawrence separately insisted that the growth of international trade is not the main cause of growing unemployment and wage inequality. Both agreed that one of the major explanations of these two trends is technological advancement demanding high-skilled labour (Krugman, 1996: 164–6). Lawrence added that technological innovation is not a response to higher international competition, as highly competitive, internationally oriented sectors are more likely to cut back on investments in response to competition than to stimulate technological innovation (Lawrence, 1996: 172). The economic recession of the 1970s was also offered as an explanation of unemployment and wage inequality. However, Krugman noted that even though demand has recovered since the late 1980s, unemployment and wage inequality are still high (Krugman, 1996: 165–6).

As Chapter 3 will show, the exact impact of trade on unemployment and wage inequality is extremely difficult to estimate. It remains one of the most disputed topics in the debate on the social clause and therefore provides both opponents and proponents with strong arguments either way.

Decreasing membership

While recession, technological development and increasing competition have contributed to expanding unemployment, they are also partly responsible for a trend that results in sleepless nights for many trade union officials: decreasing trade union density levels.[4] A combination of the above factors and related other factors explain this development: the decline of manufacturing sectors (in developed countries), the rise of economic activity in sectors where unions are traditionally weak (service sector in developed countries, informal sector in developing countries) and the increase in the number of temporary workers, part-timers and home workers. All have led to an increase in a flexible work organization, which in the majority of countries led to a diversified and splintered workforce whose interests are less represented by trade unions. Labour market decentralization and the decline of social democratic policies have further aggravated the decline of unions (Spyropoulus, 1987: 36–41; Hobsbawm, 1995; Western, 1995).[5] These trends have also affected trade unions in developing countries. In developing countries an additional challenge occurs where the labour force has an agricultural background. Such workers are often difficult to organize.

EPZs

Many countries in the developing world have adopted export-promotion strategies, with the formation of EPZs as an integral part. EPZs are areas within countries that are designed to attract export-oriented industries.[6] These industries are often offered a package of duty-free imports of products to be used in the production process, waivers on foreign ownership restrictions, special investment incentives and, most importantly for this book, investment-favourable working conditions. Production in these zones concentrates on textile, garment, leather and electrical products (Dicken, 1998: 130).

Although initially the EPZs attracted investment and created employment, the quality of both leave something to be desired. Employment often involves low-skilled and low-wage labourers, while the connection, and therefore the technology transfer, of EPZs with the local economy is often limited. A second problem is that technological innovation also takes place in these EPZs, and therefore long-term employment is not at all guaranteed. Third, due to competition among EPZs, there is a continued pressure to make the incentives even more attractive, and therefore less advantageous for the country in which the EPZs are located (ILO, 1998a: 1–2).

Among the most controversial issues related to EPZs are working conditions and wage levels. According to the ILO (1996a), in some EPZs governments have actively created bad working conditions and low wages, while in other zones they just refrained from penalizing these practices. Despite low wages, in general it appears that the average wage in an EPZ is no less favourable than those offered by employers operating outside the zones (although the average wage throughout a country may be too low to provide a decent living altogether). TNCs operating in the zones are generally willing to pay more than minimum wages.

The quality of the working conditions is an issue of major concern in most EPZs. Some countries, such as Pakistan and Bangladesh, have erected legal barriers that suspend the application of (certain) labour laws in EPZs. In general, employers refuse to give written contracts, hire apprentices instead of workers and ignore minimum standards concerning hours of work, health and safety (ILO, 1996a: 1–10).

An interesting observation of the ILO study is that it is not the EPZ status as such, but the low degree of unionization, that determines the low level of labour standards. Due to both legal barriers and non-legal ones, unionization tends to be low. Companies may promote company unions or other forms of organization to increase their control over workers, even though unions are legally admissible. Other problems reported are intimidation, dismissals and arrests to circumvent union organization. If one adds to this the long working hours, the overriding concern of keeping a job under all circumstances and the short-term contracts, it is not surprising that unionization is low. Low unionization means that there are also fewer collective agreements, even without legal barriers to such agreements. Without such agreements, problems related to working conditions, such as compulsory overtime or health and safety, tend to be much greater (ILO, 1996a: 1–14).

Informalization of the formal sector

Also linked to the growing competition in international markets is the informalization of formal sector employment all over the world, and especially in developing countries.[7] By reducing formal sector employment (and increasing the availability of a flexible labour force), the costs attached to labour are significantly reduced. Available figures suggest that in Latin America informal sector employment grew between 1990 and 1994 at an annual rate of 4.7 per cent, while employment in the formal sector grew by 1.1 per cent. In the same period, 84 per cent of new jobs were in the informal sector.[8] In Asia, estimates indicate that the informal sector absorbs about 40–50 per cent of the urban labour force. In Africa this percentage is about 61, while in the 1990s, 93 per cent of additional jobs were generated in the informal sector (ILO, 1997a: 178–9).

Decreasing state authority

The World Labour Report of the ILO (1997a) summarizes the effects of economic internationalization on state authority as follows:

> it is the potential for speculators to trigger a run on the currency that disciplines monetary and fiscal policies. It is the potential for firms to disinvest that triggers favourable tax and regulatory treatments. It is the potential for firms to relocate or outsource that dampens wage bargaining or even union organization. In short, capital may well be less mobile than its potential, but it is the potential for mobility that determines real outcomes, and that is a destabilizing factor for industrial relations systems.
> (ILO, 1997a: 76)

These possible effects of economic internationalization are exactly what concern the ICFTU. In 1996, its Sixteenth World Congress focused on the challenges of globalization of trade unions. One of the major problems identified by the ICFTU was the global reduction of governmental policy that lets interest rates respond to market demands. The ICFTU saw this as a consequence of both the financial deregulation of the 1980s and the political decision to prioritize low inflation above low unemployment. Changes in the global financial market have allowed companies to become speculators instead of investors. Governments, increasingly fearful of loss of capital, have resorted to deflationary policies and exchange rate stability in order to attract investment and increase exports. Although some Asian countries have benefited from the growth in FDI, the dark side of their economic growth is union repression and unhealthy working conditions (ICFTU, 1996a).

That state authority is weakening is a view held by many authors.[9] Trends in the global economy as described in this section illustrate that the authority in the international economy is increasingly shared between states and markets. However, the declining power of the state does not mean that markets are beyond governance. On the contrary, the declining power of the national state is reflected in the growing authority of other international institutions, or of local and regional bodies (Strange, 1996). Hence issues of public governance remain important. Even TNCs prefer financial stability to chaos, laws that settle property rights and a regulated labour system (Hirst and Thompson, 1996: 187).

The decreasing governing powers of the state have also led to a new international political environment in which intergovernmental arrangements play a larger role. National and intergovernmental arrangements for policy-making are linked through the participation of national governments in international decision-making, and through the implementation of international decisions by national governments (Reinalda, 1994: 1–3).

On five different levels, governance remains important: (a) through agreements between the major industrialized states such as the G7 or the OECD; (b) through international regulatory institutions, such as the WTO; (c) through regional economic blocks, such as the European Union (EU); (d) through national-level policies that help to create compromises between firms and social interests; and (e) through regional-level policies that provide collective services to industrial districts (Reinalda, 1994; Hirst and Thompson, 1996: 189). In sum,

> If such mechanisms of international governance and re-regulation are to be initiated then the role of states is pivotal. Nation states should be seen no longer as 'governing powers', able to impose outcomes on all dimensions of policy within a given territory by their own authority, but as loci from which forms of governance can be proposed, legitimated and monitored . . . the degree to which the world economy has internationalized (but not globalized) reinstates the need for the national state, not in its traditional guise as the sole sovereign power, but as a crucial relay between the international levels of governance and the articulate publics of the developed world. (Hirst and Thompson, 1996: 191)

While there is no doubt that the state will remain important, it is unclear what role there is to play for the older international organizations of social policy, such as the ILO. This is an important issue, since these organizations are much more sensitive to influences from non-governmental organizations (NGOs), such as trade unions, than the institutions that have a larger role in the new framework, such as the WTO (Reinalda, 1994).

Regulating Labour Standards across Borders

The shared authority between states and markets has made public international authorities an increasingly important focus for the activities of the ICFTU. This attention is especially important in an integrated economy, where the fate of workers cannot be determined solely on a national level, and where international or transnational strategies are important to limit competition that works at the expense of social conditions of work. As the decisions of the Sixteenth World Congress of the ICFTU show, one of the union's main priorities is to stimulate a social dimension to the work of international financial institutions (ICFTU, 1996b: 32–5).

There are a number of alternative ways for trade unions to promote labour standards, either through direct action or through influencing public authorities that are increasingly involved in designing schemes to promote labour standards on an international or transnational level.[10] These include ILO activities, codes of conduct, credit conditionality, donor support, consumer labels, socially responsible investment, technical and financial support, international labour courts, regional labour regulation and unilateral trade legislation.

The *ILO's standard-setting activities* are the most prominent attempt to develop guidelines for social development for governments. This will be extensively discussed in Chapter 7.

Codes of conduct are a well known way of trying to upgrade labour standards and rights. International organizations have designed codes of conduct like the OECD's Guidelines for Multinational Enterprises and the ILO's Tripartite Declaration of Principles Concerning Multinational Enterprises and Social Policy. Additionally, international respect for workers' rights has been promoted through nationally developed codes of conduct, such as the Sullivan Principles for US businesses working in South Africa, the MacBride Principles for US corporations doing business in Northern Ireland and the Maquiladora Standards of Conduct. Although the codes may have little direct effect on the real labour conditions in a country, they might influence companies to adopt similar principles and might even influence the legislators in a host country (Perez-Lopez, 1993: 1–47). Increasingly workers' organizations together with enterprises and their organizations are involved in creating *joint codes of conducts* that address labour provisions. An example is the International Union of Food, Agricultural, Hotel, Restaurant, Catering, Tobacco and Allied Workers' Associations (IUF), which signed an agreement in 1999 with the International Tobacco Growers' Association to work on the ban of child labour in the tobacco-growing industry (IUF, 1999).

The World Bank and IMF exercise *credit conditionality* in areas other than labour standards, such as the banning of genital mutilation. The punishment is clear (no banning, no loan). The chance of labour standards playing a more important role within these financial institutions in the future increased in 1994, when the US Congress passed a law requiring US directors of multilateral financial institutions to integrate core labour standards in the negotiations with the prospective borrowing countries. The law also requires that an annual report be made to the US Congress considering the progress in this area (OECD, 1996b: 177). If labour standards were to become a condition for credits, it is obvious, as Dorman rightly stipulates, that only those countries depending on loans would be affected (Dorman, 1995: 42).

Donor support is another area through which, indirectly, the respect for labour standards can be promoted. Most aid agencies will have some programme aimed at investment in primary education or poverty to relieve the burden on children to work (OECD, 1996b: 163–4). In addition, some NGOs are actively involved in financing projects aimed at the freeing of slave labourers. Again, this measure only involves a specific group of countries, the aid recipients.

Another option is the use of *consumer labels*. Such labels are attached to products or to companies, and facilitate the consumer in making the choice to buy products that are produced under certain conditions, such as those manufactured without child labour. The initiators of such labels are consumer groups, other NGOs or companies. Examples of such labels are 'Max Havelaar', a label under which food products are sold, or the Rugmark label, which ties together carpet manufacturers who do not make use of child labour. Consumer labels can be achieved through actions taken by consumer groups, as is currently the case, but in the future they might also become an international mechanism, with an international agreement stipulating objective conditions in order to obtain a label. A specific problem that affects consumer group induced labels is that the information needed by such organizations to monitor the conditions under which a product is produced might be hard to obtain, especially if subcontractors are involved. Additionally, the voluntary nature of this measure may not be sufficient to convince consumers to pay more (Dorman, 1995: 43). Another consideration is that the voluntary nature of labelling may work better for labels targeted at highly emotional matters, such as child labourers, but less for issues like fair pay or freedom of association. The same applies to consumer boycotts.

Yet another way to promote labour standards is *socially responsible investment* (SRI). This may occur either through the screening of investment funds or through initiatives of shareholders. The screening of investment funds gained renewed attention in the 1970s, especially with respect to investment in South Africa. In the 1970s and the beginning of the 1980s, this instrument was quite popular in the USA, UK and France, but spread to other developed countries in the late 1980s. Those involved are, among others, pension funds, universities and religious groups. The effects of such measures are disputed, mainly because of the lack of standardization criteria, the lack of leverage of investors in one company and the lack of monitoring expertise. However, if combined with other measures (such as codes of conducts) they tend to be more fruitful. Shareholder initiatives also occur in developing countries, and often concern companies that outsource parts of their production. Again, it is mainly institutional investors that are involved in this activity, including trade unions. Similar considerations, as noted above with respect to success, apply to this initiative (ILO, 1998b: 22–5).

If inadequate labour rights are not a matter of weak legislation but a matter of weak enforcement, *international labour courts of appeal* may offer a solution. Using the route of appealing in an international court might improve the enforcement of labour standards. Since both national laws and international agreements can serve as a basis for the court's jurisdiction, the mandate of such a court exceeds the ILO's mandate. It would require a sanctioning mechanism to make it truly effective. The advantages of such a court would be, among others, that a country could be sanctioned independently of trade relations (it would avoid the implication of economic bias) and it would be open to individual complaints (Dorman, 1995: 44–5).

This brings us to the *regional attempts to transnationalize labour regulation.* One of the earliest steps towards the design and implementation of international labour standards was a conference held in Berne in 1905, where seven European countries signed a Convention that prohibited night work by women. Progress was also made at a 1927 conference on the abolition of import and export prohibitions and restrictions, where the members of the League of Nations (predecessor of the United Nations) agreed to allow import restrictions for goods produced by prison labourers (Hansson, 1981: 7–15; Charnovitz, 1987: 569–72).

Currently, the EU is most advanced in regulating labour affairs on a regional level. Most of the EU efforts in the area of labour are directed at setting minimum standards, rather than harmonizing collective labour legislation. Through so-called 'pre-emptive legislation', certain parts of treaty provisions as well as regulations directly apply to the citizens of the member states. The idea behind this legislation is that it draws up uniform rules for specific labour standards that exceed national legislation. Through harmonization, the EU stimulates member states to ally their separate labour laws to each other. The most common way to do so is through EU directives, a form of regulation enacted by the Council, which requires the member states to transform their domestic laws within a certain time frame. The 1992 Maastricht Protocol on Social Policy provides that labour directives of the EU can be implemented through collective bargaining agreements, and through legislation and administrative regulation. It also empowers the EU to legislate on the basis of majority voting in several areas, including the area of working conditions. The gap between directives and pre-emptive legislation is closing, since court rulings stipulated that member countries can be held liable to individual workers for restitution in case of failure to enact labour directives (Van Wezel Stone, 1995: 998–1006). Several agreements of the EU with third countries stipulate provisions on labour standards.

Another regional attempt to regulate labour is found in the North American Free Trade Agreement (NAFTA). This trade agreement includes labour standards in a separate ('side') agreement. It contains restrictions on the use of child labour, promotional measures in the area of health and safety standards and minimum wages (Venture Dias, 1995: 23). It differs from EU regulation in the sense that neither Canada, the United States nor Mexico will attempt to change the labour laws of the other countries. The basis of the side agreement is the separate labour laws of the three countries. The monitoring and enforcement procedures permit one country to enforce another country's labour laws in a multilateral tribunal. There is a provision to apply sanctions that enforce the enacting of labour laws, but the conditions are too general to be effective (Van Wezel Stone, 1995: 1006–11). The United States has retained its right to use domestic trade laws with respect to labour issues not covered under the NAFTA (Venture Dias, 1995: 23)

Unilateral trade legislation is another option. The United States is one country that has introduced aspects concerning labour standards in its trade laws. In the 1980s, trade and investment policies were linked to labour conditions in four laws. The Caribbean Basin Initiative (CBI) between the United States and selected Latin American and Caribbean countries provides in some cases for additional trade preferences to Caribbean and Latin American countries. Reasonable working conditions and the right to organize and to bargain collectively can be taken into account when trade preferences are allocated. When the US Generalized System of Preferences (GSP) was renewed in 1984, respect for workers' rights was included as a condition for duty-free access for a number of products from developing countries. A country can lose its status under the GSP if it does not undertake steps to grant certain labour standards to its workers. Section 301 of the 1988 Omnibus Trade and Competitiveness Act enables the United States to undertake measures against countries that refuse to grant workers certain rights (freedom of association and the right to collective bargaining, prohibition of child labour, minimum employment age and minimum working conditions and pay levels) (Van Liemt, 1989; Caire, 1994: 303–8; Venture Dias, 1995: 23).

INTRODUCTION

Trade-enforceable Labour Standards in the GATT/WTO

Of a different order are the attempts to ensure that labour standards are regulated via systems of global governance. The focus in this respect has been on the inclusion of a social clause in the multilateral framework of the GATT/WTO. In other words, the labour standards issue can also be regulated through a system of global governance. Global governance refers to efforts to bring orderly and reliable responses to social and political issues that go beyond the capacity of the state to address individually (Gordenker and Weiss, 1995: 357).

The first time such a possibility was mentioned was in the period between 1946 and 1948, when governments discussed the establishment of the International Trade Organization (ITO). The ITO, the predecessor of the GATT that never saw the light of day,[11] included articles on labour standards:

> The members recognize that unfair labour conditions, particularly in the production for export, create difficulties in international trade, and accordingly, each Member shall take whatever action may be appropriate and feasible to eliminate such conditions within its territory. (Charter ITO agreement, cited in Charnovitz, 1995: 170)

Instead of the ITO, the GATT was established, which contained only one reference to labour standards, i.e. that governments may take measures against goods produced by prison labour (article XX). This article has thus far never been used (Interview with WTO: 2 March 1999).[12]

One of the GATT's objectives was to establish procedures for the voluntary trade negotiations between its members. Initially, the GATT was concerned with tariff reductions. Domestic policies, such as subsidies or technical barriers, became increasingly important after the Tokyo Round negotiations (1973–9). It was also during this Round that the United States tried to include labour standards, but failed (Cappuyns, 1998).[13]

In September 1986, the GATT Uruguay Round was initiated in Punta del Este. One of the most significant issues decided upon was the establishment of the WTO, a legal entity, unlike the GATT. Four principles lay at the foundation of the WTO: (a) non-discrimination; (b) reciprocity; (c) market access; and (d) fair competition. The non-discrimination principle has two components. The first is the most favoured nation (MFN) rule, which means that members are not allowed to discriminate between goods on the basis of their origin or destination. In other words, goods should be treated equally. The second component is that foreign products cannot be treated less favourably in terms of taxes and other measures than domestic goods (national treatment rule). Exceptions to the MFN rule are free-trade areas, customs unions and preferential treatment of developing countries. Reciprocity refers to the exchange of market access commitments, and is perceived as a tool to achieve liberalization. Market access and fair competition are the objectives of the system. Both principles tend to have a strained relationship (Hoekman and Kostecki, 1995: 24–32; WTO, 1999a).

The main function of the WTO is to administer the multilateral agreements in the area of trade in goods, the General Agreement on Trade in Services (GATS), the Trade-related Aspects of Intellectual Property Rights (TRIPs) and the Agreement on Trade-related Investment Measures (TRIMS) (Hoekman and Kostecki, 1995: 19; Wilkinson, 1999b: 166).[14] Besides administering the agreements, the WTO serves as a forum for trade negotiations, handles trade disputes,[15] monitors national trade policies, provides technical assistance and training for developing countries and stimulates cooperation with other international organizations. As of February 1999, the WTO had 134 members, covering about 90 per cent of world trade. Among the absent countries were China, Taiwan and the Russian Federation (WTO, 1999b).

The fact that during the Uruguay Round negotiations the scope of the GATT/WTO was dramatically expanded towards non-good sectors provided new ammunition to the proponents (notably the United States and France) of a social clause. As Wilkinson rightly points out, 'there has also been a general movement towards the regulation of trade-related areas; that is, those aspects of the production process that are intrinsic to the production of goods and services for trade, but in themselves do not constitute, in the normal sense, tradable entities' (Wilkinson, 1999b: 166). In particular, the TRIPS agreement has assigned a role for the WTO to regulate trade by introducing, rather than by removing, barriers to trade (Wilkinson, 1999b: 166–7).

The possibility that a social clause would be integrated into the WTO was fuelled not only by its broadened scope. There were other good reasons for the proponents of such a social clause to be optimistic. The world economic recession of the 1970s had replaced the tendency towards liberalized economies with more protectionist attitudes. The emergence of successful exporting developing countries also made developed countries aware of the dangers of differences in labour standards (Hansson, 1981: 32–6; Benería, 1995: 48). Moreover, in addition to economic internationalization, internationalization had also taken place in the sphere of norms and values. As

Zolberg pointed out, 'Perhaps most important, globalization also has fostered the dissemination of liberal norms regarding persons, expressed in the remarkable emergence of a widely shared notion of universal human rights' (Zolberg, 1995: 37). However, the expectations about the inclusion of a social clause did not materialize. From the early start of the negotiations in 1986 until the Singapore Declaration ten years later, the United States, with strong support from France, tried to gain recognition for a social clause, or at least to get a working party set up to study possibilities. In 1986, the United States submitted a proposal to the Preparatory Committee stating that: 'Ministers recognize that denial of workers' rights can impede attainment of the objectives of the GATT and can lead to trade distortions, thereby increasing the pressures for trade-restrictive measures' (GATT, 1986).

The United States further urged the contracting parties to review the relationship of workers' rights to the GATT objectives and instruments. When the US delegation did not succeed in including labour standards in the Ministerial Declaration that launched the GATT Uruguay Round, the Americans announced they would keep putting the issue of international labour standards on the agenda. Later that year, the European Parliament subscribed to the US commitment (Charnovitz, 1987: 565).

At the beginning of 1990, Dunkel, then Director of the GATT, warned the American Federation of Labor and Congress of Industrial Organizations (AFL-CIO) that all his attempts to create an opening to discuss a social clause were rejected by the GATT's executive council. He therefore suggested a more cautious approach, i.e. an emphasis on a social clause as a concern with human rights rather than with working conditions. He urged the AFL-CIO to clarify the issues concerning possible obligations of the countries that had ratified the ILO Conventions versus those that had not, and concerning the kind of supervisory mechanism foreseen (ICFTU, 1990).[16]

In September 1990, just before the ministerial meeting in Brussels, the United States again attempted to get a working group established. This time, it clearly defined the workers' rights in question as those rights that include freedom of association, the right to organize and bargain collectively and freedom from forced or compulsory labour. While the United States received support from the EU, the Nordic countries, Switzerland, Canada, New Zealand, some East European countries and Japan, this was not enough to gain a favourable decision (GATT, 1990).

While Dunkel did not reject a social clause beforehand, his successor Sutherland was opposed from the outset. In March 1994, just before the GATT ministerial meeting in Marrakech that marked the end of the Uruguay Round, Sutherland argued that:

> Different approaches to policy in areas such as environmental protection or social welfare are proving to be a touchstone for claims that these countries wield unfair trade advantages in the global marketplace, and that these must be met though trade restrictions if domestic industry is to survive and domestic standards are not to be dragged downwards. Simplistic demands for drastic trade remedies against so-called eco-dumping or social dumping sometimes bear a sticking similarity to more conventional forms of protectionist rhetoric, but in many respects ill-thought out measures can be more dangerous because of the popular emotional appeal that they appear able to carry with them . . . the welfare of trading nations will increase if each plays to its specific area of comparative advantage. (Sutherland, 1994)

He went on to argue that:

> The direct effect of imposing trade restrictions against exports from a developing country or industry which is unable to meet industrialized country standards, for example, will fall first and foremost on workers themselves, threatening their jobs and livelihood. (Sutherland, 1994)

In April 1994, at the Marrakech meeting, the United States tried and failed again to get a paragraph included in the final declaration that suggested the establishment of a working party to study the relationship between trade and labour standards. Prior to the Marrakech meeting, the Group of Fifteen developing countries met and decided to take a common stand against such an inclusion. The only feasible compromise in Marrakech was that the countries supporting a social clause could address the social clause issue in the Preparatory Committee. The purpose of this Committee was to ensure the transition from the GATT to the WTO (ICDA, 1994: 1; 1995: 12). In the end, however, the Preparatory Committee only vaguely referred to the discussion on labour standards by agreeing 'To discuss suggestions for the inclusion of additional items on the agenda of the WTO's work programme' (Decision on the Establishment of the Preparatory Committee for the World Trade Organization, 1994). This compromise was the result of a meeting between the United States, the EU, Brazil, India, Malaysia and Singapore in the framework of the Trade Negotiations Committee (Raghavan, 1994: 2).

The social clause has remained a sensitive issue ever since. During the first Ministerial Conference of the WTO in Singapore, December 1996, some developing countries exercised pressure to withdraw an earlier invitation of ILO director Hansenne to address the Conference. Again, it was the US delegation that pushed strongly for the inclusion of labour standards.

INTRODUCTION

Resisting the inclusion of a social clause were not only developing countries, but also some of the industrialized countries, such as the UK and Germany. In addition, Argentina was one of the isolated countries supporting further discussions on labour standards in the WTO (WTO, 1996c).

Before agreement on the text of the Singapore Declaration, several Draft Declarations were circulated. While the first drafts made a reference to the Universal Declaration on Human Rights, the final version omitted this reference. Other drafts referred explicitly to the labour standards in question, but the final version did not include such a reference (WTO, 1996a, b).

Finally a compromise was reached between the most vocal antagonists. According to newspaper reports, the United States was prepared to drop the social clause issue in exchange for an agreement on the liberalization of the information technology market (Bogaerts, 1996a: 2; Christern, 1996: 16). On the other hand, Malaysia gave up its resistance to a reference to labour standards in the Declaration, understanding that it would not have any consequences. Several developing countries followed the Malaysian lead (Bogaerts, 1996b: 2). The result was a Declaration that speaks of a renewed commitment to the promotion of labour standards, but at the same time appoints the ILO as the competent body to deal with it.

Trade Unions and the Social Clause Debate

It soon became clear that the Declaration's text could be interpreted in a number of ways. While Malaysia and India declared that the issue was no longer on the agenda, the United States and France announced that the issue would remain important within the WTO (Khor, 1997). That the issue is far from resolved has been demonstrated not only by the fact that it was again discussed during the 1998 WTO Ministerial Conference in Geneva and the 1999 Ministerial Conference in Seattle; it has also become part of the trade policy review mechanism (TPRM) of the WTO. The purpose of the TPRM is to increase the transparency in, and knowledge of, the trade policies and practices of WTO members. Each member has to submit reports that will be discussed by all members. While the mechanism was introduced in 1989, it was limited to the trade in goods. Since 1995 it covers new areas, such as trade in services and intellectual property rights (WTO, 1999c).

The ICFTU was campaigning for both a social clause and the use of the TPRM. At the start of the Uruguay Round, the ICFTU released a statement including a reference to a social clause: 'The contracting parties agree to take steps to ensure the observance of the minimum labour standards specified by an advisory committee to be established by the GATT and the ILO' (ICFTU, 1986: 3). At that time, the ICFTU emphasized standards related to freedom of association, collective bargaining, minimum age for employment, occupational health and safety, labour inspection, non-discrimination and the abolition of forced labour (ICFTU, 1986). Around 1993, the ICFTU dropped labour inspection and occupational health and safety in order to increase the chances of the proposal being accepted.

The ICFTU proposed to include these labour standards in the GATT, and suggested letting a GATT/ILO advisory body undertake regular reviews on the basis of specific complaints. These reviews should show the extent to which the GATT/WTO contracting parties fulfilled the social clause requirements. In case of non-fulfilment, the body could make recommendations, and the ILO could offer technical assistance. If, after about two years, it was concluded that the contracting party was falling short in its efforts to meet the obligations, sanctions could be applied by importing countries on exporting countries' exports (ICFTU, 1989a: 3; 1989b: 3). Alternatively, the GATT/WTO would also be able to suspend a country's right to access certain GATT/WTO services (ICFTU, n.d.a: 4).

As early as 1989 the ICFTU advocated the idea of making labour issues part of the TPRM of the GATT. As the United States would be the first country to be reviewed, the AFL-CIO asked the US trade representative Hills to include the question of labour standards (ICFTU, 1989c: 8; Interview with ICFTU: 15 September 1998).[17] However, until 1996 questioning labour standards was a little used instrument. This is due to the fact that the TPRM was much more applied from 1996 onwards, as well as to the fact that the Singapore Declaration as such acknowledged the importance of labour standards. The first country to be honoured with a scrutiny of its labour standards policy was Fiji. The ICFTU prepared a report reviewing the observance of labour standards in Fiji. As the Confederation cannot take part in the Trade Policy Reviews, it was in the fortunate position that Denmark, one of the official discussants of the country's trade policies, was willing to use the report of the ICFTU (ICFTU, 1997c; Interview with ICFTU: 11 July 1997). The Trade Policy Review discussant from Denmark specifically asked what action had been taken by the government to abide by the core labour standards as referred to by the Singapore Declaration, inquired on the position of women labourers and the effects of the country's trade policy on labourers in general. These issues were also dominant in the ICFTU report. Surprisingly enough, the US delegation reacted more positively to Fiji's efforts in the area of core labour standards, although it addressed some issues concerning ILO Convention 98. Not surprisingly, representatives from Hong Kong and

Pakistan and Fiji itself did not regard the TPRM as the appropriate forum to discuss these matters. They were joined by Australia, Colombia, Cuba, Mexico, New Zealand, Peru and Singapore. However, Canada and Japan supported the idea that the TPRM could be used to ask questions on labour standards (TPRB, 1997b).

After the review on Fiji, the ICFTU published similar reports on other countries that were planned to be reviewed by the Trade Policy Review Body (TPRB). Despite the opposition to discussing labour standards in the TPRM, some delegates continued to do so. In June 1998, for example, Nigeria was criticized during a review for violations of the CFA. The US delegate asked whether the authorities intended to cooperate with the ILO Commission of Inquiry (an issue also raised in the ICFTU review of Nigeria), and whether core labour rights would be enforced in the newly developed EPZs. The Norwegian delegate supported her. However, there was no agreement on this approach and India claimed that this was not the right forum to discuss these matters (TPRB, 1998a; ICFTU, 1998c).

Discussing labour standards within the TPRB may make governments and citizens – through media coverage – more sensitive to accepting labour standards as an integral part of trade negotiations.[18] However, reforms within the WTO are also needed to give labour standards more weight. According to Wilkinson, there are a number of possibilities for the WTO to give the social clause a place in its framework. First of all, it could give meaning to a cooperative relationship with the ILO, as it has also done with the IMF and the World Bank. Second, it could acknowledge the importance of the labour standards issue in the same way as it has done with environmental issues. As this is of very little legal consequence, the third and most far-reaching option would be to adopt an Agreement on Trade-related International Labour Standards (TRILS), following a format similar to that of TRIPS (Wilkinson, 1999b: 181–7).

Unions' activities were not limited to the WTO. Although operating within a contested economic and political framework, involving the United States and the then Soviet Bloc, the ICFTU has a long tradition of questioning labour conditions and TNCs. In the 1960s and 1970s, the organization campaigned to reverse the increasing power of TNCs by promoting the standardization of labour conditions. This standardization had to take place either through the promotion of international collective bargaining agreements within TNCs or through regulation of TNC activities. The regulation of TNC activities became a prominent aim of the ICFTU. While within the UN system the ICFTU was not very effective in obtaining this goal, it was more effective, together with the OECD's Trade Union Advisory

Committee, within the OECD. In 1976, both trade union organizations were instrumental in the acceptance of the OECD's guidelines of conduct of TNCs. However, the fact that the guidelines were voluntary in nature and only concerned activities of TNCs reduced their potential impact (Gumbrell-McCormick, 2000: 377–96).

What Hampers Unions?

We can conclude from the above observations that trade unions have several alternatives at their disposal to respond to the increasing economic interdependence of national economies. Besides having the choice between several regulatory alternatives, one would expect that the unions would also have the motivation. Unions increasingly face difficulties at a national level, reflected in declining union membership and their increasing marginalization in the polity (Fairbrother and Yates, forthcoming). One response by unions has been to focus their activity at a transnational level.

However, unions' transnational activities are constrained in many ways, some of which are intrinsic to the nature of their organization. As referred to above, one of the most important barriers is that powerful intergovernmental institutions such as the WTO do not allow direct access by NGOs. Therefore, trade unions have to rely on their governments to represent their interests. A second barrier is that there is a high degree of diversity and fragmentation between unions of different countries. Strong unions are afraid of being exploited by the weak, and weaker ones try to resist the dominance of the strong ones. Third, there is diversity in national interest representation. Unions have different links with the political system of which they are a part, and they tend to remain locked into national patterns of interest intermediation. Despite common trends in the international economy (internationalization of production and finances, unemployment, etc.), affecting all trade unions, cross-national differences among unions have in some aspects widened because these common trends do not affect all unions equally, owing to differences in objectives, alliances and power resources (Ebbinghaus and Visser, 1994: 4, 12–16). As this book will show, such differences between trade unions are illustrated in the social clause debate. Some, originating from developing countries, perceive a social clause as a mechanism to restrict them from enjoying their comparative advantage, which is lower labour standards, expressed through lower wages. They also view the actions of their fellow unions as a way to 'export' their problems of high unemployment.

From the moment it entered the social clause debate, the ICFTU had to deal with these contradictory opinions. While the ICFTU tried to increase the legitimacy of the social clause call by emphasizing that it was also supported by trade unions from developing countries (ICFTU, 1994a), there were in fact differing opinions. Trade union federations from Sri Lanka, Pakistan, Nepal, Singapore and India argued against a social clause, which led to hostilities with the ICFTU headquarters in Brussels (CTU, 1994; South Asian Consultation on Social Clause/Labour Rights in Multilateral Trade Agreements, 1996: 18–19). The ICFTU Economic and Social Committee commented that 'It was extremely damaging when trade unions spoke against the social clause and even tried to justify child labour. *All* ICFTU affiliates must present a united front in favour of the social clause and emphasize the lack of any protectionist intent' (ICFTU, 1994b: 3). In 1994, the Australian Council of Trade Unions (ACTU) wrote a letter to the Indian National Trade Union Congress (INTUC) expressing its concern about the lack of support for a social clause (ACTU, 1994). The INTUC replied: 'You will appreciate that perceptions differ between the "haves" and the "have-nots". While yours is the perception of the "haves", mine is of the "have-nots"' (INTUC, 1994a).

Not only did some of the Asian affiliates come into conflict with the ICFTU about a social clause, so did the Organization of African Trade Union Unity (OATUU). While the OATUU is independent from the ICFTU, the two organizations do have overlapping membership. To the dismay of the ICFTU, OATUU's secretary-general argued during the WTO Singapore meeting that the ILO is a better body to deal with labour standards than the WTO because of the former's tripartite structure (OATUU, 1997). On top of that, OATUU had signed a 'joint NGO statement' asking governments not to endorse WTO work on a social clause. This angered the ICFTU, as it had claimed that its African affiliates had always supported a social clause. The ICFTU told OATUU that:

> By your action, you broke the unity of the Workers' Group [in the ILO] stand on labour rights and trade, which could have weakened our position not only in terms of the strength and efficiency of our action but also in the eyes of the anti-labour governments, employers and other right wing forces who were leading the battle in Singapore against our workers' rights proposals. (ICFTU, 1997a)

Because of the three above-mentioned reasons – barriers to access to international organizations, differences in power among unions and diversity in national interest representation – the possibility of international interest mediation is not high (Ebbinghaus and Visser, 1994: 4). However, it can be argued that if unions do not cooperate across national borders, they might face an even stronger decline. This is especially true because business has fewer difficulties in aggregating transnational interests. Moreover, in the sectors that are dominated by a few large companies, business is able to act alone, outside a coordination structure, which gives them an advantage over labour (Greenwood *et al.*, 1992: 239–42).

Plan

The current pressures facing trade unions and workers in general include their continued oppression in parts of the world, the resistance of governments to trade unions and pressures related to the internationalization of the economy. This chapter surveyed some of the possible ways for trade unions to face these pressures and the limitations to the implementation of such solutions.

This book deals with issues arising from the social clause debate among unions and between unions and other actors, such as states, employers' organizations and other NGOs. In contrast to many other studies of the social clause issue, this book takes actors as a point of departure. Similarly, this book contributes to the understanding of how and with what success unions from different political, cultural and economic systems have tried to counter what they perceive as policies harmful to their workers.

The key questions this book will answer are:

1. How have selected unions attempted to influence the debate on the inclusion of minimum labour standards in the WTO agreement?
2. What accounts for their success or lack of success?
3. What conclusions, with respect to the effective behaviour of trade unions in the construction of international policy, can be drawn from these experiences?

Chapters 2 and 3 present the theoretical approach of the book. Chapter 2 explains the relevance of this discursive approach, and shows how this approach combined with other approaches helps us to understand the effects of trade unions on global governance. It also explains the rationale for the national and international union studies. Chapter 3 shows how proponents and opponents of a social clause can make use of different theoretical and normative arguments to substantiate their claims. Five subject claims are discussed. Each claim illustrates arguments for and against a social clause. The chapter concludes with an outline of two discourses, composed of the different claims. These two discourses serve as recurrent themes through the remaining chapters.

Chapters 4 and 5 cover national union studies. An analysis is provided of trade unions' discussions and their influence on the debate about a link between trade and labour standards, especially with reference to the United States and India.

Chapters 6 and 7 consider the influence of international workers' organizations, predominantly the ICFTU, on the debate within two international settings: the OECD and the ILO.

Finally, in Chapter 8 conclusions are drawn from the union studies.

Notes

1. Labour standards and labour rights are used interchangeably throughout this work. The same is true for the terms 'core', 'minimum' and 'fundamental' labour standards.
2. In 1999, Convention 182 on the worst forms of child labour was added to the list of core Conventions. As this research deals predominantly with the events before 1999, Convention 182 will be ignored.
3. The global shifts described are the result of three interrelated processes. The first process concerns the increasing importance of transnational corporations (TNCs), which can control and coordinate production chains across borders. By means of international trade and intra-firm trade, TNCs are currently responsible for about two-thirds of the world exports of goods and services. Second, states have liberalized their national markets, privatized the main sectors of economic activity and shifted their regulatory focus to levels above the nation state. Third, technological developments, especially in the area of information technology, are considered the most important factors stimulating the internationalization processes (De Groep van Lissabon, 1994: 58–60; Hirst and Thompson, 1996; Dicken, 1998: 42–6, 426–7).
4. See for data on trade union density the World Labour Report of 1997. It shows that only a few trade unions experienced increased levels of trade union density in the period 1985–95. In Africa, only South Africa and Zimbabwe show rising trade union density levels. In the Americas, this is only the case in Chile. Hong Kong and the Philippines are doing

reasonably well in Asia. In Europe, only a few trade unions have seemed to escape the declining rate of trade union density, among them those of Spain, Sweden and Slovakia (ILO, 1997a).

5. Note that declining union density tells us something about the diminishing strength of unions. According to Visser, the comparison of unionization levels of countries is tricky. For example, even if the figures are accurate, it is still unclear who is included in the figures. Therefore, it is useful to take into account the other indicators of union strength, such as the levels of collective bargaining, the occurrence of strikes, access to political circles and the level of fragmentation of the workforce (Visser 1992; see also Western, 1995; Locke *et al.*, 1996; ILO, 1997a).

6. Although in some countries one can really speak of separate territorial zones, in other countries the incentives related to 'zones' are offered to all export-oriented companies, regardless of their location within the country (ILO, 1996a: 1).

7. The growth of the informal sector is attributed not only to the intensified international competition, but also to the rapid increase of the urban labour force and the structural economic adjustment which decreases public sector employment and real wages (ILO, 1997a: 178–9).

8. The informal sector can be defined as: 'very small-scale units producing and distributing goods and services, and consisting largely of independent, self-employed producers in urban and rural areas of developing countries, some of which also employ family labour and/or few hired workers or apprentices; which operates with very little capital or none at all; which utilize a low level of technology and skills; which therefore operates at a low level of productivity; and which generally provides very low and irregular income and highly unstable employment to those who work in it. It also includes activities that are carried out without formal approval from authorities and escape the administrative machinery responsible for enforcing legislation and similar instruments' (Salter, 1998).

9. For an overview, see Ruigrok and van Tulder (1993: 13–56).

10. International level refers to the relationship among states, while transnational level refers to the relationship between non-state actors across borders.

11. Because most governments waited to ratify the ITO until the United States had made a move, the US Congress's decision to reject the ITO meant that the organization suffered a premature death. The reasons for the US Congress to do so are analysed in Low (1993).

INTRODUCTION

12. The WTO, the successor of the GATT, has a similar provision in article XXIII.
13. The United States submitted its request to include labour standards in the Uruguay negotiating round at the GATT Council meeting in 1987 (Cappuyns, 1998: 666).
14. Agricultural trade, textiles and clothing were also included in the trade negotiations.
15. It is in the area of dispute settlement that one of the innovations has occurred. While under the GATT agreement the parties had at their disposal the ability to block the formation of a dispute settlement panel or the ruling of the panel, in the WTO reports can only be blocked by a consensus, and a special body has been established to deal with appeals in the area of legal interpretations (Hoekman and Kostecki, 1995: 46–8).
16. Support of GATT–WTO directors to get a specific issue on the table is important. While their room for manoeuvre is not large, directors are important in influencing the agenda setting of the GATT–WTO meetings. Besides Dunkel, Director Rugiero was perceived as being sympathetic to a social clause (Interview with ICFTU: 11 June 1998).
17. Addressing this issue in its own trade policy review was the result of a strategic move of the AFL-CIO, which urged the then US trade representative Hills to be the first to make such a move, as an example of the seriousness of the US proposals to inlcude workers' rights in the GATT (*Inside US Trade*, 11 August 1989: 4–5).
18. Thus far, public awareness of the issues involved in liberalizing the world market has attracted most attention through the events in Seattle during the 1999 WTO meeting. This time, it was less hotly debated within the WTO, but more so outside on the streets. Farmers, environmentalists and Third World and labour activists joined hands to show the WTO member states that liberalization must have a social face.

2 Trade Unions and Global Governance

Whether trade unions have been able to insert their claims into the debate on labour standards is the theme of this book. This chapter explains the rationale behind the union studies, defines the central notions and outlines a framework for measuring the influence of trade unions.

Conceptualizing Trade Unions and Their Activities

The selection of the trade union studies

The World Trade Organization (WTO) does not allow trade union representation within its decision-making process. Therefore, the influence of trade unions on the WTO debate must be analysed in other international or regional bodies that influence decision-making in the WTO. The institutions discussed in this book are the International Labour Organization (ILO) and the Organisation for Economic Co-operation and Development (OECD). These bodies have been selected for two reasons. First, they have held extensive debates on the social clause, and have undertaken action in this field. The OECD entered into the debate with a study of the relationship between trade and labour standards, providing a mix of scientific data and political considerations. The ILO was chosen because of its intrinsic involvement in the debate: the organization is the prime international body dealing with labour standards, and linking these standards to trade sanctions would have altered the organization's nature considerably. The debates held within these international bodies can be seen as practices for WTO negotiations.

Second, the three organizations differ with respect to union representation. Within the ILO, trade unions are part of the decision-making machinery. Within the OECD, trade unions have been able to use their advisory status to influence the adjustments of the OECD study.

It is, however, not sufficient to examine the relationship between trade unions and international bodies because policy decisions on a social clause are also made at the national level. Trade unions also develop their position in relation to national governments. So as to open up the question at all levels, two union movements with strongly contrasting views of the social clause question were selected. In India, the international pressure for a social clause provoked an unlikely alliance between national trade union federations and the successive governments against the international enforcement of labour standards. In the United States, an alliance emerged between the federal trade union, the American Federation of Labor and Congress of Industrial Organizations (AFL-CIO) and the successive governments *in favour* of a unilateral or multilateral social clause. By looking at these two trade union movements, this book traces the influence of trade unions from Delhi and Washington at the international level.

The trade unions examined in this study are five Indian national trade union federations and the AFL-CIO. So as to locate the development of an international trade union position, the International Confederation of Free Trade Unions (ICFTU), and related organizational groups, i.e. the Trade Union Advisory Council (TUAC) of the OECD and the workers' group of the ILO, are studied. The ICFTU, one of the main advocates of a social clause, occupies a strategic position among the unions. Organizing about 125 million members from 145 countries, it is the single largest international trade union confederation (ICFTU, 2000). As such, it dominates both the workers' group in the ILO and the TUAC.

Trade unions, shared interests and political action

The national trade unions are secondary organizations, in the sense that they are federations of member-based primary organizations. The ICFTU is a tertiary organization (Gordenker and Weiss, 1995: 381). In other words, they are organizations of organizations. These secondary and tertiary trade union organizations are interest groups, comprising people who are jointly engaged in political action aimed at achieving common ends (Lehman Schlozman and Tierney, 1986: 10). Two components of this definition – common ends and political action – need further explanation.

One has to bear in mind that the common ends (or shared interests) are not always clearly defined and may change over time. In this study, the trade unions are organized units that represent a more or less broadly defined set of sectional interests. Sectional interests comprise both the current and the potential membership of unions. Sectional interests can be more specifically defined at the local and national levels than at the international level. The higher the level of aggregation of organization (secondary and tertiary organizations), the higher the level of aggregation of perceived interests and the greater the potential distortion in the representation of these perceived interests (Immergut, 1998: 7).

The political action of the unions studied here mainly takes the form of trying to influence the decision-making process. This direct strategy has a public element (applying pressure) and a non-public element (lobbying). At times, trade unions also make use of more indirect strategies, such as organizing protests. The difference between pressure and protest is that the former is directed towards decision-makers or their staff, while the objective of the latter strategy is to influence public opinion (Huberts, 1988: 18). Because of the international nature of the issue under study, the dominant strategy of the trade unions studied is a direct one, aimed at influencing policy-makers at both national and international levels. The dimensions of trade union influence are depicted in Table 2.1.

Table 2.1 *Dimensions of influence of secondary and tertiary trade union organizations*

Strategy of direct influence (internal and external modes)	Formal	Informal	Success
Non-public: lobbying	Advisory positions, decision-making	Meetings with policy-makers	Sensitizing and substantive (reactive or proactive)
Public: applying pressure	Testimonies	Conferences	

By advocating certain goals through lobbying and applying pressure, trade unions make use of what Gordenker and Weiss (1995: 379) call internal and external modes. Internal modes are lobbying and applying pressure in the national arenas in an attempt to influence the formulation of foreign policy. The direct pressure activities considered here are public formal strategies – such as testimonies – and public informal strategies, such as conferences organized around a specific theme. Formal non-public lobbying activities include participation in advisory councils and decision-making processes.

Informal non-public activities involve meetings with policy-makers (decision-makers and staff members); external modes involve carrying out similar activities at the international level.

The trade unions studied here are insider groups (Smith, 1993: 2–3), in the sense that policy-makers at national levels and within the OECD and ILO generally regard them as legitimate representatives of workers. This means that they are regularly included in one way or another in national and international decision-making processes. Of course, the degree to which they are treated as legitimate representatives differs according to the institutional setting. In the United States, the government consults the AFL-CIO more regularly than is the case for trade union federations in India. At the international level, trade unions have been credited with decision-making authority in the ILO, while in the OECD their official position is much weaker.

The attempts by trade unions to influence policies related to the debate on trade and labour standards through lobbying and applying pressure may be successful in two respects. The first is that they may achieve *sensitizing* successes in a political arena. Hence, they may succeed in changing the perceptions of other consequential actors. The result is that certain issues are included on the agenda. Consequential actors are actors whose actions or potential actions are taken into account by other actors (Laumann and Knoke, 1989; Knoke *et al.*, 1996: 13). The second success they may have is *substantive* in nature: they may succeed in influencing policies. These successes can be reactive in nature, i.e. foreclosing certain outcomes, or proactive, i.e. introducing new issues (Kriesi *et al.*, 1995: 210–11).

The Relation between Demands and Effects: An Analytical Model

Substantive success is measured by establishing whether trade unions have been able to achieve their concrete goals through their own intervention. The degree to which trade unions have been able to influence the perception of the other consequential actors (sensitizing successes) will be examined with the help of a discursive approach. The outcomes may be linked, but not necessarily so. It is more likely that substantive success follows on from sensitizing success, rather than vice versa.

The role of discourses in the policy process

One of the key ways of analysing how trade unions try to exert influence is to consider the discourses within the policy process. A discourse is a 'specific ensemble of ideas, concepts, and categories that is produced, reproduced, and transformed in a particular set of practices and through which meaning is given to physical and social realities' (Hajer, 1995: 60).

The practices referred to in this study are the institutional debates that preceded the decisions made in the organizations studied.

Discourse analysis as employed by Hajer (1995) is based on the assumption that problems are socially constructed. Although this does not mean that the existence of facts is denied, it does mean that the way these facts are perceived and acted upon can differ. In order for policy to be formulated, an issue has to become a problem and the problem needs to be defined, and in turn this definition requires political consequences. Hence, a problem needs a definition upon which policy-makers can act. This is what Hajer calls *discursive closure*. Looking at the stage of discursive closure, one can see which aspects of a problem are included and which are left out. In addition, policy-making implies finding ways to contain potential social conflict, i.e. to achieve *social accommodation*. This adds to the understanding of the way in which problems are positioned in the contexts of some social developments and aspirations, while others are deflected. The third element of a process is *problem closure*, which shows whether a strategy of regulation helped to achieve certain goals (Hajer, 1995: 21–44).

An important notion in discourse analysis is the concept of discourse coalitions. Coalitions are formed around specific sets of arguments on the definition of a problem and the best way to solve a problem. This gives these coalitions power (Hajer, 1995: 13). These discourse coalitions differ from conventional coalitions in the sense that 'the actors have not necessarily met, let alone that they follow a carefully laid out and agreed upon strategy' (Hajer, 1995: 13). As is the case with many discourses, discourses about labour standards are interdiscursive. The specific sets of arguments that sustain a discourse coalition are often drawn from various knowledge domains (economics, law, social sciences, ethics).

A discourse can be considered dominant when actors are required to use the ideas, concepts and categories of that discourse in order to be taken seriously, and when that discourse is translated into concrete policies (Hajer, 1995: 60–1). In this research, I refer to these two conditions as the sensitizing and the substantive success of a discourse. Hajer does not envisage dominance of a discourse as the result of the power of a particular group.

Instead, it can be the product of an argumentative interplay between a variety of social forces that have converging ideas about the nature of a problem (Hajer, 1995: 264). Politics – the process in which certain definitions of issues are organized in while others are organized out – is based on arguments (Hajer, 1995: 59).

An advantage of discourse analysis is that it provides a tool for a multilayered analysis, one that takes into account the specific outcome of a process not only in terms of goal achievement, but also in terms of enhancing the future legitimacy of certain policy options. A drawback of discourse analysis is its limited explanatory value; why certain discourses become dominant, or gain acceptance, is less explored. Therefore, in this research the concept of discourse is mainly used to describe changes that have taken place with respect to perceptions of reality and the extent to which they have been included in the debate. Because of its limited explanatory value, it is combined with other approaches, which are discussed in the next sections.

Contextual approach

The ability of unions to be influential will rely on the *characteristics of the discursive context*. This context is the way in which consequential actors perceive the larger political power relations and global economic developments. It is assumed that if the goals of trade union actors fit in with the perception of the persons these actors want to influence, trade unions will have a higher chance of achieving success.

In this research, the interpretation of global economic developments serves as a contextual discursive factor, i.e. the way in which actors perceive the relationship between the internationalization of the economy and the position of nation-states. The important issues – important because they are central to the social clause debate – are whether economic internationalization causes regulatory competition and unfair trade, and whether nation-states are able to formulate policies that are beneficial for workers.

Another discursive contextual factor of importance is that of the existing regimes. The most commonly accepted definition of regimes is 'sets of implicit or explicit principles, norms, rules, and decision-making procedures around which actors' expectations converge in a given area of international relations' (Krasner, 1983: 2).

Several terms in this definition need further clarification. Principles are defined as beliefs of facts, causation and rectitude; norms refer to standards of behaviour (rights and obligations); rules refer to the specific prescriptions for action; and decision-making procedures refer to the practices that make collective decisions and their implementation possible (Krasner, 1983: 2).[1] These principles, norms, rules and decision-making procedures do not have to be effective, but they must be recognized in order to have continuing validity (Keohane, 1993: 28). In this research, four regimes are considered to be relevant. These are the trade regime as rooted in the WTO, the human rights' regime as embedded in declarations of the UN, the labour rights' regime as embedded in the ILO and the trade and labour rights' regime as embedded in national and regional trade agreements.

The fact that a regime exists may make alternative options that contradict this regime less legitimate, while it might legitimize and strengthen those options that fit into an existing regime (Arts, 1998: 66–7). I argue that while regimes enable and constrain options, which options are facilitated or discouraged depends on: (a) the dominant interpretation of a regime; and (b) the dominant regime where more than one regime covers an area.

It is commonly accepted that regimes only change when their principles and norms are changed. Changes in rules and decision-making procedures should be interpreted as changes within a regime, not as changes of a regime. Nevertheless, certain changes in rules are interpreted by some actors as limited changes, and thus within regimes, while other actors regard such changes as affecting the norms, and thus a change of a regime itself. An example is the Generalized System of Preferences industrialized countries have developed in order to provide a differential treatment for developing countries. Developed countries have maintained that this system is a change of the rules that help developing countries to deal with underdevelopment, and as such it is a temporary deviation from the WTO's most favoured nation principle. However, developing countries have chosen to interpret this change as a change of norm, and treat it as a way to gain legitimacy for their argument that the basic WTO norms should be redistribution and equity, rather than non-discrimination and efficiency (Krasner, 1983: 4). Hence, because the interpretation of existing regimes differs, ideas about the options that fit best into a regime may also differ. Or, as Haggard and Simmons argue, although regimes may by their very nature limit some policy options and make other options available, how actors interpret these constraints and options depends on history, knowledge and purpose (Haggard and Simmons, 1987: 511).

The second reason why one cannot assume that regimes simply enable or constrain options is that different regimes may coexist peacefully while being mutually contradictive. Take the example of the labour rights regime and the trade regime. If these regimes were to become interconnected, the norm of voluntarism of the former would contradict the mandatory norm the latter prescribes, and vice versa. Whether actors would be willing to change such norms would depend on their evaluation of one regime *vis-à-vis* the other. And this evaluation would in turn be governed by perceptions of the principles and norms of regimes. Thus, the fact that there are more regimes available to govern certain relations, and that the principles and norms governing the regimes are open to interpretation, weakens the assumption that regimes *as such* regulate constraints and options.

In sum, the concept of discourse has a descriptive value and an explanatory value: explanatory, as it adds to the understanding of why certain policy options are considered valuable and others are not. Hence, as an explanatory tool, discourse analysis helps one to understand why ideas, or perceptions of reality, have become consensual to such an extent that they help to formulate policy.

Explaining success and failure

Union bodies have developed differing positions on the social clause, with varied levels of success. To understand why trade unions have or have not succeeded in achieving their goals, one cannot look only at the larger context in which unions operate. Factors have to be specified through which the demands and ideas produce successes or failures. I have selected three groups of factors, based on Huberts (1988).

The first group comprises the *characteristics of the political process*. These are the differences of opinion between the policy-makers and the freedom of policy-makers to choose between the alternatives presented. Another characteristic of the political process is the availability of formal procedures for exercising influence, such as the existence of advisory groups (Huberts, 1988: 75–7). These characteristics of the political process comprise the 'logic of influence' (Streeck, 1992: 105). The logic of influence refers to the institutional environment that provides both constraints and opportunities for unions in the form of formal and informal rules unions have to take into account. These rules include strategic considerations, rules of political prudence and norms of reciprocal political exchange.

The second group comprises the *characteristics of the interest group*, such as strength in terms of the ability to increase legitimacy or to generate trust and credibility, and the similarity between the perceptions of such interest groups and policy-makers (see also Hajer, 1995: 59; Knoke *et al.*, 1996). Large membership and resources are regarded as being of secondary importance in this research (Van Roozendaal, 2001: 53–5).

Credibility is defined as the quality of being believable and is therefore closely related to trust. Trust is defined as the quality of being reliable and responsible. Trust is related to the overall perception of an actor, while credibility is connected to the specific actions of an actor. Behaviour that elicits trust or credibility should be perceived by the target of that behaviour as relatively costly for the sender and as voluntarily provided (Jönsson, 1993: 207–8). Legitimacy is defined as the correctness of an issue according to the opinions of most people. Being able to increase the legitimacy of policy decisions may enhance unions' opportunities to play an important role, even though they lack legal authority (Willetts, 1982: 17–24). In addition, internal legitimacy, which refers to the amount of support a decision by union leadership receives from its members, is important because internal divisions make unions less interesting in terms of providing legitimacy for the decisions of policy-makers. Moreover, the lack of broad internal support hampers an articulated attitude towards international issues.

The third group of factors through which the demands and ideas of trade unions produce successes or failures comprises the *characteristics of collective action*. It is assumed that the more concrete and moderate the demands of the trade unions, the stronger their influence. In addition, the strategies employed by trade unions will be of importance. In my research, the strategies considered are those outlined in Table 2.1, i.e. the public and the non-public strategies. These strategies can be conducted alone or in alliance with other actors (Huberts, 1988: 69–71). Needless to say, having allies helps groups to be successful, especially if these allies control decisions (Tarrow, 1995: 88).

Table 2.2 summarizes and regroups the factors for the success of the trade unions involved that have been discussed so far. It also specifies the assumptions under which I expect the success of trade unions to be greater. These assumptions provide the focus of this study.

The Question of Influence and Interests

This book attempts to determine how trade unions have influenced the national and international debates on the inclusion of labour standards in multilateral trade agreements (social clause). Influence is exercised when 'the activities of trade unions have persuaded policy makers to take into account the policy goals of trade unions better than would have been the case without the activities of trade unions' (Huberts, 1988: 20). Activities mean all formal, non-formal, public and non-public strategies of trade unions. The policy goals in question are non-static expressions of interests

Table 2.2 *Preconditions for the success of trade unions*

Factors	Assumptions
Access to decision-making actors, which allows taking advantage of differences in opinion between policy-makers.	*Accessibility effect*: the greater the access to and the greater the differences among policy-making actors, the higher the probability of success
Ability to generate legitimacy, trust and credibility. Availability of resources. Ability to generate common interests with other NGOs.	*Power resources effect*: the greater the power resources, the higher the probability of success
Ability to create common interests among trade unions.	*Internal unity effect*: the stronger the common interests of trade union members, the higher the probability of success
Nature of demands.	*The moderation effect*: the more concrete and moderate the demands, the higher the probability of success
Combination of national and international interest representation.	*The double pressure effect*: if international and national strategies are combined, the chances of success increase
Perceptions of global developments. Perceptions of compatibility of existing regimes. Perceptions of the nature of regimes.	*Compatibility effect*: the greater the compatibility between the goals of trade union actors and the perception of other consequential actors (such as policy-makers) of the discursive context, the higher the probability of success

and perceptions. These policy goals are co-determined by time, institutional context and the consequential actors involved, and are therefore subject to change.

Influence is equated with success. Success and influence both refer to achieving the wanted or parts of the wanted and preventing the unwanted. Impact (or effects) concerns the whole of outcomes of a debate or a policy process, including the unwanted ones.

In general, there are three major debates on the issue of interests (Lehman Schlozman and Tierney, 1986: 14–37; Hajer, 1995: 51; Knoke *et al.*, 1996: 79–81). The first concerns the question of the basis of interests. Many scholars, originating from both Marxist and neo-classical traditions, conceptualize interests mainly in economic terms. However, this is insufficient. Social and political ideas and belief systems also shape interests. If this were not the case, the rise of certain interest groups, such as animal protection groups or environmental movements, would be very hard to explain.

The second debate concerns whether interests should be determined subjectively or objectively. The first approach equates interests with preferences, while the second envisages interests as observable from the outside, without them being explicitly expressed. The latter approach has the advantage that it becomes possible to distinguish between altruistic and self-interested behaviour, and it enables a researcher to identify when groups are not acting in their own interest (for example, because of a lack of information or capacity to determine their interests). Not surprisingly, there are some problems with the approach of perceiving interests in an objective manner. When determining objective interests, a researcher assumes that he or she is able to define objectively the interests at stake. But approaching interests as objective fails to account for differences in taste and the multiple roles of individuals or groups (Lehman Schlozman and Tierney, 1986: 16–23). The latter factor is something a researcher may miss when determining objective interests.

Closely related to this is a third debate, which revolves around the question of how individual interests add up to collective interests. Pluralists maintain that it is possible to speak of aggregated interests, while neo-institutionalists contend that the mechanisms that aggregate interests do not result in a sum of all interests, but reshape them (Immergut, 1998: 7). Staff members of organizations can to a large extent shape the interests of the larger group of members in a way they see fit for their rank and file.

To resolve the contradictions apparent in these last two debates one should accept that there is a difference between potential and expressed interests, instead of one between real and expressed interests (Immergut, 1998: 25). Expressed interests are time- and context-related, and are shaped by institutions. Potential interests are equally plausible alternatives (Immergut, 1998: 7, 25).

Conclusion

This book addresses three main questions. The first concerns the issue of how selected unions have attempted to influence the debate on the inclusion of minimum labour standards in the WTO agreement. In this chapter I explained that the trade union activities most relevant to this study are those associated with lobbying and applying pressure. In the remainder of this study the importance of these activities is analysed in the context of the national and international union studies

The second main question concerns what accounts for their success or lack of success. In this chapter I explained that the results of the above-mentioned activities should be analysed in terms of sensitizing and substantive effects. Where trade unions have been able to achieve concrete goals through their own intervention, I call it a substantive effect; where they have been able to influence the perception of reality of the other consequential actors, I call it a sensitizing effect. The chapter continued by explaining that the discursive context, as well as the characteristics of the political process, of the interest group and of the collective action, affect the degree of success of trade unions.

The third and last question of this research is what conclusions with respect to the effective behaviour of trade unions in the construction of international policy can be drawn from these experiences. This question is answered by three kinds of comparisons. The first compares the influence of national trade union federations within the ICFTU. How are the different union interests represented at the level of the ICFTU? The second comparison is between the influence of trade unions at the national level and that at the international level. Whether the lack of trade union influence at the national level is compensated for by influence at the international level, or vice versa, is studied. The third comparison focuses on the differences in influence of trade union organizations in the ILO and the OECD. What the policy decisions made in these organizations have in common is that they all deal directly or indirectly with the social clause debate, and that trade unions have played some role in determining the outcome of decisions. However, making a comparison between the reasons for success of trade unions within the two institutions is difficult, especially if one considers the large differences between the policy decisions studied in these organizations (i.e. the OECD's report on labour standards and the social clause debate in the ILO). Therefore, this comparison mainly adds to the understanding of the responsiveness of the different international arrangements to the demands of trade unions.

Note

1. See, for an assessment of regime theory, Haggard and Simmons (1987).

3 CLAIMING POSITIONS: DEBATES ON LABOUR STANDARDS

What role do labour standards play in the process of economic development? Are trade measures an effective means to enforce labour standards? Are labour standards universal? These are only a few of the questions dominating the international debate on labour standards. In this chapter, I argue that a variety of opposing claims is available to answer these questions.[1] It is because scientists cannot agree on the answers to these questions that proponents and opponents of a social clause can make use of different theoretical arguments to substantiate their claims. Five claims and their associated theoretical and normative arguments are discussed: universality/relativity, socio-economic, effectiveness/ineffectiveness, spillover/exclusion and sovereignty/interventionist.[2]

This chapter shows that the combination of certain claims supports a particular discourse. It is not the purpose of this chapter to present the 'right' perception of the issues involved in the social clause debate. It is aimed at helping the reader to put the claims and supporting arguments used in the debate into perspective. Where do the claims come from? What kinds of evidence do those who make use of such claims have to support them? Hence, this chapter first helps the reader to grasp the complexity of the debate. It concludes with an outline of two discourses, assembled from opposing arguments. These two discourses provide a recurrent theme throughout the rest of this book.

Universality and Relativity Claims

A prominent question in the debate on labour standards is whether *some* labour standards are universal. Universality would imply that these standards, or rights, are applicable to countries with different levels of development and social/cultural structures (Van Liemt, 1989: 437). If one examines the body of international declarations one certainly gets the impression that certain labour standards are widely accepted and can thus be considered universal.

The most important declaration concerning human rights is the Universal Declaration on Human Rights, as adopted and proclaimed by the UN General Assembly Resolution on 10 December 1948. The articles relevant to labour rights are:

- no one shall be held in slavery or servitude; slavery and the slave trade shall be prohibited in all their forms (Article 4);
- everyone has the right to freedom of peaceful assembly and association (Article 20);
- everyone has the right to work, to free choice of employment, to just and favourable conditions of work and to protection against unemployment (Article 23);
- everyone, without any discrimination, has the right to equal pay for equal work (Article 23);
- everyone who works has the right to just and favourable remuneration ensuring for themselves and their family an existence worthy of human dignity, and supplemented, if necessary, by other means of social protection (Article 23);
- everyone has the right to form and to join trade unions for the protection of their interests (Article 23);
- everyone has the right to rest and leisure, including reasonable limitation of working hours and periodic holidays with pay (Article 24).

The Declaration is universal in the sense that every state is bound by it, whether it has ratified it or not. The Declaration is complemented by two Covenants, which are only legally binding to those states that have accepted them by ratification or accession.[3] The Covenants also cite rights that are related to labour rights. The first Covenant, the International Covenant on Economic, Social and Cultural Rights, recognizes the right to work (Article 6), to the enjoyment of just and favourable conditions of work (Article 7) and to form and join trade unions (Article 8). The second Covenant, the International Covenant on Civil and Political Rights, maintains that no one is to be held in slavery or servitude or required to perform forced or compulsory labour (Article 8).

Several United Nations organizations and other international arrangements have also drafted specific declarations and documents on labour standards. In this context the most important ones are those by the United Nations World Summit for Social Development (1995), the OECD report on Trade, Employment and Labour Standards (1996), the WTO Singapore Declaration (1996), and the Declaration of the ILO (1998).

The UN World Summit, organized in 1995, recognizes a need for 'quality jobs, with full respect for the basic rights of workers as defined by relevant International Labour Organization and other international instruments' (United Nations, 1995). It stipulates that respect for basic workers' rights should be promoted, thereby specifically referring to the prohibition of forced labour and child labour, freedom of association and the right to organize and bargain collectively, equal remuneration for men and women for work of equal value and non-discrimination in employment (United Nations, 1995).

In 1996 the OECD undertook a study on trade and labour standards. The study selects freedom of association and collective bargaining, the elimination of exploitative forms of child labour (i.e. bonded labour and unacceptable conditions related to health and safety considerations), prohibition of slavery and compulsory labour, and non-discrimination in employment as core labour standards. The following selection criteria were used. First, the above-mentioned core labour rights correspond, as we have seen, with the provisions laid down in the Universal Declaration. These human rights are considered to be universal, transcending political, economic, social and cultural conditions. The OECD study also specifically refers to the outcomes of the Social Summit. Second, the OECD report regards these rights as enabling, thereby stipulating that these rights help workers to determine their own working conditions (OECD, 1996b: 26–8).

In 1996, the WTO member states at Singapore, after lengthy discussions, agreed to renew their commitment to the observance of internationally recognized core labour standards. The agreement pointed to the ILO as the competent body to set and deal with these standards (WTO, 1996a).

Encouraged by these developments, in 1998 the ILO adopted the Declaration on Fundamental Principles and Rights at Work, based on the principles of some of its conventions (see Chapter 7). The purpose of this Declaration is to promote the universal application of certain fundamental rights and reconfirms that:

> all Members, even if they have not ratified the Conventions in question, have an obligation arising from the very fact of membership in the Organization, to respect, to promote and to realize, in good faith and in accordance with the Constitution, the principles concerning the fundamental rights which are the subject of those Conventions. (ILO, 1998c)

The fundamental rights in question are: the freedom of association and the effective recognition of the right to collective bargaining; the elimination of all forms of forced or compulsory labour; the effective abolition of child labour; and the elimination of discrimination in respect to employment and occupation.

Other sources also confirm these basic labour rights. Reviewing eight different proposals concerning international labour standards, Van Liemt concludes that the freedom of association, the right to organize and bargain collectively and a minimum age for the employment of children are mentioned in all of them. The freedom from discrimination in employment and occupation on the grounds of race, sex, religion, political opinion, etc., the freedom from forced labour and occupational health and safety are mentioned in six out of eight proposals (Van Liemt, 1989: 437).

Although it may be tempting to conclude from these sources that there is an international consensus that these labour rights are applicable under all circumstances, this is far from true. Three objections to such a conclusion can be raised: (a) the notion of universality does not mean uniformity; (b) universality is not always recognized in practice or in principle; and (c) even if they are universal, there exists no agreement on the best way to enforce these labour standards.

Starting with the first objection, universality does not mean uniformity, but merely means that rights are drafted in such a way that all countries can implement them. This also means that the specific Declaration, Convention or Covenant allows for flexibility (Campbell and Sengenberger, 1994: 388). The Universal Declaration on Human Rights, for example, states that:

> in the exercise of his rights and freedoms, everyone shall be subject only to such limitations as are determined by law solely for the purpose of securing due recognition and respect for the rights and freedoms of others and of meeting the just requirements of morality, public order and the general welfare in a democratic society.

Several articles in the International Covenant on Civil and Political Rights provide that the rights in question shall not be subject to any restrictions except those which are prescribed by law and are necessary to protect national security, public order or the rights and freedoms of others. With respect to labour rights, the freedom from enslavement or servitude seems to be the only true universal right, since suspension is never allowed, not even in emergency situations. The International Covenant on Economic, Social and Cultural Rights states that the rights provided for therein may be limited by law, but only insofar as it is compatible with the nature of the rights and solely to promote the general welfare in a democratic society (Article 4). In addition, in 1977 the Assembly passed a resolution, supported by developing countries, that civil and political rights are dependent on economic, social and cultural rights (Krasner, 1985: 279).

The ILO considers its Conventions as being universal. However, the obligations that are part of the ILO Conventions allow for a certain degree of flexibility (ILO, 2000a). For example, when the first ILO Conventions came into force, some countries were exempted because their economic development was less advanced (Servais, 1989: 425). Okogwu states that:

> There is now a general consensus that the ILO standards should continue to be drawn up on a universal basis and that differences in national conditions and level of developments should be taken into consideration by the appropriate flexibility devices as provided by the ILO Constitution. (Okogwu, 1994: 154)

The ILO Declaration clearly considers the rights mentioned as universal and does not allow for flexibility. The Office of the ILO has argued that the real issue of the Declaration is

> not to impose on all ILO Members a single level of social protection, regardless of their respective levels of development and their particular historical and cultural circumstances and contrary to the Organization's philosophy. The issue was rather to ensure that those concerned would have the necessary means, taking into account the resources and particular conditions of each country, to claim an equitable remuneration for their labour. The fundamental rights have an obvious relevance in this context, since they represent a guarantee that employers and workers can freely demand, individually and collectively and without any discrimination, a just share of the fruits of progress. (ILO, 1998d)

The rights mentioned in the Declaration are therefore considered

> as being fundamental to the rights of human beings at work, irrespective of levels of development of individual member States. These rights are a precondition for all the others in that they provide for the necessary implements to strive freely for the improvement of individual and collective conditions of work. (ILO, 2000b)

Despite the truly universal character of this Declaration, the fact that the rights mentioned in the Declaration mainly give individuals the tools to demand their own conditions of work makes the outcome of the implementation of these rights less than uniform.

Turning to the second objection, some question universality as a principle and as a practice. It has been argued that since the overall ratification rate of ILO Conventions is low, they are not universal. Even though the eight Conventions that embody the core labour rights may have been ratified by a large majority, they have not been ratified by all (Myrdal, 1994: 342–5). Srinivasan (1994) argues that in most countries, including the developed countries lobbying for a social clause, freedom of association is limited by law and in practice, showing that universality cannot be taken seriously (see also Chapter 4). Bhagwati also argues against universal labour rights. He points out that many developed countries do not practise 'universal' labour rights and, moreover, he maintains that many countries have signed the ILO Conventions because they are, in effect, not binding. He challenges the principle of universality by maintaining that differences in labour rights reflect 'not necessarily venality and wickedness, but rather diversity of cultural values, economic conditions, and analytical beliefs and theories concerning the economic (and therefore moral) consequences of specific labor standards' (Bhagwati, 1994: 59).[4]

Bhagwati implicitly argues that it is likely that many countries have signed these declarations because they lack enforcement mechanisms. Countries might not have signed them if they could have been forced to observe them. All over the world states are violating the basic principles embodied in the various declarations, but this has almost never had repercussions for relations among states. This might change if these principles, or rights, were enforceable through trade measures. Punishing violating states through economic measures could be a way to ensure respect, but there are many arguments against such enforcement. These arguments are the subject of the next sections.

In sum, two opposing claims can be distinguished. The first is a relativity claim, which argues that core labour standards in principle and in practice cannot be uniform owing to differences in culture and economic development. This contrasts with the second claim, the universality claim, which states that core labour standards should be regarded as universal principles, although practices may be allowed to vary under certain specified conditions.

Socio-economic Claims: Rejecting and Supporting a Social Clause

The socio-economic claims voiced in the debate on international labour standards are among the most controversial ones. They deal with questions relating to the effects of labour standards on national economies and international trade, and on the compatibility of economic and social development. The main socio-economic claims that I discuss are summarized in Table 3.1.

These socio-economic claims are defended from different theoretical

Table 3.1 *Socio-economic claims*

Claims rejecting international labour standards	Claims supporting international labour standards
Labour standards policy intervenes in the market process and leads to all kinds of distortions, such as efficiency and labour allocation distortions.	Disparities in labour costs, social security and workers' rights lead to unfair competition. A level playing field would ensure fairer competition.
Labour standards imposed by developed countries limit the ability of non-unionized domestic firms and foreign countries with lower labour costs to compete. They are therefore protectionist.	Disparities in labour costs, social security and workers' rights lead to a race to the bottom/social dumping (i.e. social degradation among trading nations).
Labour standards depend on economic growth. They are a luxury good that can be afforded in certain stages of development.	Markets are man-made, and interference in markets is common practice; the question is only what kind of interference.
	Labour standards make enterprises more efficient, because of the internalization of costs (enabling constraints argument).
	Development means both economic and social progress, and conditions need to be in place that ensure the involvement of social actors.

Source: Emmerij (1994), Feis (1994), Freeman (1994), Portes (1994), Sengenberger (1994c).

47

perspectives. Importantly, these perspectives justify or condemn certain types of government intervention in the economy. As we will see, from a neo-classical perspective state intervention in the labour area has limited justification. If economic distortions that prevent trade cannot be removed directly, they should be tackled by subsidies and taxes (Gilpin, 1987: 180). Non-neo-classical economists see a stronger role for state intervention, and perceive this intervention as a justifiable means to create comparative advantage or to prevent social dumping or a race to the bottom.

Northern slowdown and Southern low labour costs

A claim often heard in the debate on international labour standards is that workers in the North need to be protected from low production costs in the South. The justification of this claim is that disparities in labour costs, social security and labour standards between the North and the South are responsible for high unemployment and decreasing wages in the North.

Various studies have looked into the relationship between economic slowdown in Northern economies and increased imports from Southern economies.[5] The outcomes are far from conclusive. Data show that wage increases in Western Europe have been 'paid' for by unemployment, while in the United States less growth in unemployment has been 'paid' for by a decline in real wages and an increase of wage inequality. During this same period, exports from developing countries to developed countries increased (Dorman, 1995: 6–7). For example, in the 1980s exports from China to the United States increased by 915 per cent (Mead, 1990; cited in Portes, 1994: 162).

Although increased labour market stress and increased imports took place in the same period, causally linking these two developments appears to be a difficult task. Whereas there is certainly a positive relationship between imports of specific goods in specific sectors, Dorman shows that several studies of the relationship between overall imports and the overall employment/wage decline come to different conclusions, varying from low to high impacts of trade (Dorman, 1995: i).[6]

As we have seen in Chapter 1, Kapstein argues that trade (i.e. increased imports from Asian countries), in combination with technological innovation, is the most important cause of unemployment and wage inequality (Kapstein, 1996: 23–5). Lawrence concludes that if the entire trade deficit of the United States with developing countries were eliminated, it would raise hourly wages by only 0.07 per cent (cited in Dorman, 1995: 9–10). Wood

(1994) shows that the impact of trade on wage inequality and unemployment is large. He calculates that the cumulative effect from the 1960s to 1990 reduced demand for labour in Northern manufacturing industries by about 12 per cent of the actual employment in these industries. This was accompanied by an increase of about 5 per cent in economy-wide demand for skilled labour relative to unskilled labour. Wood argues that these calculations do not even take into account the effects of trade on other, non-trade sectors that, for example, deliver supplies to the trade sectors, or the responses of employers in terms of the introduction of new technologies to the trade (Wood, 1994: 167). Although Katz and Murphy (1992) found that the growth in wage inequality could only be partly explained by trade, they did conclude that the relative decline in demand for labour of female high school dropouts in the United States could to a high extent be explained by trade (Katz and Murphy, 1992: 24–32).

In short, research does not provide an unambiguous answer to the question of the nature and size of the impact of imports on labour markets.[7] However, this lack of consensus has not hampered the public appeal of either claim.

Flow of capital and low labour costs

While the previous section examined the impact of increased imports from developing countries on developed countries' wages and employment structures, a related question is whether low labour standards are an important incentive for companies to shift investments from developed to developing countries. Hirst and Thompson (1996) argue that the level of foreign direct investment (FDI) from developed to developing countries is higher in periods of economic depression in developed countries. With depression being the push factor, are the low wages in developing countries the pull factor? Overall, labour costs constitute only 20 per cent of the total costs of the final manufactured product in developed countries. Therefore, for many products cheap labour cannot be considered to be the decisive factor influencing the decisions of companies to relocate their production.[8] Probably, the decision is made on the basis of a number of considerations, such as quality assurance and transportation costs. The increased use of robotic and information technology is a much greater threat to employment in developed countries than the low wages in developing countries (Hirst and Thompson, 1996: 115–20).

Even though there is not much empirical evidence that low labour costs are crucial in attracting FDI, the threat is part of the everyday political discourse (Langille, 1997: 32). This supports the claim for a level playing field through a mechanism such as a social clause, and supports the counterclaim that the comparative advantage of nations is negatively affected if they have to raise their standards.

If the competition between developed countries and developing countries for FDI is only in small part attributable to low labour costs in developing countries, can the same be said about the competition between and among developing countries and NICs? According to Sengenberger, competition among these countries for FDI in labour-intensive production has intensified since the 1980s, as labour costs in a second group of NICs (such as Thailand, Malaysia and Indonesia) are lower than in the original NICs. A third group of countries (Vietnam, Cambodia and Bangladesh) is now competing with the second tier (Sengenberger, 1994b: 399). It seems a logical conclusion that since labour-intensive production is more common in developing countries and NICs than in developed countries, low labour costs will play a more important role between and among developing countries and NICs. Interestingly enough, the competition between developing countries and NICs has thus far played no significant role in the debate on international labour standards. The argument of a level playing field is put forward by some Northern countries and by none of the 'threatened' Southern countries.

Do labour market policies hamper or stimulate economic development? Neo-classical and neo-institutionalist perspectives

Two different theoretical perspectives dominate the debate on labour standards and the consequences of neglecting or promoting them: the neo-classical and neo-institutional perspectives.[9] The *neo-classical* perspective emphasizes that markets determine economic outcomes. Setting labour standards is a function of the labour market; raising them prematurely through public intervention would create economic distortions on income and the creation of jobs.[10] The role neo-classical economists perceive for labour rights is, first, that they respond to market failures or preserve some public goods, or, second, that they arise out of organized interests in the absence of market failure (distributive function). The normative perspective of neo-classical economists is that they only see the first role of labour standards as legitimate. On the issue of wages, for example, neo-classical economists argue that raising standards through public intervention negatively affects wages: when non-monetary benefits rise, they have to be paid for by the decrease of monetary benefits (Dorman, 1995: 25–31).[11]

Neo-institutional economists, on the other hand, start with the premise that markets are incomplete and require mechanisms to adjust to changes. Labour standards influence socio-economic development, but the nature of such influence would depend on the way policy-makers apply them. In addition, without public intervention, workers cannot uphold their interests (which will affect their motivation and physical abilities), thereby inhibiting productivity growth and demand increases. Neo-institutionalists therefore advocate regulation that facilitates the operation of both economically dynamic and socially acceptable labour markets (Herzenberg *et al.*, 1990: 4; Amsden, 1994: 185; Dorman, 1995: 25–6).

An example of a neo-classical perspective on the effects of labour market intervention is provided by Fields (1990). He argues that labour standards should not be judged by process (direct government intervention to determine labour standards) but by outcome. The economic growth of NICs shows that although labour standards were severely restricted, the growth as such has resulted in increased employment and higher wages, and hence better standards. If wages had been above market level from the start, unemployment would have been the result. Moreover, 'Labour standards raised directly by the government or indirectly through protection of associational and collective bargaining rights are likely to protect one segment of the work force at the expense of the remainder' (Fields, 1990: 31).

Others emphasize that a premature adoption of social policies creates social segmentation. Portes (1994) argues that because of the availability of surplus labour, the introduction of extensive labour legislation may lead to a rise of the informal sector. Part of this informal labour is absorbed by the formal sector (for example, through subcontracting), which leads to a 'segmentation of the working class into a relatively high-paid and protected minority and a mass of unprotected workers occupied in manifold informal arrangements' (Portes, 1994: 164). Srinivasan (1990) argues that premature adoption leads to 'an island of labour aristocracy in the organized sectors . . . in a sea of poor self-employed as well as wage labour in agriculture, service and small-scale industrial sectors' (Srinivasan, 1990: 64).

For neo-institutionalists, dualism in the labour market is the result of an unequal distribution of labour standards (i.e. the concentration in the modern sector) and not of labour standards as such. Contrary to neo-classical economists, they argue that the suspension of formal sector labour legislation will not automatically result in increased productivity and wages in the informal sector (Herzenberg *et al.*, 1990: 10).

In addition, the trade-off between labour standards and economic development is viewed differently by neo-institutionalists. Even though not everyone agrees that raising labour standards results in increased efficiency, non-neo-classical economists emphasize that efficiency will not increase by keeping labour standards low (De Castro, 1995: 12). Piore (1990) observes a positive relationship between labour standards and economic development. Industrialization and economic development require capital-sensitive industries, and labour standards facilitate the shift from labour-intensive to capital-sensitive production. Low labour standards occur in industries where productivity and quality are not an issue. As Piore writes, 'As soon as capital costs become important, the employer begins to have an interest in the hourly productivity of the labour force, even if wages remain low since high worker productivity increases the productivity of capital' (Piore, 1994: 23).

For industrialized countries, facing a shift from mass production to more flexible production systems that rely on high quality and variety, procedural labour standards such as collective bargaining may help to prevent a fall back to the older production forms. In addition, they may facilitate greater worker involvement, which is needed to maintain quality. In addition, in the NICs labour standards will help to increase demand, which is needed to create employment (Piore, 1990, 1994).[12]

Piore also takes a position against the general neo-classical idea that once wages rise, non-monetary benefits will decline, and vice versa. On the contrary, Piore maintains that low-wage establishments often care less about health and safety regulations, while high-wage establishments tend towards the opposite (Piore, 1990: 36).

Some neo-institutionalists argue that some labour standards can have negative economic effects, but instead of calling for fewer labour standards they call for more, or at least for better combinations of standards. Sengenberger (1994a) argues that those who emphasize negative economic effects resulting from labour standards usually divide the international labour code (the sum of the ILO Conventions and Recommendations) into separate pieces of legislation whose effects are determined separately. However, one should take into account the effects of the packaging character of the standards, since they have a mutual effect upon each other. For example, if there is a lack of active policies to consult workers on production issues, these workers will be more likely to demand to be protected from the negative consequences of industrial change. Or the abolition of child labour may not have the desired effects if, simultaneously, no other measures are taken to compensate for the lack of income for poor families, such as the provision of better social security (Sengenberger, 1994a: 51–4).

While the bulk of this discussion is about labour standards – such as wages – on or above 'market level', one can also look at the effects of labour standards being suppressed below market level because of government intervention. A key focus in the debate has been the relationship between this type of intervention and economic growth centres, experienced in the NICs. At stake is whether the economic growth in these countries was related to the absence (neo-classical) or the presence (non-neo-classical, not necessarily neo-institutional) of *direct* governmental regulation and wage policy. Neo-classical economists, such as Fields (1990), maintain that the absence of directly set labour standards by governments and a market wage policy were responsible for the enormous economic growth in the NICs during the 1980s.[13] In contrast, in countries such as Colombia and Jamaica, wages set above market levels have caused an economic slowdown in manufacturing (Fields, 1990: 27–8). Strangely enough, Fields mentions the repression of trade unions, as has occurred in some of the NICs, but does not seem to regard this development as direct intervention. Moreover, while he acknowledges that the governments of Singapore and South Korea at times did not leave wages to the market (but instead repressed them), that does not seem to have influenced his general conclusions. In this respect, Harris states that:

> The neoclassical economists were hypersensitive to the deleterious effects on markets of workers combining to try to protect wages and conditions, but cavalier when it came to governments interfering in labour markets to enforce low wages, regardless of whether these reflected real scarcities or the number of police truncheons. (Harris, 1986: 131)

Several case studies on different NICs arrive at different conclusions from that of Fields. You (1990, 98) contradicts the neo-classical thesis that South Korea was able to grow because of a free labour market. He argues that the repression of trade unions was partly motivated by political considerations. Nevertheless, low wages during periods of depression did stimulate economic growth. However, since in the long term Korea's economic success depended not as much upon labour-intensive exports as upon raising productivity, as well as upon the growth of capital- and skill-intensive production, wage increases during periods of less repression have had a positive effect: 'much of the impetus for technological development came from import-substitution policies and rising labour costs, while the phenomenal growth of exports helped provide the resources required for it' (You, 1990: 112).

Lim (1990) suggests that the experience of Singapore shows that there was no free labour market but active government intervention; for example, holding down wages below the market level in the recession of 1974–5, and a high-wage policy in 1979 to foster capital- and skill-intensive development. When this did not have the desired effects, shelter was sought in wage constraints, later followed by higher wages. Other interventions by the state included a wide array of social investments. Therefore, Singapore does not show the virtues of a free labour market. However, nor does it show that repression was the motor behind its economic growth. The dominant motivation for the repression was political, and Lim argues that Singapore would have attracted similar investments without repression, as the economic context was favourable in the late 1960s (Lim, 1990: 73–90).

The interpretation of the NICs' experience is of importance because it might shed light on the relationship between labour standards and economic development. Besides the discussion of whether a free labour market has been responsible for the NICs' economic growth, the question poses itself as to whether political exclusion of labour is beneficial for economic development. Although the scope of this chapter does not allow a full exploration of this issue, one should take into consideration at least two issues. The first is that even if labour is excluded from politics, a state may still develop labour legislation that is cost increasing. As we have seen, opinions are divided on whether direct intervention is beneficial to economic development or not. The other issue is whether exclusion as such facilitates economic planning.[14] Although exclusion might do this, it is also argued that unions help to channel conflicts, thereby preventing socio-political and economic instability (Banuri, 1990: 59–60; You, 1990: 100).

Challenges to neo-classical theory and their consequences for perspectives on labour standards

The neo-classical and non-neo-classical economists make different claims about issues such as social dumping, the race to the bottom and the so-called level playing field.[15] Let us first consider the point made about social dumping and the need for a level playing field (see Table 2.1). Although there is lack of evidence supporting the claim that low labour costs are crucial to attracting FDI, they do play a substantial role in the competition between labour-intensive industries. However, according to neo-classical theorists, harmonization of labour laws is not required at the international level to prevent a race to the bottom (that is, increasing competitiveness through

Debates on Labour Standards

lowering labour standards). The first reason is inherent to the nature of neo-classical theory, namely that the lack of a level playing field creates comparative advantages (Langille, 1997: 25). The second reason is that there are ways to avoid a race to the bottom other than restricting labour rights, such as exchange rate adjustments that make imports more expensive and exports cheaper (Dorman, 1995: 15). Neo-classical trade theory suggests that exchange rate adjustments make a lowering of labour standards avoidable and in general the theory denies that trade can lower the aggregated income of a country. For these reasons the claims of social dumping, the race to the bottom and the level playing field are not defendable from this perspective (Dorman, 1995: 15).

Freeman (1994) maintains that government intervention can help countries to adjust to regulatory competitive pressure resulting from lower labour costs. If a country wants higher labour standards, it can have them if it is willing to pay. The way to pay for these standards is not only through exchange rate adjustments, but also through lower wages for labourers that benefit from standards, or through taxes (Freeman, 1994: 87–8). Common among these arguments is the idea that there is no such thing as an unavoidable pressure resulting from lower labour costs abroad, although it must be clear that the measures proposed can be more easily applied in wealthy developed countries than in poor developing countries.

All these domestic measures proposed by neo-classical thinkers may pose other problems, though. For example, the adjustment of exchange rates has its limits, as Dorman points out (Dorman, 1995: 20–4). This example of a two countries–two goods–two factors of production model on which the exchange rate argument is based does not represent the real world. Adjustments in currency rates might be good for trade with one country, but bad for trade with another. Therefore, adjustments may worsen the overall terms of trade. In addition, the adjustment of exchange rates has become more difficult than before; for example, because of the movement towards common currencies in economic blocks.

Non-neo-classical economists emphasize that neo-classical trade theory is being reshaped by the increased mobility of capital and the subsequent regulatory competition. This, combined with the fact that labour, and its regulation, is relatively immobile, has created a different situation in the international trade arena. Due to these developments, neo-classical trade theory has come under significant pressure since the mid-1980s. Its continued emphasis on explaining comparative advantage through the relative availability of production factors, based on the assumption that capital and labour are internationally immobile (the *ceteris paribus* assumption), has become less relevant, and the importance of industrial organization has been recognized.[16] Industrial organization theories try to explain why most trade is between advanced countries with similar industrial structures, why it tends to be intra-industry trade and why this intra-industry trade has not been accompanied by an increase in trade disputes (Gilpin, 1987: 177-8). Strategic trade policy models assumed that not only natural endowments create comparative advantages, but that government intervention can also create comparative advantages. These strategic trade policy models not only show the possibilities for governments to interfere and create comparative advantages (for example through the protection of certain industries), but they also show that the efficient allocation of resources alone cannot explain trade policy. Rather, it is a mixture that also includes domestic military or socio-political considerations, and its explanation should therefore include bargaining models (Ruigrok and van Tulder 1995, 202-205; Gilpin 1987, 221).

Closely related to this is the debate on the protection of declining industries. The rise of the NICs was threatening the old industries in the North, with the NICs using what were thought of as unfair tactics (for example, low wages). Some economists, even the more neo-classical-oriented ones, sought arguments to protect these industries.[17] In general, it was thought that the neo-classical theory of specialization was being overtaken by rapid global changes, specifically the acceleration of changes in comparative advantage. Since the adjustment costs of comparative advantage have increased, it has been argued that these industries needed protection (Gilpin, 1987: 188-9). For example, Feis (1994) argues that although it may be theoretically right to maintain that international competition is beneficial to all those countries engaged in this process, in real life the effects can be destructive. Many countries, especially the old industrial ones and those that are overpopulated, are unable to adjust quickly to shifts in their competitive position, i.e. their labour and capital are not blessed with strong mobility (Feis, 1994: 55).

Effectiveness and Ineffectiveness Claims

Claims of effectiveness or ineffectiveness relate to three questions. First, will a social clause decrease protectionist policies, or will it be a protectionist instrument in itself? Second, is a social clause the right expression of solidarity with oppressed workers? Third, will a social clause weaken or strengthen the ILO? Each is examined in turn.

Decreasing or increasing protectionist policies?

The claim related to effectiveness is that an international agreement on a specific set of labour standards neutralizes the forces behind protectionist measures. Claims related to ineffectiveness maintain that a social clause: (a) has a protectionist purpose itself; and (b) is not very effective as a protectionist instrument.

The effectiveness claim is expressed, among others, by the former Director General of the ILO. The reasoning underlying this claim is that there are a number of countries that use unilateral economic measures against countries that violate labour standards, or have engaged in trade agreements that include a labour component. In addition, since in many Northern countries there are strong feelings about 'unfair' competition with Southern countries, the tendency to shelter economies through all sorts of unilateral measures may increase. The argument is therefore that an international agreement on labour standards will decrease the use of these unilateral measures.

This claim is based on the observance that there is no such thing as free trade, and that many forms of protectionism still exist. Old Protectionism, the domain of tariffs and quotas, has from the early days of the GATT been the primary focus of international negotiations. Since its initiation the GATT has organized eight negotiating rounds to reduce tariff barriers to international trade, in which it largely succeeded. Before the establishment of the GATT, average import tariffs in nine major industrial countries were around 35 per cent, while in the 1980s this was reduced to 5 per cent (Ruigrok and van Tulder, 1995: 224). For some countries the difference is even greater: the average level of US tariffs for manufactured imports was 53 per cent in the early 1930s, and 4.9 per cent in the late 1970s (Oxley, 1990: 4, 9).

Nevertheless, the GATT did not entirely lift the barriers to free trade. Besides the fact that there were important exceptions to the elimination of tariffs and quotas through the GATT (for example, in the case of balance of payment problems), New Protectionism consisting of non-tariff barriers, such as administrative measures, subsidies and voluntary export restraints (VERs), gained importance when tariffs decreased. The main stimulation for the erection of non-tariff barriers was the developments that took place in the 1970s, such as increased energy prices, increased competition from some Asian countries and, related to that, the increasing closure of the European Community as a bloc. Although the GATT tried to address these issues in the Tokyo Round of negotiations (1973–9) in order to curtail rising protectionism, the use of non-tariff barriers continued to increase (Gilpin, 1987: 190–204).

This growing use of non-tariff barriers was most visible in the form of VERs and anti-dumping regulations. VERs, previously negotiated outside the GATT mandate, were concentrated in a few sectors (such as services and automobiles), in which they had considerable impact. These sectors were usually characterized by a strong union presence and endured strong competition from NICs and Japan. In the early 1990s, VERs affected around 15 per cent of the world trade. About 33 per cent of Japanese exports to the EU and the United States were covered by VERs (Ruigrok and van Tulder, 1995: 229).

The claim that if countries were to observe certain labour standards then lower trade barriers could be used as a reward has become less significant. The WTO has reached an agreement on abolition of VERs and similar measures. During recent WTO trade policy reviews of the two trading blocks, it was concluded that in the case of the EU the most favoured nation (MFN) tariffs on industrial products are low and declining. And while tariffs on agricultural products are still high, they are also in decline. The review also concluded that in certain areas, such as consumer electronics, textiles and automobiles, high tariffs, along with intensive anti-dumping measures, still exist (TPRB, 1997a).[18] In the case of the United States, zero tariffs apply to one-third of the tariff lines, while MFN tariffs declined in the period 1995–9 from 6.4 to 5.7 per cent. The report also noticed fewer anti-dumping measures (TPRB, 1999).

Because of this steady lowering of tariff and non-tariff barriers one could argue that progress in the WTO will take away a part of the validity of the claim that a social clause is an effective instrument for lessening protectionist policies. However, this may be too optimistic a view on the progress of the liberalization of world trade, for four reasons.

The first reason is that while world trade is liberalized, it is far from free. Tariff and non-tariff barriers still exist in some areas where North–South competition is strong, such as cars, textiles and consumer electronics. For example, in the United States three times the overall average tariffs are applied on certain products, such as textiles and clothing (TPRB, 1999).

The second reason is that in certain areas liberalization may not change the position of the trading partners significantly. For example, the abolition of quotas in the area of textiles and clothing under the Multi-Fibre Arrangement (MFA) will probably not entail a drastic change for Northern importers. In the past quotas were not very effective because of their country-specific nature. This meant that every time an exporter became successful, it attracted quotas, which resulted in a dispensation of trade from the initially successful exporters (mainly large Asia countries) to other low-wage exporters, until these new ones faced quotas. This means that even though quotas will be abolished, Northern concerns about textile and clothing imports will remain in place (ODI, 1995).

The third reason why one should be cautious in thinking that liberalization will continue is that economic setbacks may block liberalization. For example, while its members generally respect the WTO commitments, some Latin American countries have increased certain tariff barriers and introduced administrative and technical measures against imports (TPRB, 1998b).

The fourth reason is that some WTO regulations, such as anti-dumping regulations (which prohibit lowering the prices of goods introduced on a foreign market below the normal value), remain open to interpretation and can still discriminate against low-cost producers (ODI, 1995). Given these reasons, the claim that a social clause could be an effective instrument to reduce the need for protectionist policies may remain valid.

A counter claim argues that a social clause is an ineffective instrument for decreasing protectionist policies because it has a protectionist potential itself (Herzenberg *et al.*, 1990: 4; Dorman, 1995: 25). As Bhagwati puts it, 'A social clause is . . . a way in which fearful unions seek to raise the costs of production in the poor countries as free trade with them threatens their jobs and wages' (Bhagwati, 1994: 60).

There can be no dispute about the fact that certain *unilateral* social clauses include such an aim. For example, the US Overseas Private Investment Corporation (OPIC) offers US companies insurance on their investments in 'friendly' developing countries against matters like the risks of war. When in 1985 the mandate came up for renewal, the AFL-CIO criticized the OPIC for exporting jobs by reducing the risks of foreign investments. Therefore, the US Congress decided to include an amendment that the OPIC should only insure or finance a project if the host country is taking steps to adopt and implement laws that apply internationally recognized labour standards to the domestic situation (Van Liemt, 1989; Venture Dias, 1995: 23). Yet, even though protectionist or foreign policy sentiments may drive a social clause, non-neo-classical economists are more willing to distinguish between protectionist instincts and legitimacy. To quote Langille, 'While it may be true that *some* who argue for international labour rights may be animated by protectionists instincts – that still does not affect the legitimacy of the message – it only tells us something about the messenger' (Langille, 1997: 20).

However, some argue that it is possible to distinguish between fair and protectionist labour standards legislation. According to Mandel, protectionist labour standards legislation would entail laws to prevent the import of *specific goods*. On the other hand, labour legislation promoting fairness would focus on distortions resulting from anti-labour policies and actions. In other words, a comparative advantage in trade should not be allowed to rely on artificially depressed labour standards, which harm workers (Mandel, 1989: 453, 459–60).

If protectionist intentions are the driving force behind a social clause, the question arises as to whether it would be an effective instrument. Hansson argues that from the point of view of protectionism, only social clauses that are cost raising in export economies, and that result in price increases, are beneficial. For the latter requirement to be fulfilled, the export economy must have enough market leverage actually to influence world market prices. He therefore concludes that 'if protectionism is the main aim, there are other more efficient measures to be found in the arsenal of traditional trade barriers as well as among those measures that are associated with "the new protectionism"' (Hansson, 1981: 175). Hence, Northern countries that are mostly concerned with protecting domestic industries may not have an incentive to replace remaining trade-regulatory tools with a social clause, even more so because the application of social clauses is limited to a certain practice (work conditions), while the other tools, such as tariffs, are potentially more far-reaching. This, combined with the fact that a social clause interferes with domestic policies, makes it difficult to imagine that countries would choose social clauses above other measures. De Castro points out that a social clause is ineffective from a protectionist point of view since an improvement of labour conditions in developing countries will not serve as a solution to unemployment in the developed countries. The reason is that in developed countries the share of low-skilled labour costs in the total costs is on the decline, while capital costs, research and development costs and marketing costs are increasing (De Castro, 1995: 11).

Social clause as an expression of solidarity

In the previous section I discussed the claims concerning the possibilities of using a social clause as a protectionist instrument itself. In this section the claim that a social clause is an act of solidarity with oppressed workers is addressed. I review the claims as to whether a social clause is an effective or an ineffective way to express solidarity. The main thought behind the claim that a social clause is effective in this respect is that improving labour standards will not necessarily result in a sharp reduction of economic outcomes.

Hansson claims that enabling labour standards (the ones that are better defined as rights, such as freedom of association) can be seen as an act of solidarity with workers worldwide.[19] This is because the economic effects are dependent on how workers choose to use such rights. Therefore, there are no economic reasons to deny people such rights. However, where other labour standards are sought, such as minimum wages, this would not be a clear act of solidarity, since workers in the formal sector might be better off, but those outside will probably be worse off.[20] Hansson regards a social clause that prohibits child labour as doubtful from the point of view of workers' solidarity, since, if it were enacted without complementary social policies, it would increase the pressure on large-size families. Similarly, the effects of a social clause on working hours are probably negative, even for workers in those export sectors covered by a clause. This is because although wages might increase, the new mix of working hours and wages could also be negative. With respect to health and safety, workers that remain employed in the formal sector might again be better off, but the resulting unemployment is negative for the rest of the workers. In sum, if solidarity is limited to workers in export industries, all standards discussed will have positive effects or keep the status quo, with the exception of hours of work (and probably child labour). The fact that a social clause will concentrate on standards only in the export sector has negative effects for workers outside this sector. However, Hansson claims that if an exporting country is able to increase the international price of its exporting goods, the negative effects of a social clause will be reduced (Hansson, 1981: 175–9).

A similar study applying trade theory to international labour standards was conducted by Brown *et al.* (1993; cited in Dorman, 1995: 17–18). They conclude that exporters of labour-intensive goods can profit from higher labour standards. The reason is that higher labour standards decrease the availability of labour as a factor of production, which is translated into higher wages and subsequently increased prices. For example, countries that forbid the previously condoned practice of using forced labour in labour-intensive industries will increase costs. Again, however, increased prices will only occur if such an exporting country is able to transfer its high costs into high prices, which for most goods is only possible if exporting countries join hands. In addition, higher labour costs may stimulate capital-intensive industries – only located in a country to be closer to consumers – to move production to other parts of the world (Van Beers, 1996: 999).

In sum, Hansson has shown that a social clause may improve the situation of those working in the export sector, but at the same time it may worsen the situation for workers in other sectors. Since working conditions in the export sector are often better than those in the rest of the economy (Edgren, 1979: 525; Caire, 1994: 304), one can doubt whether a social clause will improve working conditions significantly. This has led some to claim that a social clause is an expression of solidarity with a limited part of the population, and that this selective solidarity will be at the expense of workers in other parts of the economy (FIAN, 1995). Moreover, a social clause will be more effective in improving working conditions in countries that rely heavily on export (De Castro, 1995: 13–14).

The effectiveness of a social clause as an expression of solidarity is further complicated by the question of whether it can rectify the abuse of workers. The problem referred to here is that the non-enforcement of certain rights is not only because governments do not care, but also because the social structures underlying work conditions are so persistent that they cannot be changed easily. An often-cited example is child labour. Besides the fact that child labour is only partly linked to export activities, a problem mentioned above, a related problem concerns the question: what happens to family welfare if children are denied work in certain sectors (Srinivasan, 1994: 37)? Some fear that they will find work in even more hazardous employments, such as prostitution (De Castro, 1995: 13). The argument is that if child labour is only tackled from a legal angle, without provisions that help families to cope with poverty and children to obtain education, a trade-related measure to force governments to end child labour may not be effective. On the other hand, there are some countries, such as Pakistan or Myanmar, which are persistent violators of human rights (including labour rights). In these countries, it is mainly the lack of will rather than the lack of ability that induces the government to deny rights.

A strengthened or weakened ILO?

The third effectiveness claim is that the solidarity of developed countries with workers in developing countries requires multilateral labour standards. If labour standards are voluntary, which is the basis of the ILO, developing countries will hesitate to implement labour standards because of a fear of losing competitiveness (Emmerij, 1994: 323–4). It is therefore claimed that some force is needed to make developing countries adopt labour standards.

In contrast, it is claimed that such enforcement would only decrease the adoption of labour standards. Since the ILO is based on the principle of voluntarism (meaning that the Conventions of the ILO need to be ratified by countries in order to evoke any action by the ILO), a link between the ILO and the WTO may have a negative impact on the level of ratification of the ILO Conventions. This claim will only be true if countries ratifying a Convention have no intention of implementing it and are suddenly forced to do so under the threat of sanctions. In addition, the chain of events that took place recently has overtaken this claim. The ILO Declaration on Fundamental Principles and Rights at Work that was discussed above has made the principles underlying the eight core Conventions applicable to all member states of the ILO, irrespective of ratification. Hence, while the specifics of the eight core Conventions still need ratification, the underlying larger principles do not.

Spillover and Exclusion Claims

As discussed above, non-tariff matters have been on the agenda since the Tokyo Round of the GATT. The start of the GATT Uruguay Round in 1986 provided a landmark with respect to the number of new non-tariff issues that have entered the international trade agenda. These issues are Trade-related Intellectual Property Rights (TRIPs), Trade-related Investment Measures (TRIMs), environmental regulations and the General Agreement on Trade in Services (GATS). As Esty notes, 'as one field of nontariff barriers is cut down, another one springs up as protectionist interests find new ways to bend the rules of the trading system for their own benefit' (Esty, 1994: 24).

For some, these developments provide justification for a claim in favour of a social clause. They interpreted the trading system as allowing for the inclusion of labour standards. For others, the inclusion of non-tariff issues does not provide any grounds to include labour standards. The spillover claim consists of four arguments.

First, it is argued that because the mandate of the WTO has been enlarged compared to that of the GATT, there is a new incentive to consider the inclusion of labour standards.

Second, the spillover claim argues that even though some of these new issues are not trade-specific (i.e. they are not tradable), they are trade-related. The inclusion of TRIPs and environmental issues in the WTO are aimed at alleviating the negative effects of intellectual piracy and the negative effects of economic development on the environment. Labour would also be classified as trade-related, and not as trade-specific (Hughes and Wilkinson, 1998: 380–1).

Third, the prime reason why the new issues have been brought up in the GATT/WTO framework, especially the TRIMs, is that they are considered to be trade distorting. In the spirit of neo-classical trade theory, these issues were tackled in order to eliminate policy obstacles to perfect competition (Hirst and Thompson, 1996: 56–7).[21] The question is whether differences in labour standards are trade distorting. Those in favour of a social clause may give an affirmative answer: 'Denial of worker rights takes unfair advantage of the world trading system' (Pease, 1994: 51).

Fourth, in practice labour standards are already regarded as trade issues. As we have seen in Chapter 1, the GATT allowed governments to take measures against goods produced by prison labour (Article XX). The WTO has a similar provision in Article XXIII. In addition, there is unilateral and regional trade legislation that includes labour provisions. These are most prominent in the United States. The fact that there already exists legislation in this area demonstrates that labour standards are regarded as trade-related issues.

On the other hand, the exclusion claim argues that the case for the other non-tariff issues is a distinct one when compared with the case for a social clause. Bhagwati argues that a social clause, unlike provisions on intellectual property rights (IPRs), is not about economic efficiency. Moreover, in contrast to labour standards, these issues are trade-related since, for example, they refer to trade in technology (in the case of IPRs) or resurrect rules that are parallel trade rules (such as the avoidance of local content rules in the case of TRIMs) (Bhagwati, 1994: 57–8). The exclusion claim is also put forward by some developing countries, like India. It is argued that the non-tariff issues should not have been incorporated in the first place, so why consider additional non-tariff issues (Wilkinson, 1999a: 6–7)?

The pursuit of a labour standards provision seems to be analogous to the question of environmental provisions. There are some interesting parallels between the two issues, especially with respect to notions such as fairness and morality (Charnovitz, 1994: 21–2). However, it is often pointed out that there is one important difference between the two issues. Environmental issues may have physical externalities, while labour issues are perceived not to have these (see Charnovitz, 1994). Because of these externalities, free traders (neo-classical economists) and environmentalists tend to see intervention on behalf of the environment as legitimate. Many neo-classical economists envisage trade as a tool to enforce international environmental agreements aimed at addressing global or transboundary pollution spillovers (Esty, 1994: 51). The fact that physical transboundary effects are not perceived to be important as far as labour standards are concerned makes a similar consensus between neo-classical economists and labour rights activists difficult to conceive.[22]

Sovereignty and Interventionist Claims

Not interfering in the domestic affairs of other states is a strong guiding principle of international relations. A social clause interferes with the domestic affairs of a country, and will thus limit the regulatory freedom of an individual country. Not surprisingly, countries with lower labour standards often put forward this objection to a social clause (Emmerij, 1994: 324).

However, claiming sovereignty can go hand-in-hand with supporting a social clause. The argument in this case goes as follows. Because of increased internationalization of the economy and mobility of capital, the regulatory power of states has been limited, or is perceived to be limited (see Hirst and Thompson, 1996). One way of dealing with this (perceived) decreased autonomy would be to reclaim sovereignty by entering into multilateral standard setting arrangements that avoid regulatory competition (Langille, 1997: 34).

The Discourse of the ICFTU

The significant role the ICFTU played in all three organizations demands a description of the ICFTU's four main claims in defence of a social clause. The first claim is a spillover claim and is based on two arguments. The first argument maintains that the fact that the GATT has recognized a relationship between trade and 'non-trade' issues, such as intellectual property rights, has created a precedent for labour standards (ICFTU, 1986). The second argument for a spillover claim is that the GATT/WTO already interferes in national policies to ensure fair trade; for example, in the form of anti-dumping provisions (ICFTU, 1989b: 1–2).

The second claim is the universality claim. It is argued that standards proposed by the ICFTU are among the most widely ratified ILO Conventions, and can therefore not be considered to be developed countries' standards (ICFTU, 1995c).

The third claim is a sovereignty claim, countering the argument that a social clause is a breach of national sovereignty. The ICFTU argues: 'A workers' rights clause would restore sovereignty by allowing policy to be determined through negotiations – providing a counterweight to the enormous economic muscle of TNCs. Its aim is not to limit power [of governments], but to limit the abuse of power' (ICFTU, 1998a: 28).

The fourth claim is a combination of an economic and an effectiveness claim. The argument is that a social clause will be beneficial for developing countries. It will not hurt countries' comparative advantage or stimulate protectionism. The reason is that a social clause does not include a global minimum wage but will support workers in choosing their own working conditions. Minimum standards would help to ensure that competition facilitates social development instead of exploiting workers (ICFTU, 1994c: 4): 'The primary beneficiaries would, in fact, be the developing countries wishing to ensure balanced social development and most vulnerable to cut throat competition on the basis of labour exploitation' (ICFTU, 1994c: 4).

Through the elimination of exploitation, competition will be focused on improving productivity rather than on decreasing wages and working conditions. In this way, a social clause will contribute to constructive competition because a minimum floor will reward good employment practices (ICFTU, n.d.a: 6). In addition, the Confederation has produced the argument that protectionist pressures will be harder to resist without the introduction of a social clause (ICFTU 1986). Political support for trade liberalization might break down if nothing is done about differences in labour standards:

> In many countries, of both the industrialized and developing world, political leaders are under pressure from various groups that perceive their jobs to be threatened by foreign competition. Political support for trade liberalization is fragile when electors are being invited to, in effect, back a vague but general promise that increased competition will improve the general welfare while a large number of specific groups of workers face worsened conditions of employment or redundancy. (ICFTU, 1994c: 2)

This line of reasoning is not restricted to trade liberalization, but extends to democracy as a whole. Rising unemployment, poverty and social disintegration create a fertile ground for anti-democratic forces, the ICFTU argues. Democratic leaders should use trade policy to show that they are aware of the necessity to combine social security and economic flexibility (ICFTU, 1994c: 2–3). To gain support from its members in developed countries the ICFTU emphasizes that labour standards are a necessary component of trade liberalization, since pressure on wages inhibits the development of global demand and the growth of consumer markets in developing countries. The growth of consumer markets will result in rising employment. Because of the growing interdependence of countries, respect for core labour standards should be a worldwide process (ICFTU, 1994c: 2–3; n.d.a: 6).

Noteworthy is that in most circumstances the ICFTU tries not to be associated with the argument that a social clause solves the problem of unemployment in the North resulting from the competition in labour standards. Therefore, it refers to a *perceived* threat to jobs (see citation above). However, an exception to this is found in the comments of the ICFTU on the OECD report on labour standards.

Conclusion: Two Discourses

In the previous sections I discussed the theoretical and normative considerations that form the basis of claims and counter-claims that characterize the debate on labour standards. In this concluding section, the claims are organized and brought under the umbrella of two discourses.

The first discourse is that of interventionism. The phrase 'interventionist discourse' is chosen to emphasize the differences from the phrase 'neo-liberal discourse', which is the second one. It does not imply that neo-liberal policy-making cannot include interventionist strategies. In the end, however, the differences between the two perspectives are more ideological than practical: whether non-tariff barriers such as subsidies are chosen, or whether tariff barriers, such as quotas are chosen, or whether it is chosen to refrain from this kind of intervention is ultimately a decision made by governments to ensure their goals (Langille, 1994: 332–3).

The *interventionist* discourse is characterized by a number of claims in favour of a social clause. First, the universality claim maintains that some labour standards are to be respected under all circumstances, even though there should be space for flexibility. Second, the socio-economic claim, based on a variety of arguments, maintains that disparities in labour standards lead to industrial and financial relocation on the basis of unfair practices. Third, the effectiveness claim tells us that if core labour standards are left to the discretion of individual governments, they will not be enacted because of the fear of losing competitiveness. Fourth, the spillover claim argues that there is little or no difference between issues such as labour standards, environmental standards or IPR standards with respect to possible inclusion in the WTO. Fifth, the sovereignty claim maintains that national legislation is under pressure from international economic developments, which have limited the ability of states to regulate domestic affairs. A social clause would be a way to reclaim this sovereignty.

The *neo-classical* discourse argues against a social clause. First, the relativity claim entails that human rights, including labour rights, are not equally valuable in all societies. Second, socio-economic claims are based on the argument that the setting of labour standards is a function of the free market. Third, the ineffectiveness claim provides four basic arguments against the social clause. The first is that if it has positive effects, they will be limited to the export sector. In addition, the non-enforcement of labour standards is the result not of the lack of goodwill, but of the lack of abilities. Moreover, the enforcement of a social clause will be unevenly spread because of prevailing power structures, and it threatens the ILO, as this organization is based on voluntarism. Fourth, the exclusion claim holds that there is no place for labour standards in the WTO, since they are not trade-related issues. Finally, the sovereignty claim stipulates that a social clause would be at odds with the notion of sovereignty.

One has to keep in mind that the two discourses outlined are ideal types. Even though some claims are more mutually compatible than others, they are not necessarily equally supported by the propagators of a certain discourse. For example, even among those who see a positive role for labour standards, who seem to accept that there are core labour rights and who believe that social and economic development should take place simultaneously, preferences regarding the specific tools of promoting these rights differ.[23] In addition, many of those supporting a social clause do not support the theory that wage inequality and unemployment are caused by low labour standards in other countries.

Moreover, supporting certain claims of a neo-classical discourse with respect to a social clause does not mean that these claims are also used on other occasions. In the international arena, states that make use of a neo-classical discourse are at the same time carrying out interventionist policies at home.

Throughout this book, I refer to the role that the two discourses play in the debates in the different national and international arenas (practices). The two discourses simplify the reality. Therefore, they should be understood as a way of classifying arguments into certain theoretical and normative contexts.

Notes

1. Claims are statements presented as true for a fact, but lacking sufficient proof or disputed. These claims are supported by arguments, which are statements to support a claim, in order to convince others of the correctness of a claim.
2. Others have also tried to make sense of the vast amount of arguments circulating at present. See, for example, Langille (1997), who classified the arguments in groups of human rights, efficiency, collective action problems, sovereignty, pragmatic, political consistency, institutional and 'rock bottom' issues.
3. Together the two Covenants and the Declaration form the International Bill of Rights.
4. However, even he sees the prohibition of slavery as a universal right (Bhagwati, 1994: 59).
5. References to 'imports' or 'trade' include imports from industries relocated to low-cost countries and imports originating from locally owned industries. In addition, trade often takes place between subsidiaries of the same company. In this section, these issues are not further specified, as they do not affect the nature of the relationship between employment, wage inequality and trade. However, in the next section, relocation is further considered as it provides an often-heard argument in favour of a social clause.
6. An example of a positive relationship is the production of clothing. Because of its high labour-intensity, low labour costs are an important factor determining comparative advantage (Van Liemt, 1992: 456).
7. According to Dorman, differences in the outcomes between most studies can be explained by the assumptions, methodologies and quality of the data (Dorman, 1995: 1).
8. An exception is labour-intensive production, which will relocate more easily to low-wage countries than capital-intensive production (Hirst and Thompson, 1996: 117–18).
9. The call for international labour standards is not necessarily supported by all those that fall into the category 'neo-institutionalists'. In addition, one could undoubtedly think of many other perspectives on the debate, but these two tend to dominate the labour standards–trade debate.
10. Nevertheless, neo-classical economists would also agree with a minimum list of labour standards (Herzenberg *et al.*, 1990: 4).
11. Note that there are differences among neo-classical economists too. For example, Ohlin suggested in 1956, in a report studying the social aspect

of European integration, that free trade could be helped by adopting a minimum level of labour standards (Charnovitz, 1995: 10). However, his (and his group's) remarks were very cautious (Hansson, 1981: 20–1).
12. Srinivasan argues that hourly wages above the market-clearing wage would result in unemployment (Srinivasan, 1990: 67–70).
13. Direct government intervention refers to legislation on workplace issues, such as collective bargaining, or improving employment earning opportunities (Fields, 1990: 21).
14. This argument is put forward by some non-neo-classical economists (Herzenberg et al., 1990: 7–8).
15. Note that these notions have a strong psychological dimension. They are metaphors that help to stimulate certain sentiments. For example, the term social dumping seems to refer to the general issue of dumping, a generally rejected measure (Myrdal, 1994: 349).
16. Among these are theories concentrating on the explanation of intra-industry trade, the oligopolist nature of corporations and technology gaps between countries (see Gilpin, 1987: 176; Ruigrok and van Tulder, 1995).
17. Some neo-classical economists could see merit in the arguments supporting the protection of declining industries, since they are analogous to the protection of infant industries, which some neo-classical economists find legitimate (Gilpin, 1987: 183–9).
18. In 2000, the EU was criticized by the WTO for its high tariffs on textile, clothing and agricultural products (TPRB, 2000).
19. Hanson's study includes the effects on labour-surplus economies and full-employment economies. I refer only to the conclusions with respect to labour-surplus economies, as they are most relevant for developing countries.
20. This is in line with the neo-classical argument made earlier about the dichotomy between the formal and informal sectors.
21. Hirst and Thompson have argued that: 'to a large extent the way GATT has treated the TRIM issue derives from an intellectual milieu that no longer conforms either to the features of the evolving international economy or to a robust theoretical orthodoxy' (Hirst and Thompson, 1996: 57).
22. I deliberately use the word 'perceived', as bad labour conditions can stimulate workers to work in countries where they may be treated better, even if their work is illegal. Some may argue that this is a physical externality.
23. Tools other than a social clause include better terms of trade and the restreaming of public capital, as in aid or lending (Caire, 1994: 304).

4 THE FAIR TRADE DISCOURSE ON INTERNATIONAL LABOUR STANDARDS: THE CASE OF THE UNITED STATES

Since the early 1980s the US government, supported by the trade unions, has pursued the inclusion of labour rights in national trade legislation or in international agreements. In the period between 1985 and 1990 alone, Congress introduced more than 40 Bills related to trade or financial aid and labour standards, albeit with an enormous variety in subject matter. Sometimes a Bill concerned nothing more than, for example, a prohibition of import of motor vehicles from Yugoslavia until internationally recognized workers' rights were afforded (HR 3853). In other cases, it concerned the definition of the denial of workers' rights as an unfair and unreasonable trade practice (S 497). Frequently, the bills introduced targeted the former Soviet Union's and China's forced labour practices (see, for example, HR 1331, HR 2468, HR 4812 and S 1420) (Thomas, 2000).

Even though the inclusion of workers' rights in trade agreements became an important topic for the AFL-CIO, the fact that in the 1980s the labour rights issue started to play an important role in US trade policies had reasons beyond the AFL-CIO's influence, such as the increasing trade deficit. In 1984, this deficit was estimated to be US$123 billion, of which about one-third was with Japan alone. The sheer amount of dollars involved made trade not only a top priority, but also an important issue in elections (Destler, 1992: 88–9; O'Shea, 1993: 43).

The first issue addressed in this chapter is US domestic enforcement of core labour standards. While the American rhetoric on the importance of labour standards is strong, the actual labour standards situation in the United States leaves a lot to be desired. The United States has ratified fewer Conventions than India, and its federal laws show gaps with respect to the coverage of the content of the ILO Conventions.

The next section analyses the efforts of the AFL-CIO to include labour standards in a number of unilateral and multilateral trade laws. Discussed are: (a) the 1984 Generalized System of Preferences (GSP) renewal; (b) the conclusion of the NAFTA (1990–4); and (c) the Trade and Omnibus Act 1988 in connection to the GATT negotiations and the Uruguay Round Agreements Act (1986–94). The last part of this chapter addresses the influence of the AFL-CIO on the debate and the trade legislation that has been enacted.

Core Labour Standards: *De Jure* and *De Facto*

The United States sets one of the worst examples when it comes to the ratification of the ILO's core labour standards. It has only ratified two out of the eight Conventions that refer to core labour standards: Convention 105 on the abolition of forced labour and Convention 182 on the abolition of the worst forms of child labour. However, even if not ratified, the content of most core standards is (partly) covered by domestic legislation.[1]

The Fair Labor Standards Act 1938 (FLSA) regulates child labour in the United States. It stipulates that children under eighteen years of age employed in non-agricultural occupations are not permitted to work in hazardous employments, while children between the ages of fourteen and sixteen are not allowed to work more than three hours a day. Children under fourteen years of age are not allowed to perform any industrial work. Both the federal and state laws offer less protection for children working in agriculture than in other occupations, as the FLSA does not cover work on family farms. Children above sixteen are allowed to work in all hazardous agricultural employment, and between twelve and fifteen they are allowed to work unlimited hours in non-hazardous forms of employment. While about four million children (under eighteen) are legally employed in the United States, one to two million children are illegally employed (American Academy of Paediatrics, 1995: GAO, 1998a: 22–4). About 14,000 children under the age of fourteen are said to work in sweatshops (ICFTU, 1999: 10).

Agriculture is seen as the most dangerous area where children work. Because of its strenuous and seasonal character, it has negative effects on children's education (NCL, n.d.a; GAO, 1998a: 8). Estimates of the number of children working in agriculture vary widely. In 1997, around 155,000 children between fifteen to seventeen years old worked in US agriculture. More than a third of these were illegal children who entered the United States unaccompanied by their parents (GAO, 1998a: 15–16). Other estimates say that about 800,000 (!) children under sixteen work in agriculture as seasonal and migrant workers (NCL, n.d.a). In 1998, President

Clinton announced the start of the Child Labor Initiative to combat abusive child labour and to increase education opportunities (GAO, 1998a: 10).

There is a vast amount of law prohibiting job discrimination. Examples on the federal level are the following. Title VII of the Civil Rights Act 1964 prohibits employment discrimination related to race, colour, religion, sex or national origin. The Equal Pay Act 1963 aims to protect males and females who perform equal work in the same establishment from discrimination based on sex. People aged 40 and over are protected against age discrimination (the Age Discrimination in Employment Act 1967). Finally, disabled people are protected against discrimination not based on qualification through Title I of the Americans with Disabilities Act 1990 and Section 501 of the Rehabilitation Act 1973 (US Equal Employment Opportunity Commission, 1998a).

Despite the numerous laws in place, they are not sufficient to prevent discrimination occurring in practice. Immigrants and ethnic minorities are discriminated against on the US labour market (Bendick, 1998). While most discrimination complaints are settled through private law suits, others are brought before public commissions. In 1998, the Equal Opportunity Commission received almost 80,000 complaints about discrimination, of which more than 36 per cent were related to race (US Equal Employment Opportunity Commission, 1998b). An even larger category was a 'combined' category of practices covered by 'retaliation against an individual for filing a charge of discrimination, participating in an investigation, or opposing discriminatory practices'. The percentage here is almost 46 (US Equal Employment Opportunity Commission, 1998b).

Despite the prohibition of forced labour by US law and by ILO Convention 105, unions argue that it does occur in the form of prison labour. The reason for this is that 21 states have statutes that compel prisoners to work, while other states punish those who do not work by, for example, denying earlier release (AFL-CIO, 1997a; ICFTU, 1999).

Freedom of association in the United States, as in many countries, is a complicated matter. Large numbers of American workers, in the public and private sectors, are prevented from enjoying trade union rights and participation in collective bargaining, either by law or by fact. In the public sector, the Federal Labor Relations Act and the Civil Service Reform Act deny more than two million federal employees the right to strike or to enter into collective bargaining over hours, wages and other forms of economic benefits (ILO, 1993; ICFTU, 1999). On the state level there are large differences, but almost half of all state employees (about seven million) are not allowed to bargain collectively (ICFTU, 1999). The ILO Committee on Freedom of

Association confirmed in 1993 that the exclusion of public servants from collective bargaining rights is performed on too broad a basis (ILO, 1993). In the private sector, the ICFTU has estimated that about one in every ten workers is illegally fired because of union campaigning, suggesting that the law does not sufficiently protect workers. Access to employers' property to inform workers about joining a union can be legally denied. Agricultural and domestic workers are not covered by federal legislation (ICFTU, 1999), although some states have special laws covering these categories of workers.

Trade Unions and the Emergence of the Fair Trade Discourse

The interest of trade unions in 'fair' trade

For three decades after the Second World War the United States was one of the strongest supporters of free trade. However, in the 1980s the increasing trade deficit led to a dominance of aggressive unilateralism over non-discriminatory multilateralism. This aggressive unilateralism, i.e. the strategy of threatening to close the US market to competitors who do not want to open their own or who make use of unfair practices, was expressed in a number of trade remedy laws (Destler, 1992: 21, 125). The notion of trade remedy refers to procedures, developed in the 1930s, to protect US interests against imports through, for example, anti-dumping regulations. These laws were designed to lessen the effects of 'unfair' foreign competition on US firms (LAC, 1988: 9; O'Shea, 1993: 41; Salvatore, 1993: 312–13). Among these laws were those dealing with labour standards.

One of the discourses upon which the strategy of aggressive unilateralism was based was that trade should be fair. The fair trade discourse included the economic claim that the 'playing field' of trade relations needed to be levelled in such a way that countries could compete without foul play, such as deliberately lowering labour standards to decrease production costs and therefore consumer prices, or limiting market access (Low, 1993: 27–8). This fair trade discourse came to dominate US trade policy and helped to contain the rising social conflict over trade. On the basis of this discourse the road was paved for greater government intervention in trade-related areas. However, the interests behind these interventions were diffuse. While there were those who linked their own economic interests to the welfare of workers abroad, for others the fair trade discourse was a welcome diversion from the fact that protectionism, rather than fairness, was the most important motive.

Not only were the interests diffuse, the shape of the government intervention was also a matter of dispute. In some cases the US government used the fair trade discourse to justify threats and actions against foreign countries to protect US industry; in other cases it was used to force foreign countries to increase their liberalization efforts. More specifically, while most called for 'fair trade', not all agreed that the increasing trade deficit had to be fought by protectionist policies against foreign competitors (Low, 1993: 14–15, 27–8). For example, President Clinton used the trade deficit as a call for opening up foreign markets in his 1992 election campaign, and this was also the position of Republican governments in the 1980s. On the other hand, Lane Kirkland, the President of the AFL-CIO, wanted to solve the trade deficit through changes in trade policy, which should include effective workers' rights provisions and provisions to curb other unfair trading practices. At the same time he maintained that the 'competitive advantage in trade should not be derived from the denial of the right to freedom of association, the refusal to ensure a safe work environment, the exploitation of child labor and other such reprehensible practices' (Kirkland, 1987: 12).

The fear of liberalization had not always been characteristic of the AFL-CIO. After the Second World War the AFL-CIO supported trade liberalization as a means to combat communism, and was equipped with enough confidence to be fearless of the potential competition from low wages. When the AFL-CIO started to embrace the fair trade discourse, as illustrated by the demands for trade-related labour standards and trade adjustment assistance, this was done out of a mixture of genuine solidarity with workers in other countries and self-interest (Hecker, 1993: 356–64).

There was certainly reason for the AFL-CIO to be fearful of foreign competition. Two of its strongest affiliates, the Union of Needletraders, Industrial and Textile Employees (UNITE!) and the United Automobile, Aerospace and Agricultural Implement Workers of America (UAW) were both experiencing the hardship of global competition. In the area of textiles, major production growth had taken place in some of the Asian economies since the 1980s, mostly at the expense of Japan, the United States and European countries. The United States, although still considered to be a leading exporter, developed a major trade deficit in textiles (US$3.1 billion in 1995). While the United States is still the second largest employer in the clothing sector, in 1995 this sector had a trade deficit of US$34.7 billion, with a growing proportion of these imports coming from Mexico and the Caribbean. Between 1970 and 1993, a total of 700,000 US jobs were lost in these industries (Dicken, 1998: 286–311).

However, while imports from countries with low wages have an adverse impact on employment, there is still doubt about the importance of this factor compared to that of other factors, such as productivity changes. For example, in the area of textile production, recent technological innovations in spinning speeds alone have decreased the requirement for labour by about 40 per cent. While the increase in productivity has partly been a response to increased competition, much of this competition came from other developed countries (Dicken, 1998: 311–12). Dicken concludes that:

> There is no doubt at all that such imports have adversely affected employment in the textiles and clothing industries of the industrialized economies. But it is misleading to attribute all – or even, in some cases, most – of the blame directly to this single cause. (Dicken, 1998: 311)

On the other hand, UNITE! believes that economists tend to underestimate the effect of trade. Rapid changes in information technology have made it unnecessary for producers to be located close to consumers, the union argues. UNITE! estimates that in 1999, 100,000 jobs were lost due to increased competition (interview with UNITE!, 4 February 2000).

The automobile industry has also experienced strong shifts in production. In the 1970s and 1980s, Japan became the single largest producer of cars. While still being the second largest producer, the United States saw its world share of production decrease from 51.4 per cent in 1960 to 17.1 per cent in 1995. US car companies moved the largest part of their production abroad. In the 1980s, employment in the US automobile industry fell by 24 per cent. Less than in the textile and clothing industry, these changes are attributable to a shift of automobile production to developing countries because of low wages.[2] Employment decreases are mainly caused by the slow growth in demand, the inability of the USA to produce small and fuel-efficient cars, the expansion of US car manufacturers in – mainly – other developed countries and the high import penetration of Japanese cars (Dicken, 1998: 316–50). Another factor responsible for the transnationalization of the US car industry has been the attempts of auto manufacturers to limit the bargaining power of labour. When, in the 1980s, the US car manufacturers expanded into Canada and Mexico, this was 'not only an attempt to reduce costs but also to circumvent . . . domestic bargaining partners and search for more compliant trade unions and governments in neighbouring countries' (Ruigrok and van Tulder, 1993: 407).

While one can question the impact of the individual factors on the production shifts of US companies in the areas of textiles, clothing and car manufacturing, it is logical that US unions, representing workers in the sectors affected by shifts, would look at the role of labour rights in these shifts. That is why the UAW and UNITE! have been actively involved in supporting the inclusion of labour rights in trade agreements.

For the AFL-CIO, campaigning for the inclusion of labour rights in trade agreements has been an important field of activity. In 1985, two unions representing textile and clothing workers – later merging into UNITE! – had about 438,000 members, making it the ninth single largest union of the AFL-CIO, with more than 90 affiliates. In the same year, the UAW accounted for 974,000 members, making it the second largest affiliate (AFL-CIO, 1995: 220–1). The decreasing employment in both sectors is reflected in the membership numbers for 1999. In that year, UAW counted 745,000 members, while UNITE! counted only 210,000 members. This made UAW in 1999 the fifth largest affiliate of the AFL-CIO, and UNITE! the eighteenth largest affiliate. Illustrating the rising importance of new sectors, the third largest affiliate in 1999 was the International Union of Service Employees. This union grew between 1985 and 1999 from 688,000 members to 1,104,000 members (AFL-CIO, 1999: 96–7). In 1999, the AFL-CIO had 68 affiliated unions (AFL-CIO, 1999: 96–7).

The fact that UAW and UNITE! declined in importance has also been reflected in the AFL-CIO expenditure on international affairs. While in 1995 the international affairs division had more than US$5 million to spend, this was halved in 1998. This cut mainly benefited field mobilization, which saw an increase in its expenses from more than US$12 million in 1995 to almost US$19 million in 1998 (AFL-CIO, 1997b: 52–3; AFL-CIO, 1999: 82; interview with UNITE!, 4 February 2000).

In addition to the decreasing importance of the old industrial unions there are two other reasons for this decline in funding. For one, the leadership of the AFL-CIO has changed, and so did priorities. Second, with the end of the Cold War the international usefulness of the AFL-CIO for the US government has decreased. While the government used to fund many of the Federation's international activities, it is far less willing to fund the AFL-CIO's critical attitude towards globalization (UNITE!, 4 February 2000).

This decreasing attention to international affairs does not necessarily mean that labour standards and trade relations receive less attention than in the past. Without the Cold War to dominate the international agenda of the AFL-CIO, the international affairs programme was able to concentrate on other matters, such as supporting workers' interests in international financial institutions (AFL-CIO, n.d.).[3] In addition, some of the industrial affiliates, such as UNITE!, have increased their own international activities' funding (UNITE!, 4 February 2000).

Trade unions and the Democratic Party

From the mid-1970s onwards, the changing attitude towards trade was also noticeable in the Democratic Party. Traditionally one of the strongest supporters of free trade, the Democrats became increasingly in favour of protection of domestic production (Hecker, 1993: 356–64).

The Democratic Party is very important for the trade unions. Trade unionists believe that Democratic Party weakness affects their position (Dark, 1999). It is a mutually beneficial relationship, as trade unions have some capabilities that make politicians of the Democratic Party susceptible to their demands. First of all, Democratic candidates can rely on union members to work as volunteers in their campaigns. Second, the AFL-CIO has 13 million members (5 per cent of the total US population), and when the unions endorse a candidate – which is almost always one with a Democratic background – this candidate can count not only on the votes of the largest part of these members, but also on some of the votes of the members' families (Interview with AFL-CIO, 31 January 2000). Peter D. Hart Research Associates' survey concluded that in 1992 twice the number of union members voted for Clinton as for Bush (compared to all adults) (Peter D. Hart Research Associates, 1993). The third reason why congressmen of the Democratic Party may be more susceptible to trade unions' wishes is that trade unions finance part of their campaigns. The AFL-CIO maintains that the

> spending by big business overwhelms the AFL-CIO's campaign. Corporate interests are – and always have been – far outspending labor in all areas of the political arena, including PAC [Political Action Committees] and individual campaign contributions and so-called 'soft' money contributions, as well as in voter education. (AFL-CIO, 1996)

This does not mean that the financial side can be neglected. Unions' soft money contributions (money spent outside the federal regulatory framework on, for instance, issue advocacy) are estimated to be in the billions of dollars. Hard money, spent on federal candidates, is believed to be much less. Still, in 1996, labour PACs spent about US$48 million on federal candidates (22 per cent of PAC total), compared to the US$141 million (65 per cent of PAC total) of business PACs (Cantor, 1997). Also important is that unions spend their money much more strategically than business PACs. Unions predominantly spend their money on Democrats, while the other PAC donations have less uniformity (Dark, 1999: 149–50). In 1996, Democrats received about 92 per cent of all labour PACs donations. In contrast, most money from business PACs goes to Republican candidates (Cantor, 1997). Finally, of the many interest groups operating in the US political arena, trade unions are among the easiest for the Democratic Party to work with. Not only are the unions willing to support Democratic policies, because of the wide variety of issues that unions represent they are also willing to make compromises and to work on issues that are not their first priority (Dark, 1999: 148–9). The willingness to make compromises was illustrated during the 1992 Clinton election campaign. When the unions endorsed Clinton, this showed that 'Disagreements over trade were offset by Clinton's decision to place health care reform at the center of his campaign and by his call for an increase in the minimum wage' (Dark, 1999: 162).

The 1984 GSP Renewal

In the 1980s, one of the first initiatives for legislation around labour standards concerned the GSP. The GSP gives duty-free access to some products from some developing countries. In 1984, during the renewal process of the GSP, it was determined that those countries wishing to benefit from these preferences should guarantee certain internationally recognized workers' rights within their territory.

The inclusion of workers' rights in the GSP was preceded by a similar inclusion in the Caribbean Basin Initiative (CBI). However, this programme is more limited than the GSP because of the number of countries eligible under the programme and because of the lack of petition rights for interested parties (Lawyers Committee for Human Rights, 1988: 34–7). The 1984 renewal of the GSP was accompanied by a heated discussion. Besides the fact that the renewal itself gave cause for debate, as the Republicans were more in favour of renewal than the Democrats, the inclusion of workers' rights was quite remarkable, since in the 1980s the USA was governed by the Republicans.[4]

Resistance to the GSP renewal: 1984

The Republican Reagan administration wanted GSP renewal, but did not want labour standards (*Inside US Trade*, 23 November 1984: 7). The main reason for the support for renewal of the GSP was that it illustrated the USA's willingness to make sacrifices for a liberal trading system, and the

Republicans hoped that GSP renewal would create goodwill among developing countries. This goodwill was seen as a valuable asset in GATT negotiations (Destler, 1992: 84). However, the increasing trade deficit made support for GSP renewal not at all popular among those wanting to protect the domestic industries and jobs. One of the strongest voices against GSP renewal came from the AFL-CIO and affiliated unions (Interviews with House of Representatives, 9 June 1997; UAW, 31 January 2000).

Some Democrats, such as Representative Richard Gephardt, shared the fear of decreasing competitiveness if some rival trading powers were to be rewarded with easier market access. Despite this Democratic support, a labour-supported amendment of Gephardt to exclude preferences for Hong Kong, Korea and Taiwan from the GSP was defeated (Destler, 1992: 84–8).[5] Together with Singapore, these countries accounted in 1983 for 80 per cent of the GSP imports (Harvey, 1995: 2). While this made the GSP biased towards countries not really needing this originally development-oriented instrument, the GSP affected only about 3 per cent of US total imports. This was very small, even though it did concern sensitive products such as textiles and shoes (Destler, 1992: 84). It took until 1988 before the United States Trade Representative (USTR) decided to graduate the four Asian countries from the programme (Lawyers Committee for Human Rights, 1988: 36–7).

The inclusion of labour standards in GSP

While the proposal to exclude Hong Kong, Korea and Taiwan from the GSP preferences did not receive enough support, restricting access on the basis of adherence to certain conditions did get support.[6] Congressmember Donald Pease (Democrat) proposed (HR 5136) to include workers' rights in the GSP (Interview with House of Representatives, 9 June 1997). This was supported by the AFL-CIO, UNITE! and UAW. While in principle opposing GSP renewal, the unions argued that if the GSP was to be renewed, labour standards should be part of it (Interviews with AFL-CIO, 15 November 1999; UAW, 31 January 2000; UNITE!, 4 February 2000).[7] Congressmember Pease's interest in the issue of labour standards was motivated by the fact that he represented a highly unionized state (Ohio) with auto and steel industries (Interview with UAW, 31 January 2000). As he explained during the Congressional hearing, 'As I talk with my constituents . . . and as I talk with my colleagues in the House, it is clear that Americans are increasingly getting fed up with unfair trade practices on the part of our trading partners' (Committee on Ways and Means, 1986: 55). Because he was a member of the

House of Representatives, Pease's support was invaluable to the AFL-CIO. The combination of Pease's interest in trade-related labour standards and the specific Congressional political constellation helped to make labour standards a part of the GSP. In this respect, it is important that during the 1980s, the Democrats dominated the House.

The fundamental labour standards defined within the 1984 GSP were freedom of association, the right to organize and bargain collectively, the prohibition of forced labour, a minimum age for employment, minimum wages, hours of work and occupational health and safety. The GSP made no reference to the prohibition of discrimination (Lawyers Committee for Human Rights, 1988: 11–14). It was the first time that labour standards were specifically defined. The 1983 reference in CBI only read: 'the degree to which workers in each country are afforded reasonable workplace conditions and enjoy the right to organize and bargain collectively' (Lawyers Committee for Human Rights, 1988: 33–4). Trade unions were involved, just like other organizations, in the definition of the labour standards included (Interviews with House of Representatives, 9 June 1997; UAW, 31 January 2000). In retrospect, the AFL-CIO wished that it had pushed for the inclusion of the prohibition of discrimination, but at that time this was not really a political issue for the unions (Interview with UAW, 31 January 2000). As a spokesman 'explained': 'It was 1984!' (Interview with AFL-CIO, 15 November 1999). In retrospect, the AFL-CIO also wished that it had not included the minimum wage, as this appeared to be an easy target for opponents of a social clause. While the AFL-CIO's definition of a minimum wage only referred to a minimum wage that every country had to determine itself, it was easy to misinterpret as demanding a global minimum wage (Interview with AFL-CIO, 31 January 2000).

The Reagan administration had to make GSP renewal acceptable through the inclusion of labour standards. While the government did not support the inclusion of workers' rights in the GSP, it did not vehemently oppose them. The most important reason was that the inclusion of workers' rights in regular trade legislation would mean that countries – or products – were denied access to the US market. The GSP, on the other hand, involved a special kind of trade legislation, which granted duty-free access to certain products from a selected group of developing countries. Including labour rights in the GSP would therefore mean a reduction of benefits that had been granted to countries on the basis of 'goodwill'. Because of this, it was not seen as a strong protectionist instrument. One trade unionist said: 'All Reagan wanted to avoid were quota and tariffs' (Interview with AFL-CIO, 6 June 1997).

A second reason was that the inclusion of labour standards was seen as more 'fair' than 'protectionist' in nature. This is because the GSP provided possibilities for sanctions not on the basis of injury to US industry, but on the basis of violations of workers' standards. In practice, however, the cases pursued in the United States may have been motivated not by economic interests, but by foreign policy interests (Harvey, 1995).

By 1995, more than 100 petitions were filed by numerous organizations, and ten countries had been punished with a suspension of GSP benefits (Harvey, 1995: 3). The AFL-CIO remained dissatisfied with the number of countries being sanctioned because of violations of workers' standards. According to the AFL-CIO, the GSP phrase 'taking steps' – referring to the necessary action undertaken by a country – is vague and allows for too much flexibility on the side of the administration. The AFL-CIO therefore argued that it should be replaced by a reference that a country 'has adopted and is enforcing laws' (Anderson, 1995b).

Despite these criticisms, some assert that the effects of the GSP and similar programmes should be sought not only in actions resulting from the denial of benefits, but also in countries' responses to the issue. For example, the Dominican Republic, under threat of losing its GSP status, made debt bondage on sugar plantations illegal and translated the rights to organization and collective bargaining into law, although this was not particularly effective in practice. The same is argued in a 1998 Government Accounting Office report:

> The major CBI apparel shipping countries have made efforts to improve worker rights to meet international standards in recent years. The GSP annual review process has provided an important mechanism for filing and resolution of worker rights petitions and has played a role in encouraging the adoption of reforms. (GAO, 1998b)

Labour's Failure in NAFTA: 1990–4

In the 1980s, the AFL-CIO was not as deeply involved in issues concerning international trade agreements as it would be a decade later when the North American Free Trade Agreement (NAFTA) came on the table.[8] The NAFTA negotiations, which started in 1990 under the auspices of the Bush administration, were continued by Clinton and completed in 1994. While the AFL-CIO did not want the NAFTA, the Federation's second best option was for Clinton to renegotiate the agreement. However, the AFL-CIO failed to influence Clinton's position on this aspect, despite the fact that Clinton's presidency had increased labour's access to the administration.

Resisting NAFTA

After 1988, the interest of the AFL-CIO in trade legislation increased significantly (Interview with House of Representatives, 9 June 1997). The most important reason for this was that President Bush had entered into the first stages of preparation of the NAFTA, and the AFL-CIO was worried about job losses that they expected to result from integration with Mexico.

Labour's resistance to the NAFTA centred on three claims. The first was an economic claim, based on several arguments. First, the NAFTA would cause a loss of jobs in the United States when companies moved across the border in search of lower wages. Under the slogan *they are going to move our jobs to Mexico*, the AFL-CIO and its affiliated unions tried to stop the NAFTA negotiations by making an economic appeal to workers who were afraid of losing their jobs (Cowie, 1994: 19). Second, it was argued that a free trade agreement with Mexico would stimulate deindustrialization of the US economy. Because of the availability of cheap labour, enterprises would be less interested in investing in innovation. Third, free trade would result in the regression of social and environmental standards: 'A free trade agreement with Mexico, a country where wages and social protections are almost nonexistent when compared to our own, simply invites disaster for US workers' (Donahue, 1991: 4). Fourth, while it was also argued that these negative effects could be countered by increased export possibilities from the United States to Mexico, the AFL-CIO did not see much prospect in such a scenario, owing to the low purchasing power of Mexicans (Donahue, 1991: 8). Fifth, the AFL-CIO stressed the positive relationship between workers' rights and economic performance: 'The historic strength of the US economy has been based on a variety of factors, including a highly educated, productive, and well-paid work force' (Donahue, 1991: 9).

The second claim was based on solidarity, arguing that Mexican workers, especially in the *maquiladores*, were denied basic trade union rights. Solidarity was also expressed by the argument that the wages paid to Mexican workers were too low to stimulate economic development in Mexico (Donahue, 1991: 10–13). However, this appeal to cross-border solidarity fell on deaf ears, as the largest Mexican trade union, Federation CTM, not only supported the NAFTA, but even claimed that harmonizing labour law between the three countries would degrade working conditions for Mexicans (Cowie, 1994: 20–3).

The third claim was an adapted version of the environmental spillover claim and concentrated on people and drugs. It was argued that a free trade agreement between the two countries would result in a higher influx of Mexican migrant labour into the United States, as the Mexicans would try to make the free movement of labour an issue (Donahue, 1991: 13–14). Moreover, efforts to stem the flow of illegal drugs from Mexico into the United States would come under pressure (Donahue, 1990b). The alternative case for rejecting the NAFTA presented by the AFL-CIO was investing in the future of Mexico, meaning a combination of debt relief and foreign aid (Donahue, 1991: 18).

There are four points worth noting about the way the AFL-CIO organized its opposition to the NAFTA. First, the AFL-CIO did not stand alone in rejecting the NAFTA. While in the 1980s AFL-CIO-aligned unions had been working together with other NGOs on the issue of labour standards, the Federation itself had found it more difficult to do so (Interview with UAW, 31 January 2000). Other groups also had interests in rejecting the NAFTA, such as the International Labor Rights Fund, the consumer group Public Citizens, environmental NGOs (Greenpeace, Friends of the Earth and Sierra Club), agricultural organizations like the National Farmers Union and the Third World-oriented Development GAP.[9] These groups found each other in the fear of increased competition and a downward harmonization of labour, environmental and food security legislation. The AFL-CIO saw the opportunity to make workers' rights the subject of an animated debate by linking it with problems characteristic of environmental issues. Just as companies could move to avoid environmental legislation, they could also move to avoid labour legislation. Many of the above-mentioned NGOs were united in the Alliance for Responsible Trade (Interviews with ILRF, 11 July 1996; AFL-CIO, 30 May 1997).

Second, while the AFL-CIO for the first time found coalition partners among other interest groups, it was less able to stimulate solidarity with the Mexican trade union Federation CTM, also involved in the NAFTA debate. What made this solidarity difficult was the fact that AFL-CIO unions accused Mexicans of stealing their jobs, while the Mexicans were economically not in a position to refuse these jobs. To complicate matters even further, for many years the AFL-CIO had interfered in the Latin American trade union movement by means of its American Institute for Free Labor Development (AIFLD), which opposed leftist Mexican unions. These activities had not stimulated trust of the Mexican unions in the AFL-CIO and blocked the formation of a cross-national counter attack (Hecker, 1993: 359–62; Mumme and Stevis, n.d.: 44–5; Cowie, 1994: 24–9).

Third, when the anti-NAFTA coalition broadened, industry, which supported the NAFTA, also became more active. Previously, industry had not been too worried about the labour standards and trade debate, as it mainly concerned US unilateral legislation directed at other countries. This time, however, it concerned a bilateral agreement based on the consent of two parties: the United States and Mexico. In contrast to the references to labour standards in unilateral legislation, such as in the GSP, it is more difficult to discontinue bi- and multilateral agreements. This was the reason for business to become more active in both the NAFTA and later the WTO debates (Interview with United States Council for International Business, 19 June 1997).

Fourth, the nature of the discourse changed. While the fair trade discourse as carried by the AFL-CIO always had a protectionist edge, this became even more clear in the NAFTA debate. The NAFTA debate was much more specific than earlier debates, as Mexico borders the United States (Interview with AFL-CIO, 30 May 1999). In addition, the nature of the attacks was much more vigorous than was the case in the 1980s. This time Mexican migrant workers were attacked.

Fast-tracking NAFTA

The start of the NAFTA negotiations in 1990 was accompanied by a discussion on the extension of the fast-track procedure covering the Uruguay Round negotiations, as well as the NAFTA. Since 1974, the US Congress has granted the President fast-track authority. This means that a trade agreement negotiated by the President cannot be amended by Congress. Instead, the Congress is expected to decide on the negotiating objectives in advance and to vote for or against an agreement (Destler, 1992: 436). More than ever, fast-track has become an issue of contest. The reason is that non-tariff barriers are increasingly subject to GATT/WTO negotiations. This means that in many cases a trade pact will demand changes in domestic-oriented legislation. Depending on the nature of an agreement, Congress is expected to adjust domestic legislation or to pay compensation if it refuses a signed agreement (Interviews with USTR, 5 and 6 June 1997).

Together with other NGOs – for example, the NGO coalitions The Citizen Trade Watch Campaign and The Fair Trade Campaign – the AFL-CIO vigorously opposed the extension of fast-track. While the Advisory Committee for Trade Policy and Negotiations (ACTPN), a private sector advisory committee to the President organizing about 44 industry and two labour representatives, recommended fast-track extension, the labour representatives presented a dissenting view. Their trust in the government's protection of US workers had been squashed by the NAFTA negotiations. In addition, the Bush administration had in the view of labour not accomplished enough of its negotiating objectives, such as import fees to finance trade adjustment or workers' rights (Interview with ACTPN, 1991: 27–8).

The AFL-CIO's viewpoint on the NAFTA and fast-track received some support from the Democrats. Besides Congressmember Pease, Richard Gephardt, although not rejecting the NAFTA and fast-track outright, also demanded the inclusion of workers' rights and trade adjustment (*Inside US Trade*, 29 March 1991). In a later stage, Gephardt weakened his demand and backed up fast-track extension with an option to make amendments if US jobs disappeared, if workers were abused or if the environment were polluted (*Inside US Trade*, 10 May 1991). Other Democrats, such as Levin and Riegle, asked for similar provisions (Destler, 1992: 101–2).

Clinton's victory and labour's loss

In 1992, Democrat Bill Clinton won the US presidential elections. This, however, did not significantly improve the NAFTA issue for the trade unions. First of all, there was strong support for the NAFTA among US business, including exporting firms hoping to find new markets for products and technologies, and the service sector that saw its investment possibilities expanded. Clinton, first unsure whether to support the NAFTA (Hogenboom, 1998: 122–3, 207), announced two months before his election that he would support the NAFTA provided that there were labour and environmental agreements negotiated on the side. The suggestion of side agreements had already been made by the Bush administration (Hecker, 1993: 363). This attempt to equalize the playing field was meant to increase support for the NAFTA. The AFL-CIO, however, wanted Clinton to renegotiate the agreement instead of adding a side agreement (Donahue, 1993). Not only did the AFL-CIO expect a renegotiated agreement to be legally stronger than a side agreement, it also secretly hoped that demanding a renegotiation would decrease the NAFTA's chances of survival (Interview with AFL-CIO, 31 January 2000).

In contrast to the AFL-CIO, Clinton claimed that the NAFTA would have positive economic effects for US workers. First, while he did not fail to recognize the importance of increased mobility of capital and production, he argued that jobs would be created through increased trade. Second, Clinton argued that nothing that would happen in the NAFTA could make a difference to the problems already confronting the United States, namely the threat by companies to move to other countries in order to depress wages. So what was needed was a way to reconcile a high-wage economy with a world of increasing mobility and increasing competition. Skill enhancement of workers, increased investments in innovation and increased exports were the measures emphasized by Clinton. The third argument in the economic claim was strongly related to the second, and maintained that free trade does not equal economic growth: 'The issue is not whether we should support free trade or open markets. Of course, we should. The real issue is whether or not we will have a national economic strategy to make sure we reap the benefits' (Clinton, 1992). Such a strategy would involve social partners. The fourth economic argument claimed that in a world of regional trading blocks, having open relations with neighbouring countries is of crucial importance when other countries become protectionist.

The prospects of a large Mexican market seemed much better in the eyes of the proponents of the NAFTA than in the eyes of the opponents. In order to meet some of the opponents' concerns, Clinton proposed side agreements to protect US workers and the environment (Clinton, 1992). Another card up Clinton's sleeve was the inclusion of a Trade Adjustment Assistance Act, about US$4000 per dislocated worker up to 2003, based on the assumption that a total of 145,000 workers would lose their jobs.[10] This plan, however, was sharply criticized. Petersen, a Democrat Senator, argued that those 145,000 jobs would be in the first NAFTA year (*Inside US Trade*, 22 October 1993: 6–7). At that time, numerous studies were predicting different effects on US jobs due to the NAFTA. The Bush administration was sure that it would create 175,000 jobs. During the Clinton administration, these prospects were significantly reduced to anywhere ranging from 35,000 to 94,000, figures that would not make up for the job losses (Cowie, 1994: 13; GAO, 1997). Interestingly enough, Clinton did not mention improving workers' rights as an act of solidarity. To US Secretary of Labor Robert Reich, however, respect for labour rights was central to his analysis (Reich, 1994a). Reich did not expect low labour standards abroad to be the reason for the growth of low-wage work abroad, but attributed this trend largely to technological change (Reich, 1994b).

While one could have envisaged a NAFTA side agreement to be a step towards a level playing field, this was not how the AFL-CIO perceived it. It argued that the side agreement was weaker than the provisions that already existed under US law. Not only did the sanctioning part of the side agreement merely include references to health and safety, child labour and minimum wages, it also made enforcement of national labour law the basis of the agreement, instead of providing an international definition (*Inside US Trade*, 16 July 1993: 15; 3 September 1993: 20). The selection of these standards was probably the result of business and Mexican interference, who both feared enabling rights more than anything (Interview with AFL-CIO, 15 November 1999).

During testimony in 1993 before the Labor and Human Resources Committee of the Senate, AFL-CIO Secretary-Treasurer Donahue described the NAFTA as a business agreement. The side agreement he characterized as an agreement that 'rather than advancing labor rights and standards, actually represents a weakening of existing remedies available under US law' (Donahue, 1993). Other complaints concerned weak rules of origin, inadequate safeguard procedures, inequitable rules for investment and inequitable market access (Donahue, 1993: 4).

The voting on the NAFTA in 1994 was a close call. In all, 156 of the 258 House Democrats voted against NAFTA, as did 27 of the 55 Senate Democrats. The lack of influence of the AFL-CIO in the NAFTA case is, to a large extent, retraceable to the decision of the Democrats that the costs of excluding the AFL-CIO were not perceived to be high (Mumme and Stevis, n.d.: 45). This did not result in the alienation of the AFL-CIO. Despite being strongly disappointed, keeping the relationship with Clinton in shape was more important to the AFL-CIO than was the NAFTA (Dark, 1999: 171–2).

Trade Remedy and Negotiating Objectives: The Omnibus Trade and Competitiveness Act 1988 and the GATT Uruguay Round

Among the most important trade issues after the 1980s were the negotiations that took place in the framework of the GATT. While the AFL-CIO was not supporting the GATT Uruguay Round that had started in 1986 and was concluded in 1994, it hoped that the inclusion of workers' rights would ease the pain of a liberalized world market. Its pessimistic view of the new round was shared by some industries (AT&T and steel and mineral companies), which were afraid of the loss of means to protect their industries. During the second half of the 1980s, these industries and the AFL-CIO demanded the update of US trade remedy laws (*Inside US Trade*, 31 May 1985: 9–10; 12 April 1985: 12; Donahue 1986). The AFL-CIO framed the economic claim of trade deficit and job losses and the claim of universality of human rights in a widely shared fair trade discourse.

The groundwork for introducing fairness in trade policies was already laid in the Trade Act of 1974. The Act instructed, for the first time in US trade law, the President to make fair labour standards a negotiating objective in GATT negotiations. Section 301 of the Act enabled the President to undertake actions to restrict imports in case of unfair trade practices. During the 1980s, the definition of unfair trade practices was broadened to include labour standards (Baldwin, 1993: 89). In the following section, both the discussion on 'unfair' trade practices and that on the GATT negotiations – resulting from the renewed negotiating objectives in the GATT – are discussed.

Trade Remedy

In 1984, the US trade deficit was estimated to be US$123 billion (Destler, 1992: 88–9; O'Shea, 1993: 43). The ever-rising trade deficit was becoming a real problem for the AFL-CIO, as it fuelled fears about unemployment and relocation of industries. As one trade unionist argued, 'money is going out of the United States for imports; money which then isn't available for use here; money which creates jobs in other countries while the US unemployment rate remains too high' (Stone, 1985: 286).

The initial response of the AFL-CIO to the increasing trade deficit was to ask for greater trade adjustment assistance (TAA) and for revisions of trade legislation to protect domestic industries against cheap foreign imports. However, as political support for TAA improvement was lacking, and the TAA funds were cut back rather than increased, protectionist feelings within the trade union movement were fuelled (Destler, 1992: 252, 442–3).[11] Therefore, trade unions began looking at the multilateral trade negotiations of the GATT for support to change their gloomy future.[12] As a spokesman of UNITE! said, 'Reagan wanted to kill trade adjustment assistance altogether. Unions decided for another strategy, saying that at least the benefits of trade should go to the producers: the issue of labor rights' (Interview with UNITE!, 20 June 1997).

The trade deficit made trade a top one priority issue in US politics, and this led in 1988 to the creation of the Omnibus Trade and Competitiveness Act, the purpose of which included an increase of the possibilities for unilateral retaliation (Destler, 1992: 439).

The history of this Act started in 1985, when the renewal of trade legislation became an issue for the Democrats hoping to defeat the Republicans in the upcoming elections, even though protectionists, free traders and those in between were found in both parties. Reagan, until 1986, supported, at least verbally, a *laissez-faire* attitude towards trade, thus rejecting too much trade intervention (O'Shea, 1993: 41). However, in practice he strengthened the protection of some industries, such as textiles and steel (Destler, 1992: 122–4). The Democrats were able to make trade legislation an electoral issue because the second Reagan term was characterized by a lack of initiative to fight the increasing trade deficit. In fact, Reagan took steps to decrease the protection of certain industries. With elections coming up in November 1986 and with him being accused of insufficient action, Reagan was 'forced' to announce in a 'fair trade' speech at the end of 1985 the undertaking of more efforts to open up foreign markets for US producers and the initiation of unfair trade practice cases against Japan, Korea, the EU and Brazil. Nevertheless, some Democrats wanted more import restrictions than the Republican administration cared for (O'Shea, 1993: 44–5). This was illustrated by the Gephardt Amendment, which proposed to tax imports from certain competitors up to 25 per cent. This amendment passed the House of Representatives, but was replaced in 1988 by Section 301 (Destler, 1992: 237; O'Shea, 1993: 43).

What was at stake in this new trade legislation debate? First of all, it was about remedy laws that would give 'unfair' trade practices more attention. In January 1986 Congressmember Pease had written a letter to the US Trade Representative Yeutter, asking what the President had done to countries that competed on the basis of 'unfair' practices, such as disrespect for labour standards. Yeutter answered that the key to improving US competitiveness did not depend only on measures to address unfair trade practices, but also on macroeconomic policy measures (Committee on Ways and Means, 1986: 74–6). Clearly, this was only a part of the answer Congressmember Pease wanted to hear. Starting his own campaign, he wrote a letter to House members asking them to support an amendment to Section 301 of the Trade Act 1974 to treat the denial of workers' rights as an unfair trade practice. Thereby he specifically mentioned some of the USA's strongest competitors, South Korea and Taiwan (Pease, 1986). A short time later the House Ways and Means Committee approved a Bill (HR 3) introduced by Gephardt. HR 3 included references to the Gephardt Amendment, restrained presidential discretion in trade remedy cases and gave room for retaliation in case of non-reciprocation. In short, it included much of what Democrats, and some of the Republicans, wanted (Destler, 1992: 90–1). Trade unions were also relieved:

> The AFL-CIO believes the bill passed by the House in the 99th Congress made significant progress. . . . Changing trade law and policy to provide timely and predictable relief to workers and industries injured by imports are also long overdue. America's fair trade laws must be strengthened to address new discriminatory commercial practices. The denial of worker rights by our trading partners can no longer be ignored. (Kirkland, 1987: 2)

Within the administration, the ideas contained in HR 3 were not well received, but the Republican administration's options were limited since the Republican Party had lost control over Congress in 1987. In 1987, the Democrats took over the Senate, while maintaining dominance in the House, thereby gaining control over the entire Congress. New trade legislation was named a top priority (Destler, 1992: 90–1, 124–5). US Trade Representative Yeutter claimed that workers' rights were objectionable given the absence of internationally accepted trade standards for workers' rights and accompanying sanctions (*Inside US Trade*, 20 March 1987: 2). In short, the administration interpreted the existing trade and human rights regimes as totally unconnected.

Like the US Trade Representative, the Department of Labor was unhappy about an amendment to Section 301 of the Trade Act 1974. The new Secretary of Labor, former US Trade Representative Brock, who tried to convince HR 3 co-sponsor Congressmember Rostenkowski to oppose the amendment, summarized: 'A unilateral, trade-linked, American approach emphasizing punitive measures over incentives, especially through the public branding of unfairness under 301, would be counterproductive' (Brock, 1987). At the international level, the administration also condemned the coverage in Section 301 of workers' rights. Brock said in Geneva during the 1987 International Labour Conference that sanctioning violations of freedom of association and collective bargaining, compulsory and child labour and standards related to hours of work, occupational health and safety and minimum wage would invite retaliation. He added:

> We're continuing to discuss ways in which GATT-related trade sanctions might reinforce ILO efforts to encourage respect for workers' rights. I hope these efforts succeed. Because quite frankly, if we can't discuss workers' rights here and we can't discuss it in the GATT, nobody should be terribly surprised to see unilateral efforts to link worker rights and trade. (*Inside US Trade*, 24 June 1987)

Interestingly enough, Brock also made the point that a sanction on Soviet exports for not granting labour rights would result in Soviet retaliation. However, if 'the world's worst offenders of worker rights' were left unharmed, how would the application of sanctions to other countries be justified? (Brock, 1987). This statement was made around the time in 1987 when members of the House Foreign Affairs Subcommittee accused the administration of selectively applying the GSP provision on workers' rights. While it had been no trouble to remove Romania from the GSP list of beneficiaries, Chile somehow managed to stay on the list, despite continued reports of workers' rights violations. The subcommittee members explained this odd situation as one in which 'the political aims of the Administration took precedence over the actual workers' rights situation there' (*Inside US Trade*, 31 July 1987: 9).

In 1988, the Omnibus Trade and Competitiveness Act came into being. Through this Act, the President's 301 authority was extended, which gave him the power to use sanctions against countries that do not respect fundamental workers' rights. The fundamental labour standards in the Trade Act refer to the same categories as defined in the GSP Renewal Act: the freedom of association, the right to organize and bargain collectively, the prohibition of forced labour, minimum age for employment and standards for minimum wages, hours of work and occupational health and safety. Compared to the GSP, the Trade Act provided some advantages. The scale of sanctions is much greater under the Trade Act than under the GSP. Under the Trade Act, specific products can be targeted instead of whole countries. The number of countries affected is theoretically much larger, as the GSP can only involve beneficiary countries. On the other hand, Section 301 can only be enacted in the case of an economic injury, while the GSP is based on the violation of labour rights only. Finally, sanctions under Section 301 have almost never been enacted. This is because the section is considered to be powerful because of its use as a threat (Mandel, 1989: 466–9).

Even though the 1988 Trade Act responded to the interests of the AFL-CIO, the Federation was not satisfied. Making workers' rights a negotiating objective had already been done in 1974, but had not paid off internationally.[13] More importantly, the retaliation authority of the President was limited by the stipulation that workers' rights needed to be consistent with the level of economic development (Interview with AFL-CIO, 30 May 1997), a condition introduced by the Republican Senator Danfort (*Worker Rights News*, 1988: 5). This condition practically shifted the focus of labour standards from universal to relative.

While the inclusion of labour standards in Section 301 gave the AFL-CIO the opportunity to petition certain countries, neither the Federation nor its affiliated unions made use of this right. The reasons are that the discretion of the President is so encompassing that he can decide whether or not to take up a case, and President Bush was unlikely to grant such petitions. When the administration came into the hands of the Democrats in 1992, and the chances for AFL-CIO petitions to be granted increased, the NAFTA became the major issue on the agenda. This drove Section 301 to the background.

According to the AFL-CIO, it was a pity that the unions never made use of their right to petition. In the case of intellectual property rights (IPRs), which were also included in the Trade Act 1988, business petitions had made it an important trade issue for other countries to take into consideration. This resulted in the inclusion of IPRs on the international trade agenda (Interview with AFL-CIO, 15 November 1999).

GATT Moves

While trade remedy was an issue enjoying some support among business, the request of the AFL-CIO to include labour standards in trade agreements was far less supported. Nevertheless, the Reagan administration, not by conviction, but because of strategic considerations, supported the inclusion of labour standards in the GATT negotiations. The reason for this was that the administration hoped that such support would curb similar provisions in unilateral trade laws. An AFL-CIO staff member explained the support of the subsequent Bush administration for raising the issue of workers' rights in the GATT as follows:

> we were pursuing changes in trade law that would have given the executive branch authority under unfair trade statutes to take action against violation of internationally recognized labour rights and they did not want that. So their argument before the Congress and internationally as well was we do not need to do this unilaterally if we can pursue this in the multilateral context of the Uruguay Round. (Interview with AFL-CIO, 11 July 1996)

US Trade Representative Yeutter agreed that workers' rights were important, but understood from the initial responses of other GATT parties that it would not be easy to raise the issue in the GATT. Therefore, he suggested that 'international grass roots constituency-building by the unions would serve as pressure points on other governments to visit their positions on worker rights in the GATT' (Yeutter, 1986).

In Punta del Este – during the 1986 GATT negotiations – it became clear that the agenda for the coming GATT Round did not include a reference to labour standards. Therefore, in 1987 the US Trade Representative tactically decided to start with a request for a working group instead of asking for an inclusion of labour standards in the concluding text of the negotiations. Since in the past this had been a successful strategy with trade and services, expectations were high. The government asked the AFL-CIO to do the same with its counterparts in other countries (Anderson, 1987).

The prospect that a working group on labour standards would be established increased after the labour standards reference was included in the Trade Act 1988. The aim of such a working group was to study the relationship between trade and labour standards and draw up a list of internationally recognized labour standards. Although the GATT members' initial reception of the idea had been poor, bilateral talks between the United States and several countries had fuelled the expectation that such a working group could be established at the end of 1988 (*Inside US Trade*, 11 March 1988: 13–14).

Domestically, US efforts with respect to a working group were viewed positively. The Labor Advisory Committee (LAC) – a sectoral policy committee consisting of trade union representatives advising the government on labour issues – suggested the government continue pushing for a working group and reassessing the strategies of the US negotiators. The LAC argued that without workers' rights American workers would be exposed to competition with people working under the lowest conditions, American jobs would then disappear and economic growth would be limited. Even though the LAC reaffirmed that the purpose was not to impose US labour standards on other countries, or fix a minimum wage, at that time the minimum wage standard was still included in the list of labour standards (LAC, 1988: 9–12).

It took slightly more than a year to crush the US expectations that the GATT Council would agree to establish a working group. GATT Director Dunkel, wanting to break away from the impasse, had proposed establishing a joint GATT–ILO staff study on the relationship between trade and labour standards. This study, like the proposal for a GATT working group, was rejected by developing countries (US DOL, 1989a). Strategically, the LAC advised that the negotiators try to include workers' rights in the various other negotiating groups, such as the one on investments (LAC, 1989). In other words, the denial of workers' rights should be viewed as a subsidy, as an investment incentive and so on (US DOL, 1989b).

Late in 1990 a new strategy was developed to increase the acceptability of a working group. The US government, together with the AFL-CIO, decided to narrow down the definition of fundamental labour standards to forced labour, freedom of association and the right to collective bargaining and organization. By eliminating child labour, health and safety and wage standards, it was hoped that the working group proposal would be made more palatable to developing countries. US negotiators would use the GATT Council meeting to table this proposal, and the AFL-CIO would try to sell it to the ICFTU (Donahue, 1990a).

Meanwhile, the ICFTU was developing its own initiatives. During a meeting with Dunkel, personally committed to the workers' rights and trade link, it became apparent that the 1984 US changes in the GSP requirements had left ill feelings in developing countries, and were partly responsible for the lack of support for the US proposal in the GATT (AFL-CIO, 1990a). As a result, the ICFTU asked the Americans to reconsider unilateral trade provisions on workers' rights, a proposal not very well received at the AFL-CIO, since unilateral measures were all there was on offer (AFL-CIO, 1990b)

With the arrival of the Clinton administration, the AFL-CIO found a friendlier attitude in the White House towards a GATT social clause. US Trade Representative Micky Kantor was in favour of incorporating workers' rights in the GATT/WTO, and was instrumental in making it an international agenda issue. Instead of spending its energy on the administration, the AFL-CIO was now able to increase pressure on its international counterparts and to discuss labour standards with foreign politicians. The contacts with the administration were mainly devoted to coordinating activities (Interview with ICFTU, 30 May 1997).

In the first months of 1994, the draft of the Uruguay Round agreement was discussed during hearings within House and Senate Committees. UNITE! pressed for workers' rights – again including more rights, such as the prohibition of child labour – to be added to the Uruguay Round implementation Bill (Gundersheim, 1994: 232). The two main claims of the AFL-CIO-related unions were still that jobs had been lost to low-wage countries, and that the GATT agreement would mean further job losses and wage depression as US workers were subjected to unfair competition with countries which maintained low labour costs through the suppression of workers.

In addition to the two main claims of the AFL-CIO, a new claim surfaced. The fear had arisen that the establishment of the WTO would entail a loss of sovereignty for the United States. The reasons for this fear were that the WTO lacks public participation, is a forum where most of the members are undemocratic countries and as an organization could judge whether US laws, such as Section 301, were in violation of the WTO regulations (Bywater, 1994: 51–2; Donahue, 1994a: 161). In January 2000, the WTO rejected a European Union complaint that argued that Section 301 was not WTO-consistent (TechLaw, 2000).

The anti-NAFTA coalition was still in place and was extended to a worldwide scale. It was less divided than had been the case with the NAFTA because the perceived implications of the WTO were clearly regarded as a threat. Together with 300 other domestic and foreign NGOs, including trade unions, a statement was presented opposing the Uruguay Round negotiations. While the objections to the Uruguay Round were based on many more claims, claims concerning repercussions for the environment and sustainable development and the implications for national sovereignty played a strong role in these objections (Wallach, 1994: 215–18).

As was mentioned above, business became much more fearful of the incorporation of labour standards, since the issue was a multilateral agreement. Speaking on behalf of the Alliance for GATT NOW – representing about 500 US companies – business desperately wanted the Uruguay Round Agreement, since it expected major economic benefits. It robustly rejected the inclusion of labour standards (Interview with United States Council for International Business, 19 June 1997).

The LAC remained sceptical about the merits of the Uruguay Round. In 1994, the LAC gave once again a negative opinion with regard to US trade negotiations. It maintained that the GATT agreement fell short of the formal trade negotiating objectives, offered little advantage and generally disadvantaged US workers. Using the same discursive frame as President Clinton had done during his election campaign, it argued that it is not a question about protectionism versus free market, but a question about how it can be ensured that economic benefits are distributed equally. The blame was put on others:

> the US, by itself, absorbs more than half of all less developed countries' manufacturing exports. These persistent patterns of trade clearly indicate that the benefits and costs of the 'open trading system' are not borne equally. (LAC, 1994: 3)

The demands of the LAC, therefore, were more of the same. They included the inclusion of workers' rights to address trade advantages, the strengthening of US trade remedy laws and the elimination of special and differential treatment that was provided for even the most advanced 'developing' countries (LAC, 1994: 3). The LAC also maintained the economic claim that the suppression of human and workers' rights by governments to maintain comparative advantage is among the most cruel and prevalent trade subsidies (LAC, 1994: 4). Four days after the LAC had submitted its report, ACTPN submitted a report to the US Trade Representative that was more positive about the Uruguay Round negotiations than that of the LAC. The labour representative on the Committee therefore submitted an additional statement to the report, a copy of the LAC statement (ACTPN, 1994: 164–6).

On 11 March 1994, 68 members of Congress appealed to President Clinton to do his utmost to include workers' rights in the final Declaration to be signed in Marrakesh (Visclosky and Brown, 1994a). Fourteen days later, US Trade Representative Kantor sent a letter to Peter Sutherland, the then Director of the GATT, demanding that the WTO should address workers' rights, even if it was only to ensure that political support for the WTO would not be undermined. Kantor proposed the following language:

> Ministers recognize that the more open multilateral trading system resulting from the Uruguay Round should benefit workers around the world through the impact of increased trade on employment and income. They also express the view that trade gains should not come at the expense of the realization of social objectives and, in this connection, they agree to undertake early consideration of the relationship between the trading system and internationally recognized labor standards. (Kantor, 1994)

However, the administration was becoming divided over how hard to push for a working party on labour standards, as the debate also involved linking the human rights record of China to trade (*Inside US Trade*, 25 March 1994). In addition, the opposition the United States faced was too strong and therefore the proponents had to be content with the reference in the Marrakesh agreement that new issues, including workers' rights, could be further discussed in the WTO.

Domestic battles: Slowing down fast-track

In 1994, the fast-track authority of the President expired. Clinton wanted new authorization to have room to negotiate the Uruguay Round, an enlargement of the NAFTA and a Free Trade Area of the Americas (Bolle, 1996: 1). Even more than during the NAFTA preparations, the Uruguay Round negotiations coupled with the fast-track renewal heated up the debate about whether labour and environmental goals should be part of the trade negotiating objectives.

Clinton wanted to extend his fast-track authority for another seven years and introduced this proposal as part of the implementation Bill of the Uruguay Round. However, he was caught between several partly overlapping groups. On the side of both Republicans and Democrats there were objections to extending fast-track, although for different reasons. Just as developing countries had warned the US administration that its insistence on labour standards could put the trade negotiations in danger, many Republicans warned Clinton that his failing to consult Congress before pushing for labour standards in the WTO was inducing them to rethink their support for a fast-track authority renewal (*Inside US Trade*, 15 April 1994). These Republicans agreed that fast-track would be extended if the administration would promise not to pursue labour and environmental issues (*Inside US Trade*, 13 May 1994). The three specific demands of the Republicans with respect to a new fast-track proposal were: the elimination of the negotiating objectives on labour and environment; the assurance that fast-track would not be used to change US labour and environmental laws (the sovereignty claim); the prohibition of trade sanctions being used to penalize violations of labour and environmental laws abroad (*Inside US Trade*, 5 August 1994). Major business groups, such as the Business Round Table, supported these Republicans. However, there were also Republicans and business leaders who just wanted a weaker wording on trade and labour standards, or did not want fast-track at all (*Inside US Trade*, 8 July 1994).

Not only Republicans, but also Democrats, together with the AFL-CIO, started to call for a block on fast-track extension. As they were unsatisfied with the results on environmental standards and workers' rights reached in Marrakesh on 7 April (Brown, 1994), their condition for fast-track renewal was the inclusion of labour standards. What the two groups shared was the fear of a loss of sovereignty: once a trade agreement was negotiated under fast-track, both sides were afraid they would not have the right of amendment.[14]

That the sovereignty claim found a response outside political circles was illustrated by a poll conducted in November 1994. This revealed not only that labour and right-wing Republicans were opposed to the allegedly comprehensive powers of the WTO, but also that 65 per cent of the respondents found it inappropriate that the ability to enact national law to stop the import of child labour-made products was limited (Yankelovich, 1994). In addition, 57 per cent felt that the WTO agreement would contribute to the decrease of American jobs because of cheap labour (Yankelovich, 1994).

There were also Republicans who not only shared the fear of loss of sovereignty with some of the Democrats but also shared the fear that the NAFTA and WTO would weaken the US economy. A bipartisan group, called the Fair Trade Caucus, including fourteen House lawmakers, was established halfway through 1994. The participants were worried about the effects that the NAFTA would allegedly have on US workers and the trade deficit, and expressed concerns about the degradation of US environmental and other laws that were possibly in conflict with WTO regulation (*Inside US Trade*, 8 July 1994).

The worries of the different groups became part of Bills introduced in the US Congress. Visclosky, one of the US Representatives who had demanded that the administration should undertake efforts to get workers' rights included in the Marrakesh agreement, produced, in collaboration with the AFL-CIO, a new Bill (HR 4271). This Bill demanded the establishment of a working party on trade and workers' rights. In addition, Congressmen Gephardt and Richardson proposed a Bill, HR 4375, which made the extension of fast-track to the trade negotiations between the United States and Chile conditional upon the inclusion of environmental laws and workers' rights (*Inside US Trade*, 13 May 1994; Anderson, 1995a).

In 1994, business groups responded to this Bill with a proposal to include a safeguarding option in the fast-track authority, stipulating that if environmental and labour conditions were negotiated, Congress would have the right to propose amendments (*Inside US Trade*, 15 July 1994). Other opposition came from House Democrat Brown, who requested the AFL-CIO to put pressure on the Senate Democrats to decouple the Uruguay Round Implementation Bill from fast-track extension (Goold, 1994).

In August 1994, the Senate Finance Committee followed the House Ways and Means Committee by approving the expansion of trade rules as negotiated in the Uruguay Round, and the creation of the WTO. It refused, however, to consider an extension of fast-track, as President Clinton requested (*Washington Post*, 3 August 1994). Clinton thus had limited choice on what he could send to Congress. The administration decided to let go of its proposal to have fast-track covering possible changes in domestic environmental and labour law. It wanted to reserve the right to use sanctions to enforce labour and environmental agreements, but at the same time it needed to meet the Republican demands. Therefore, the administration proposed limiting the use of sanctions to existing laws, such as Section 301. In this way, Congressional approval would precede the use of trade sanctions. On the issue of whether environment and labour would be overall negotiating objectives the administration was willing to make a compromise and delete it, instead keeping some reference to it in the fast-track Bill. While industry acknowledged that the administration had come a long way in an attempt to accommodate their demands, trade unions warned the administration that they would start a campaign along the lines of the anti-NAFTA campaign to defeat the WTO if the administration gave in to the Republican demands (*Inside US Trade*, 5 August 1994, 12 August 1994). The threat of alienating the AFL-CIO if the administration went ahead with the proposed fast-track was strong enough for the administration to withdraw fast-track altogether (Interview with Department of Labor, 11 July 1996). What was left was the Bill to approve and implement the Uruguay Round trade agreement, which in December 1994 became public law. Section 1.31 of the Uruguay Round Agreements Act directs the President to seek the establishment of a working party in the WTO on workers' rights, and to keep Congress up to date on its progress (Uruguay Round Agreements Act 1994). This was the result of lobbying of the AFL-CIO at Congress (Interview with USTR, 6 June 1997).

This small victory notwithstanding, the AFL-CIO remained sceptical about the Uruguay agreement. It was afraid that the WTO's binding dispute settlement would make it more difficult for the United States to undertake actions to defend its national interest, and did not support the end of the Multi-Fibre Arrangement (Donahue, 1994b). That the WTO agreement could limit US trade policies was also acknowledged by the administration. US Trade Representative Kantor argued that the legislative initiatives, such as prohibition of the import of child labour products (the Harkin Bill), would be in conflict with WTO articles on national treatment and most favoured nation treatment (*Inside US Trade*, 2 December 1994). On the other hand, the administration did its best to contest the claim that US sovereignty was compromised. A variety of 'experts' was brought in to convince members of Congress that no international agreement could bind the United States if it did not want to be bound. Even the conservative Heritage Foundation was brought in. Its economic expert claimed that no sovereignty was lost because future amendments to the Uruguay Round Agreement have to be accepted by a member before becoming binding upon that member (Cobb, 1994: 32).

Assessment of Influence

To what extent have the debates on labour standards in the different phases of US trade politics served the interests of the AFL-CIO and its member unions with respect to the trade and labour standards discussion? In order to establish a relationship between interests, actions and impacts, the following conditions need to be fulfilled: the interests have to be expressed; there should be access for the AFL-CIO to those politically responsible; interests and impacts should be similar; there should be a short time lag between the

FAIR TRADE DISCOURSE: USA

expressed interests (goals) and the impacts; and the decision-making authority should have remained in the hands of the same individuals during the period studied (Arts, 1998: 78). In this section I examine the extent to which these conditions were fulfilled.

Defining impacts, successes and failures

For the sake of analysis, I have divided the US trade policies and the attempts of the AFL-CIO to influence these as follows: (a) the 1984 GSP renewal; (b) the NAFTA (1990–4); and (c) the Trade and Omnibus Act and the Uruguay Round Agreements Act (1986–94). In each phase, the AFL-CIO made specific demands, and in each period, different impacts occurred (see Tables 4.1 to 4.3).

Table 4.1 *Interests and impacts: the GSP 1984*

Interests	Substantive impacts	Sensitizing impacts
No GSP, or one including labour standards	Moderate: the GSP was renewed, but it included labour standards, petitions were filed and partly granted	Yes: definition of labour standards and increasing awareness for labour standards
		No: increased resistance of foreign governments against labour standards in trade agreements
Other unilateral legislation including labour standards	Yes: many such as CBI, OPIC	Yes: illustrated the importance of the issue

In the 1980s, numerous trade Bills including labour standards were introduced, meeting many of the specific interests of the AFL-CIO. However, the impact of this legislation was fairly limited. This was due to the fact that the President did not support or, in case of Section 301, was not expected to support the implementation of the legislation. Nevertheless, the very fact that in the 1980s labour standards became an issue whenever trade and related laws were considered can be seen, from the perspective of the AFL-CIO, as a sensitizing success. The response of several countries to the possibility of

101

Table 4.2 *Interests and impacts: the NAFTA 1990–4*

Interests	Substantive impacts	Sensitizing impacts
Renegotiate NAFTA	No: a side agreement was offered but labour did not consider this to be meeting their demands	Unclear
To enforce violations of workers' rights through trade actions: right to organize and bargain collectively, health and safety standards, appropriate minimum wage structure, elimination of child labour, forced labour and prohibition of discrimination	Moderate: only three were granted in the side agreement but only under specific conditions, such as persistent patterns of poor enforcement; long procedures make action improbable	Possibly: minimum wage, health/safety and child labour were included and may have become part of the public perception

Source: adapted from Donahue (1993).

being excluded from the GSP or CBI has had an effect on the perception of the governments of these countries.

However, one must recognize the failure of the AFL-CIO to define labour standards once and for all. As I have shown, the fact that the GSP in 1984 included a reference to labour standards has not stopped Democrat or Republican administrations from deviating from this definition. In this sense, the sensitizing impact of the definition issue has been quite limited. Another limitation on the impact of the debate is that it has stimulated ill feeling among governments of the affected GSP and CBI countries. This has fuelled resistance against labour standards in a multilateral setting.

During the 1990s the interests of the AFL-CIO have hardly been met. The NAFTA has materialized, and while the Clinton administration tried to accommodate the AFL-CIO concerns with a side agreement, this was only a small consolation. At the same time that the AFL-CIO interests were being partly met, the administration also accommodated business interests and Mexican considerations by limiting the possible impact of the NAFTA side agreement. As the AFL-CIO admitted, the fact that fundamental rights such as freedom of association or the right to collective bargaining are not protected through the NAFTA is a great failure of the NAFTA side agreement (Donahue, 1993).

While at first sight the efforts of the AFL-CIO with respect to the GATT/

Table 4.3 *Interests and impacts: GATT (1986–94) and the Trade Act 1988*

Interests	Substantive impacts	Sensitizing impacts
Labour standards should be part of the President's negotiating authority	Yes: it is part of the Trade Acts 1974 and 1988, and of the Uruguay Round Agreements Act	Moderate: the issue will continue to be tabled by the United States but at the same time has just a weak priority
Defining lack of labour standards as unfair trade practice (Section 301)	Moderate: unions failed to follow it up, thereby limiting the impact	Moderate: lack of labour standards was accepted as an unfair trade practice; however, level of development was considered important
No fast-track authority without labour standards	Moderate: no fast-track authority was granted, either way	–
No fast-track authority excluding the possibility of sanctions or the possibility of changes in national laws	Yes: proposal for fast-track authority excluding sanctions or possibility of changes in national laws withdrawn	–

WTO and US Trade Acts seem rather successful, the interest granted was in itself not very substantial. Labour standards had been part of the President's negotiating authority since 1974, so one can argue that, from the perspective of the AFL-CIO, the discontinuation of this negotiating objective would have been more of a failure than continuing it. Moreover, fast-track authority was not granted without labour standards, but at the same time it was not granted including them. The definition of labour standards as an unfair trade practice (Section 301) could be seen as a success. However, the fact that no follow-up in the form of cases filed has occurred made it less substantial than it could have been.

Modes of collective action

During the different phases the AFL-CIO had a variety of strategies at its disposal (see Table 4.4).

Table 4.4 *Characteristics of collective action*

Strategy of direct influence	Formal	Informal
Non-public	Taking part in the ACTPN and the LAC, two advisory committees	Contacts with and lobbying of members of Congress, including preparing legislation
Public	Testimonies, especially in Ways and Means Committee and Finance Committee	Mobilizing the public, especially through coalitions

The influence of the AFL-CIO through the two advisory committees was rather weak, even though it provided them with access to the administration. The first and most important is the ACTPN, the private sector advisory committee to the President representing about 44 industries and two labour representatives. The Committee has to be consulted before and after trade negotiations by the US Trade Representative and in the case of disputes. However, unions are not very powerful in the ACTPN because they often have a different view from the rest of the – business – members. This is illustrated by the dissenting statements that trade unions often published after the ACTPN has published its advice. The further problem between the US Trade Representative and the unions is that: 'the job of the USTR is to open up markets while the unions blame all misfortune on international trade' (Interview with USTR, 28 May 1997).

The LAC is a policy committee consisting of trade union representatives advising the government on labour issues. Correspondence between trade unions and government officials shows that the members of this committee do not always feel that they are taken seriously. When the United States was about to make commitments in the area of textiles and tariffs, a LAC representative from UNITE! wrote:

> To present us with a proposal which has already gone through the governmental interagency process for approval and is shown to us literally one business day before it goes on the table in Geneva makes a mockery of the advisory process. (Gundersheim, 1990)

The same happened with the NAFTA. In October 1990, the AFL-CIO wrote a letter to the Deputy US Trade Representative asking why the promise that the LAC would be consulted when the administration started to develop its approach to the USA–Mexico negotiations was not kept. Not only were they not involved; it had already been decided to keep environmental issues out of the negotiations (Donahue, 1990d; *Journal of Commerce*, 26 October 1990). As a spokesman of UNITE! stated: 'LAC may not be influential – depending on the President – but it is nevertheless useful because you get the most recent information on the trade negotiations' (Interview with UNITE!, 20 June 1997). In general, the ACTPN has more influence on policy than the LAC (Interview with USTR, 6 June 1997), but 'ACTPN is heavily weighted against the unions' (Interview with UNITE!, 20 June 1997).

Support from Congressmembers – gained by lobbying or testimonies – was of crucial importance for trade unions as they are responsible for introducing and voting on legislation. However, in most cases it was not possible to determine whether Congressmembers were influenced by labour's position or whether they just represented similar views. I assume that the Congressmembers' interest in labour standards is probably a bit of both. This similarity in perception made the Congressmembers more susceptible to specific proposals, such as the specific definition of labour standards. The similarity may be the result of a similar constituency for Congressmembers and the unions. It may also be the case that unions on a local level contributed to the Congressmembers' perception. As noted above, Representative Pease referred to his voting constituency as getting 'fed up with unfair trade practices' (Committee on Ways and Means, 1986: 55). Moreover, some Congressmembers realized that organized Labour – especially in the older industries – views economic internationalization as a threat. In a survey from 1993, union members identified US companies moving abroad as a serious problem, even more serious than the shortage of secure jobs or the growing inequality among incomes (Peter D. Hart Research Associates, 1993).

Judged by its elaborate lobby network in Washington (Dark, 1999: 147–8), lobbying is one of the most important practices for the AFL-CIO. In addition, some Congressmembers are very receptive to AFL-CIO demands. Until 1991, Congressmember Pease was one of the AFL-CIO's allies, and after 1991 Congressmembers Brown, Sanders and Frank were considered to be supporters of labour standards (Interview with House of Representatives, 9 June 1997). In addition, Representatives Visclosky and Gephardt were considered to be supportive from time to time (Interview with AFL-CIO, 30 May 1997).

Because trade agreements include tariff issues, testifying at committee hearings is a way to present views on trade issues. If the issue at stake requires changes in US law, it is first discussed by the Ways and Means Committee of the House, then by the House itself, subsequently by the Senate Finance Committee and finally by the full Senate. Both committees organize hearings to gather information. In general, disagreement within these committees is small, since they are all dominated by free traders. Often, real debate starts when the issues are brought to the House and Senate floors (Interview with USTR, 5 June 1997). When an issue does not require a change in US legislation, the task of the Congress (including the two committees) is to ensure that the USTR operates within the mandate given to it by the Congress. The power of Congress rests on the fact that it can vote down (parts of) a negotiated agreement, and can decide to limit or not to extend the President's next negotiating authority (Interview with USTR, 5 June 1997).

From the NAFTA on, public mobilization on the national level has played an important role in making labour standards a public issue. The fact that the AFL-CIO was able to form a coalition with other groups showed that it was not just a matter of workers fearing losing their jobs; it was also a matter of consumers fearing the health and safety aspects of products and of environmentalists fearing environmental degradation. Not only were different interest groups involved in the campaign against the NAFTA, on rare occasions some US and Mexican unions were able to organize alliances across borders, and tours were organized to take note of each other's working environment (Cowie, 1994: 26–9). The anti-NAFTA campaign, touching upon the fear of US workers losing their jobs, was the only campaign that put labour standards on the agenda of ordinary people.

Public mobilization also took place among groups willing to support the NAFTA. Among these were some environmental organizations. Their cooperation was rewarded with a greater influence over the terms of the side agreements. This facilitated access for environmental groups and also created more room for congressional passage of the agreement (Vogel, 1995: 245). This resulted in a slightly better deal for the environmentalists as compared with the AFL-CIO (for a discussion see Mumme and Stevis, n.d.).

Time lag and decision-making authority

Now that the relationship between demands and impacts and the issue of access have been established, the influence of time-lag and changes in decision-making authority should be considered.[15] During the short time span in which the debate on GSP renewal took place no major change in decision-making authority occurred. However, the AFL-CIO was fighting the GSP renewal too hard to be very influential on the content. On the other hand, aligned unions such as the UAW were said to be influential during the policy-making process (Interview with House of Representatives, 9 June 1997). Since the new GSP policy was put in place, the AFL-CIO has been important in filing petitions.

During the four years the NAFTA was on the political agenda, the Democrats came into office. This change of administration was not very important for the NAFTA discussion. Both the Republicans and the Democrats wanted the NAFTA and both supported a side agreement on labour. Again, the AFL-CIO was important in filing petitions.

In 1987, the Democrats took over Congress. This did not substantially influence the decision to keep labour standards as a negotiating objective, as the Republican administration preferred a multilateral solution to a unilateral one. The change in Congress did mean that the lack of labour standards was included as an unfair trade practice. The fact that many Democrats and the AFL-CIO wanted a labour reference in Section 301 for similar reasons classifies them as part of a discourse coalition.

Within the very short time span of a few months several decisions were made concerning the implementation of the Uruguay Round agreement and fast-track extension. The LAC proved to be very negative about the possible consequences of the Uruguay Round agreement and urged the inclusion of labour standards. Two months later 68 members of Congress demanded a similar provision, receiving a positive response from US Trade Representative Kantor. Hence, there seems to be a relationship between the demands of the AFL-CIO and the continuation of the negotiating objective of the USTR.

On the matter of fast-track legislation the AFL-CIO seems to have been influential. Within the span of one month Republicans demanded an adaptation of the proposed legislation on fast-track and the AFL-CIO gave a threatening response which led to the withdrawal of the proposal for fast track-legislation. No major change in decision-making authority had taken place.

Conclusion: Explaining Impacts, Successes and Failures

To summarize the impacts in line with the expressed interests of the AFL-CIO during the decade studied:

- the GSP and other unilateral legislation included (defined) labour standards, and received increased attention in the affected countries;
- labour standards remained a negotiating priority in the Trade Act 1988, and the issue was part of GATT meetings;
- labour standards were defined as an unfair trade practice in the Trade Act 1988;
- labour standards became a negotiating priority in the Uruguay Round Agreements Acts in 1993;
- no fast-track excluding labour standards, the possibility of changes in national laws or sanctions was granted.

As Tables 4.1 to 4.4 show, these successes were few, and the failures were many. The impacts that were conceived as failures by the AFL-CIO were:

- the GSP was renewed and labour standards were weakly enforced;
- weak support of Republican administrations for labour standards in the GATT;
- feared weak enforcement of labour standards as unfair trade practice;
- the NAFTA was signed, and the labour side agreement was weak;
- the United States has not been able to convince WTO members of the importance of labour standards.

In Chapter 2 I explained which factors could explain the successes and failures of interest groups. These referred to the characteristics of the discursive context, the interest group, the collective action and the political process. All these factors – some more than others – have influenced the impact of the AFL-CIO and its affiliated unions.

The successes of the AFL-CIO and affiliated unions were partly the effect of the economic position of the United States. The increasing trade deficit in the period studied facilitated the emergence of the fair trade discourse. The main argument of the discourse was that there should be a level playing field, which would allow equal access to markets and competition on the basis of similar conditions of production, such as the provision of minimum labour standards. While the violation of workers' rights abroad was addressed, motivated by humanitarian concerns, the fear of foreign competition was shared across political boundaries and provided an even stronger motivation.

The broadness of the fair trade discourse created bipartisan support for government intervention to reverse the increasing trade deficit. However, it did not facilitate agreement on the nature of the intervention. While some felt that the role of the government should be to protect domestic industry, others emphasized that the government should focus on opening up foreign markets. As this chapter showed, the former role was often supported by the opposition, the latter by the administration.

The AFL-CIO emphasized the contribution of unfair foreign labour practices to the trade deficit. As I have shown, many of the Federation's activities were aimed at the protection of domestic industry. In the view of the AFL-CIO, one of the ways to increase this protection was to create legislation to punish countries that did not respect labour standards. Much of the effectiveness of the AFL-CIO's activities was derived from the fact that the demand for minimum international labour standards was compatible with the fair trade discourse.

One of the clearest examples of how the fear of foreign competition created support for a social clause was in the case of the unilateral laws of the 1980s. In the case of the GSP, Democrats resisted its renewal. The fact that the Reagan administration wanted Democratic support for GSP renewal meant that they had to give something in return. Including labour standards in the GSP silenced the Democratic objections to GSP renewal. Among the unions, it was the UAW that has been most influential, as it was more supportive of the GSP including labour standards than was AFL-CIO headquarters. Even though AFL-CIO headquarters did not want GSP renewal, the Federation did influence the effects of the GSP and CBI on non-US territory. The Federation (and others) petitioned countries to be surveyed for violating labour standards, and these countries in some cases responded by adjusting their domestic laws. Hence, the AFL-CIO has contributed to a generalization of the idea that fundamental labour standards need to be taken seriously.

During all three phases researched (the 1984 GSP renewal, the NAFTA (1990–4) and the Trade and Omnibus Act 1988 and GATT negotiations (1986–94)), the Democratic Party was very important for the trade unions. As explained, this worked both ways, since trade unions do have some assets of importance to politicians of the Democratic Party, such as financial contributions, their endorsements and, ultimately, the votes of their members.

However, unions' resources in terms of electorate, money and other kinds of aid did not pay off during the NAFTA debate. Halfway through the NAFTA debate, President Clinton came into office. At that time the Democrats dominated Congress. Clinton realized that the NAFTA was strongly opposed, not only by labour, but also by other groups. Facing this opposition, but at the same time believing in the advantages of the NAFTA, President Clinton negotiated several side agreements. This time, the AFL-CIO was able to get more union members to oppose the NAFTA than it had during the multilateral trade negotiations. This happened because of its members' strong fear of Mexican competition as compared to general trade issues, thereby inducing the AFL-CIO to adopt a much stronger protectionist discourse. This increased its distance from the Democratic administration. In contrast to the AFL-CIO, some environmental organizations were willing to support the NAFTA in exchange for a greater influence on the terms of the side agreements. According to some, this facilitated access for environmental groups and also created more room for congressional passage of the agreement. As I have shown, labour was unable to develop good relations with its Mexican and Canadian counterparts on a larger scale. Therefore, it was incapable of setting up a cross-national counter attack. The NAFTA debate illustrated that not all Democrats supported the views of the AFL-CIO, and once the Democrats took office this lack of support became more visible.

The situation was different during the 1980s. On many occasions the Democrats supported AFL-CIO demands on labour standards. Even though the Democrats were in opposition, they were able to influence trade policy substantially. The reason was that while the Republicans were in office, the Democrats had the majority in the House. At the end of the 1980s this was also the case in the Senate. Another reason why labour standards were translated into policy during the 1980s was because of the strong Republican fear of unilateral, protectionist trade laws (such as Section 301). This induced successive Republican governments to be receptive to including labour standards in multilateral trade negotiations in the GATT framework.

With respect to the Uruguay Round, probably the greatest success of the AFL-CIO was to pressure the Clinton administration to refuse to go along with a deletion of environment and labour from the overall negotiating objectives. The most likely reason for this is probably that labour standards had already been a part of the general trade negotiating authority for almost twenty years, and excluding the labour element under the Clinton administration would have been too much. At the same time, a discursive coalition was formed around the issue of sovereignty. This coalition made use of the fears that the United States would have to give up the right to formulate its own policies in order to be part of the world trading community. The success of this odd discursive coalition was that it made a quick extension of fast-track unacceptable. When the Federation threatened to start campaigning against the Uruguay Agreement if labour standards were explicitly excluded from fast-track, Clinton sacrificed his fast-track authority.

What is interesting about the failures of the AFL-CIO is that many of them concern weak enforcement. This means that the AFL-CIO has been able to get the issue of labour standards on to the political agenda and translated into policy, but has not been able to influence the follow-up.

In the next chapter, the influence of Indian trade unions in the debate on a social clause is analysed. As we will see, they did not support a social clause, despite the pressures of the ICFTU to change their position. By opposing a social clause, the unions let go of an opportunity to use foreign pressure to change their own position at home. On the other hand, supporting a social clause would have contradicted the neo-liberal discourse dominating India's social clause debate.

Notes

1. Most issues the Conventions deal with are legislated on a federal level. Since state legislation is closely modelled upon federal legislation, this section covers mainly federal legislation related to child labour, discrimination, forced labour, freedom of association and collective bargaining.
2. This shift should be less in the future. While labour costs account for between a quarter and a third of production costs, they are decreasing because of technological changes (Dicken, 1998: 326).
3. One of the ways in which the Cold War orientation was reduced was by the replacement of a large part of the older generation staffing the AFL-CIO's international division by young people from other US organizations.
4. In the period 1980–8, the Republican Ronald Reagan was President of the United States. Between 1988 and 1992 the Republican George Bush was President. In 1992, the Democrat Bill Clinton became President.
5. Individual unions, such as the United Auto Workers (UAW), did support GSP renewal (Interview with House of Representatives, 9 September 1997). For some US industries the GSP programme was beneficial, since manufacturing work was partly done in GSP countries (*Inside US Trade*, 31 December 1987).
6. While excluding countries on the basis of the argument that US industry needed to be protected was not supported, the practice of excluding countries was certainly not new. When the GSP came into existence (1974), access was denied to countries that had communist governments, belonged to OPEC, harboured terrorists or had expropriated US property without compensation (Harvey, 1995: 1).
7. Pease, trying to include workers' rights in trade agreements, worked not only with trade unions, but also with human rights and church

organizations (Interview with House of Representatives: 9 June 1997).
8. This agreement, which was signed in 1994, concerned the creation of a regional trade block involving Canada, Mexico and the United States.
9. For a comparison of the labour and environmental side agreements of NAFTA, see Mumme and Stevis (n.d.).
10. This US$4000 would be used for retraining and relocation assistance (*Inside US Trade*, 11 October 1993: 6).
11. Within other segments of society the view on protectionism was mixed. Even though protectionist tendencies in US politics increased, they were not fully exploited. The reasons for this were a lessened pressure on US trade balance because of a cheaper dollar during the second half of the 1980s and the pressure against protectionism of parts of US industry whose interest it was to keep certain imports cheap, either because they were produced by their own company abroad or because they were needed inputs for domestic production (Salvatore, 1993: 327–8).
12. Included in the GATT negotiations was the aim to give contracting parties the possibility to impose a small, uniform import fee to subsidize adjustment assistance programmes, proposed by, among others, Congressmember Pease. Pease and Roth, a Republican Senator, threatened that if no other option were left, this would be done unilaterally (*Inside US Trade*, 11 August: 4–5). Similar words came from the AFL-CIO (Donahue, 1989). In 1990, the President decided that an import fee would not be in the national interest and decided not to pursue it (Donahue, 1990c).
13. The Trade Act 1974 instructed the President, for the first time in US trade law, to make fair labour standards a negotiating objective in GATT negotiations.
14. According to the AFL-CIO, the sovereignty argument did not play a strong role in the trade union movement, as an agreement always implies giving up some sovereignty (Interview with AFL-CIO: 31 January 2000).
15. The shorter the period between the attempt to exercise influence and the change of policy, the more likely it is that the influence attempt may have been successful. If a change in decision-making authority occurred during the period studied, one has to consider the possibility that a change in policy was not the result of an influence attempt but that of a new decision-maker (Huberts, 1988; Arts, 1998).

5 THE NEO-LIBERAL DISCOURSE ON INTERNATIONAL LABOUR STANDARDS: THE CASE OF INDIA

When in 1994 the United States tried to include a reference to the relationship between trade and labour standards in the final declaration of the Uruguay Round, an overwhelming majority of Indian political parties, trade unions, employers' organizations and media interpreted this as a way to deprive India (and developing countries in general) of its economic comparative advantage. Moreover, the implicit suggestion of a social clause, that it is unwillingness rather than the inability of governments to observe core labour standards, was not easy to digest for India.

Between 1994 and 1998, the period when the social clause was an important issue in India, changes have taken place in the composition of the government. In 1994, the Congress Party was in office. In the 1996 general elections, the right-wing nationalist Bharatiya Janata Party (BJP) emerged as the single largest party, but was able to stay in office for only thirteen days. After this, the United Front assumed office, supported by all the non-BJP parties. The Congress Party and the Communist Party of India (Marxist) did not participate in the government, and lent support from outside. From March 1998 to April 1999, the BJP was in office again. The position on the social clause did not change during this whole period.

The main feature of the Indian social clause debate is the absolute agreement between trade unions, employers' organizations and the government that a social clause should be rejected. The argument I make in this chapter is that trade unions not only rejected a social clause, unlike some representatives of the unorganized sector, but also failed to take advantage of the pressure on the Indian government, created by the social clause debate, to press for demands in related areas. This uncritical support for the Indian government can be explained by three factors. First, trade unions have been governed by their distrust of the international community, including fellow trade unions. Second, they have a weak domestic political position. Third, they were not interested enough in groups that could potentially have benefited from a social clause, such as the unprotected workers, to take a positive attitude towards a social clause. The distrust of foreign intentions and the lack of interest in unprotected labourers are what trade unions shared with the government and employers' organizations. These feelings facilitated a broad anti-social clause coalition in India.[1]

This chapter provides a background that helps us to understand the power of the factors that shaped the Indian social clause debate. It analyses the claims used in the debate and describes the processes of dissemination of the claims among the different groups of stakeholders in the debate.

Origins of Distrust: Counter-hegemony and Liberalization

After India gained independence in 1947, it adopted a state-planned development strategy, similar to many other developing countries. This strategy was characterized by powerful state institutions and a strong role for the state in planning. Being a large country with a high degree of political and economic autonomy, India had been able to occupy a leading position in the coalitions of developing countries as embodied in the in 1964 established Group of 77 (G-77) and the Non-Aligned Movement (NAM).[2] The influence of these Southern, counter-hegemonic coalitions expressed itself by prioritizing issues that were consistent with state-led development, such as the political and economic sovereignty of weak states. Through the principle of one nation, one vote, Southern coalitions were able to put developing countries' priorities high on the agenda of the specialized United Nations agencies, such as the United Nations Conference on Trade and Development (UNCTAD). Within the GATT, norms taking underdevelopment into account became institutionalized; for example, in the form of differential treatment of products from developing countries (McDowell, 1997: 60–3). This differential treatment was embodied in the Generalized System of Preferences (GSP), which reduced import barriers for developing countries.

The major force behind the formation of the international coalition among developing countries was the perception that many international trade arrangements were biased towards the interests of developed countries. Contributing to this perception was the design of the Multi-Fibre Arrangement (MFA), which legitimized discriminatory trading practices of developed countries by putting a ceiling on textile imports. At the same time, the negotiation of deals between developed countries on matters like export credits in other international settings, such as the OECD, was also seen as contrary to developing countries' interests. In addition, the developing countries eyed with great suspicion the growing support for 'new protectionism' and the unilateral trade measures designed by some of the leading trading nations, like the United States. Although all developing countries have made use of protectionist policies, this has in general been perceived as more legitimate because of their developmental problems (Helleiner, 1993: 396–401; McDowell, 1997: 71).

While India had taken a leading role in this counter-hegemonic coalition, its position weakened considerably in the 1980s because of the increasing differentiation of the levels of development between developing countries. The rise of the newly industrialized countries (NICs) weakened the perception of common interests among developing countries. This in turn eroded the options for those developing countries that did not choose economic development as prescribed by neo-classical economists. Moreover, international arrangements (such as UNCTAD) and international policy choices that previously had shown sensitivity to developing countries' problems were getting less support from the international community than before (McDowell, 1997: 74–5). Within the GATT, the break-up of the Southern front was visible, as is explained below.

Liberalization became the common development path of many developing countries. As in other developing countries embarking on liberalization, India's liberalization was stimulated by an economic crisis that hit the country at the beginning of the 1980s. The roots of this crisis can be traced back to the doubling of oil prices in 1979–81, to India's large imports in general and to a stagnation of exports in the period 1982–5. This increased India's foreign exchange shortage and induced heavy borrowing from the International Monetary Fund (IMF) and commercial banks to pay for the occurring deficits. The first loan was from the IMF, but with the elections on the doorstep the government decided to return the IMF loan and started borrowing commercially (Kumar, 1996: 1603). To change the situation, adaptations in the exchange rate policy were initiated in 1986, while government control of industry and investments was deregulated. The market was opened up to increase competition and to prepare Indian industries for competition in the global market (Sawant and Rao, 1993: 3–5).

Although deregulation stimulated economic growth, current account deficits increased significantly in the 1980s. The liberalization policy had induced the public sector to import more capital goods. The money to pay for these imports came from commercial banks and consisted of hard foreign exchange currencies borrowed against high interest rates. Additionally, the export situation left a lot to be desired. About 20 per cent of the exports were paid for with weak currencies from the then Eastern bloc. At the same time, exports to Western countries decreased because of the recession in those countries. The high deficits, the rising interest payment on foreign debt and the increase in imports hampered India's economic growth.

Early in 1991, India was again confronted with a severe economic crisis. Foreign exchange reserves fell, deficits increased, the burden of foreign debt was growing and there was high inflation. In response, the moderate economic liberalization was replaced by a stronger liberalization orientation through the New Economic Policy (NEP) (Kumar, 1996: 1603–4; Joshi and Little, 1996: 14–16). India adopted a Structural Adjustment Programme (SAP) aimed at reducing budget and balance of payments deficits, and economic sectors, such as trade and industry, were reformed to become more market-oriented and to facilitate integration into the global economy (Masilamani, 1995: 5). Public expenditure in sectors such as education and agriculture, which had increased significantly during the 1980s, was reduced to relieve the debt. The free inflow of capital and technology was stimulated by the relaxation of governmental controls. The number of industries reserved exclusively for the public sector, industrial monopolies and restrictive trade practices and tax regimes were reduced (Sawant and Rao, 1993: 3–5; Patra, 1993: 41–6; Joshi and Little, 1996: 249).

Indian liberalization was further facilitated by the domestic changes in interests (Kohli, 1995; McDowell, 1997). Many business organizations and the middle class started to support economic liberalization, stimulated by reduced taxes and the increase of private shares in industries. The political agenda accompanying liberalization gave a high priority to technological innovation and efficiency to stimulate economic growth (Kohli, 1995: 316–30).

Since its liberalization policy, India's stake in the international market is higher than ever. This resulted in many disputes between India (and many other developing countries) and the developed countries during the GATT Uruguay Round. These disputes involved not only more traditional issues such as textiles and agricultural trade, but also the inclusion of new issues, such as intellectual property rights (IPRs), investment, services and labour. India, together with Brazil, tried to acquire leadership among the developing countries in the Uruguay Round (Patnaik, 1997: 118).

From the start of the Uruguay Round in 1986, India opposed the discussion of IPRs in the GATT. For the first few years of the Round, India kept the issue off the table with the support of a coalition of thirteen other developing countries. The coalition argued that the UNCTAD and the World Intellectual Property Organization (WIPO), instead of the GATT, were the proper forums to discuss IPRs. One of the main reasons for many developing countries opposing a stronger IPRs regime was their interest in the protection of their strong pharmaceutical industries. These industries are able to provide cheap generic drugs. However, the coalition of developing countries was too weak to make it through the Round. Brazil, Mexico and Argentina started to adopt a more positive attitude towards discussing IPRs in the Round. Under the US threat of unilateral trade measures and in need of US support to get IMF and World Bank loans, India was forced to change its position at the beginning of 1989 (Oxley, 1990: 191; Patnaik, 1997: 127).

A similar pattern of first opposing and then changing positions is visible in the issue of trade-related investment measures (TRIMS). India, together with other developing countries, argued that the GATT was not the appropriate forum to discuss this issue, since investment issues were considered to be domestic issues. These countries especially did not want to discuss investment measures, as they were perceived to be unrelated to trade. If investment was to be discussed, India argued, the only trade-related subjects are export performance requirements and local content/manufacturing requirements (Patnaik, 1997: 133–5). Despite the objections of developing countries, the final outcome of the negotiations was the proposal for the WTO to study the subject (Jain, 1997: 102). In GATT/WTO language, this meant that services were definitely going to be included in the WTO mandate.

In 1985, just before the start of the Uruguay Round, India introduced a 'position paper' on the Round. While the paper claimed to support the Round, it argued against the inclusion of services (Oxley, 1990: 100–4). This rejection was supported by many other developing countries. Again, these countries questioned the legal competence of the GATT/WTO in this matter. The dominance of transnational corporations (TNCs) in services projected an image of neo-colonial threat. India was afraid that an agreement on services would be unprofitable for the infant industries in the developing countries, and that it would erode national sovereignty. India, which had only recently made some moderate attempts towards liberalization, feared that its heavily state-financed service sector would not survive international competition. Supported by countries like Brazil, Argentina, former Yugoslavia and Egypt (the Group of Five), India faced the question of whether to leave the GATT negotiations preparing the new Round, or to accept the compromise that the issue of services would be open for discussion. They chose the latter option under threat from the United States that it would continue to discuss services with or without the Group of Five. The Unites States also threatened not to participate in the new Round, or to withdraw the existing trade concessions from developing countries. The Indian-American economist

Bhagwati advised India to enter into the service negotiations, since its coalition partners (especially Brazil and Egypt) were tied too strongly to the United States to remain in the coalition. He argued that India should instead make sure that the freedom of movement of people was included in the agreement. The predictions by Bhagwati materialized in 1987. Threatening sanctions, and in some cases making good on the threats – for instance, in 1987 when it doubled the duties on some imports from Brazil – the United States was successful in breaking up the coalition of the opposing developing countries. But even without the US measures the coalition was beginning to disintegrate. For one, developing countries did not have the same interests. Some Far Eastern and South East Asian countries were much less opposed to a service agreement than some of the less developed countries. Moreover, developing countries increasingly recognized that it was difficult to leave out services because of the strong links with other issues, such as investment. Therefore, developing countries accepted the inclusion of services in a special negotiation group, provided that development objectives would constitute an integral part of the talks (Patnaik, 1997: 135–8; McDowell, 1997: 92–111).

Even though India had accepted the inclusion of services, in 1989 the United States continued to put pressure on the country by placing India on the list of priority countries to be sanctioned under Section 301 of the Omnibus Trade and Competitiveness Act 1988 if no agreement were reached on barriers to investment and insurance.[3]

In India, the US threat was taken seriously. As India's single largest trading partner, the United States is extremely important to India. In the period 1994–5, 10 per cent of India's imports came from the United States, while 19 per cent of its exports had the United States as destination (Government of India, 1999). In addition, the United States is India's single largest foreign investor. To the United States, India is of less, but increasing, importance. Between 1991 and 1998, US exports to India rose from US$1999 million to US$3564 million, while its imports rose from US$3192 million to US$8237 million. In this same period, India went from 27th to 24th place among the USA's top trading partners. In terms of exports, India became relatively less important, dropping from no. 30 in 1991 to no. 32 in 1998, but in terms of imports it became relatively more significant, rising from no. 25 to no. 23. The trade balance of the United States with India thus shows an increasing deficit of US$1193 in 1991 and US$4673 in 1998 (US DOC, 1999). The United States had begun to view India as an important emerging market, especially since India had committed itself to opening up its domestic market. In 1994 Clinton indicated that he wanted to increase his ties with

India because of its rapidly expanding market and its economic reforms, which had made the country more accessible. This policy orientation was illustrated by the fact that Clinton sent numerous business delegations to India (Malhotra, 1997: 432–3, 437).

Although the United States did not execute its Section 301 threat, the fear was real. Still, India did not give in easily, and in a coalition with other developing countries it managed to come up with some counter-proposals on how to deal with services. One of the main successes for India was in the area of the freedom of movement of people. Some developing countries argued that developed countries should allow the temporary entry of foreign professionals. This feature was recognized in the WTO service agreement (*Times of India*, 12 April 1994; *Telegraph*, 19 April 1994; Patnaik, 1997, 139–40).

Following the conclusion of the Uruguay Round, disputes between India and developed countries have not been resolved. For many years the United States and the EU complained about high tariffs in certain areas, such as agricultural and consumer products. Although India has committed itself since 1991 to more strongly liberalising its economy through the New Economic Policy, and its average tariff rates fell from 144 per cent in 1990–1 to 35 per cent in 1997–8, market access remains sensitive (EU, 1999). According to a survey of the European Commission, India continues to violate the Uruguay agreement on tariffs. This is due to a combination of basic applied tariffs, which remain high and are sometimes increased, and recently introduced measures like Special Customs Duty and Additional Customs Duty. Although the Special Customs Duty was abolished after complaints from the EU, others remain in place.

Developing countries also have complaints. Countries such as India protest against their limited market access to developed countries, predominantly the EU and the United States, in the areas of textiles and agricultural products. One of the sore points is the threat and actual use of Section 301 of the Omnibus Trade and Competitiveness Act 1988. India has been under surveillance by the United States for not allowing sufficient access to US financial institutions, banking and security firms, and for not providing adequate IPRs protection. The Dispute Settlement Body of the WTO has received complaints against India on insufficient application of its IPRs regime, its import duties and its quantitative import restrictions (Dhar, 1997; Jain, 1997: 102–3; *Indian Express*, 17 July 1997; EU, 1999).

In this section I have argued that during the Uruguay Round the counter-hegemony of developing countries to the liberal trading system eroded. Because of this erosion, the position of India as a leading voice among developing countries became very weak. I show in the remainder of this chapter that on the issue of a social clause, India has been able to keep its leading role, and to unite most developing countries. After developing countries had been forced to give in on many of the new issues that had entered the agenda of the Uruguay Round, the opposition to a social clause seemed all that was left to the developing countries operating as a bloc. This was, however, not enough to sustain a coalition of developing countries in the Uruguay Round negotiations. Even in this case there were differences of opinion between developing countries, as some, such as Argentina, were not opposed to discussing labour standards in the WTO (WTO, 1996c).

Core Labour Rights: *De Jure* and *De Facto*

While part of India's resistance to a social clause may have originated from its weak position in multilateral trade negotiations, it was also the substance of a social clause that worried the government. India has ratified ILO Conventions 29, 100 and 111, relating respectively to forced labour, equal remuneration and non-discrimination (see Appendix). Despite trade union demands, India refuses to ratify ILO Conventions 87, 98, 105 and 138, respectively relating to the freedom of association, the right to collective bargaining and the abolition of forced and child labour (NATLEX, 1999). The primary reason why the Indian government has not ratified Conventions 87 and 98 is that it does not want to grant these rights to certain categories of public servants, while the ILO Conventions only allow the exclusion of senior officials involved in policy-making (*Pioneer*, 1 May 1992, 31 October 1994).[4] Conventions 105 and 138 have not been ratified because forced and child labour are still used in the country.

Despite the refusal to ratify the four Conventions, the majority of the standards related to the core Conventions are part of national law and/or the Indian Constitution. Individual states may have their own provisions. Freedom of association and the right to organize are described in Article 19 of the Indian Constitution and are protected through the Trade Unions Act 1926, which allows any seven workers to form a union and protects unions against civil and criminal prosecutions arising out of disputes. India has no law that provides for statutory union recognition and collective bargaining. All attempts to change the Indian law from one stimulating dispute settlement through government intervention (adjudication, arbitration and conciliation, as provided under the Industrial Disputes Act 1947) into a system enabling and promoting collective bargaining have failed. The main opposition has come from the smaller unions (which are too weak to enforce *de facto* collective bargaining), medium-sized unions (since only the largest unions would be recognized as a bargaining agent), employers and ruling parties. Additionally, as long as disputes concerning the counting of membership are not resolved, there is a practical obstacle to this kind of recognition, and to compulsory bargaining (Ramaswamy and Ramaswamy, 1988: 197–9). The Bonded Labour System (Abolition) Rules 1976 provide for the discharge of labourers from any obligation resulting from the terms of their bond (Anonymous, 1990: 4; NATLEX, 1999). In addition, article 23/1 of the Indian Constitution prohibits forced labour (Anonymous, 1990: 8). The Equal Remuneration Act 1976 and its amendment (1987) regulate equal payment between men and women. A special commission monitors and investigates alleged abuses of minorities (NATLEX, 1999). In addition, scheduled tribes are entitled to certain development funds and government hiring quotas (ICFTU, 1998b). Child labour is regulated through the Child Labour (Prohibition and Regulation) Rules 1986, and in article 24 of India's Constitution the engagement of children younger than fourteen in certain employment areas is prohibited, and the conditions of work in other areas are regulated (Commission on International Labour Standards and Trade, 1996: 10; NATLEX, 1999).

Despite these legal arrangements, day-to-day life is an entirely different matter. The most important observation is that the above-mentioned legislation is *de facto* mainly applicable to the workforce employed in the organized sector. India's workforce is estimated to make up about 37 per cent of its population (Sinha, 1994: 774). Of this 37 per cent, only 7.5 per cent is employed in the organized sector (Davala, 1994: 5; Prasad, 1999). While overall employment increased from the early 1970s to the mid-1990s, this growth mainly took place in the unorganized sector (Kannan, 1999: 755).

Although freedom of association and the right of collective bargaining are generally respected in the organized sector, the ILO regularly receives complaints concerning violations of freedom of association from labourers working in the informal sector and EPZs, and from certain categories of civil servants that are not granted this right (ICFTU, 1998b). The absence of national law on collective bargaining does not mean that collective bargaining does not occur. The use of collective agreements has modestly grown, especially in states where government intervention to solve disputes is limited (Ramaswamy, 1992: 25–8). Still, one should note that barely 1 per cent of the organized sector workforce is covered by collective agreements on wages and working conditions (Sharma, 1996: 50).

Despite legislation, bonded labour remains a major problem in India. The country has been criticized by the ILO for its inability to implement its laws in this area. Although the estimates differ, there are about five to twenty million bonded people (ICFTU, 1998b).[5]

Female workers are, as in most countries, confronted with lower wages and worse working conditions than their male counterparts (Ghosh, 1995: 575). In many cases indigenous people and people from low castes are discriminated against and harassed (ICFTU, 1998b).

It is a well known fact that child labour is a major problem in India. In fact, India has the doubtful honour of being the country with the largest number of child labourers in the world. Their number is cautiously estimated at around seventeen million (1987 sample) (ILO, 1996c: 1). The ICFTU uses figures ranging from 22 million to 100 million (ICFTU, 1998b). Although the ICFTU still sees the government's efforts to deal with child labour as ineffective, considering the scale of the problem, the regional office of the ILO highlighted a recent increase of the government's efforts to deal with child labour (ILO, 1996c: 2; ICFTU, 1998b). Domestically, special committees have criticized the government on several occasions that its work to abolish child labour has not been sufficient. In 1994, the Parliament's Standing Committee on Labour and Welfare accused the government of not listening to the Committee's recommendations on child labour (*Pioneer*, 27 April 1994), while in the same year an official committee on labour standards concluded that India lacks the will to eliminate child labour (Commission on International Labour Standards and Trade, 1996: 58).

The Emergence of a Broad National Coalition

The largest central trade union organizations (CTOs) are the Bharatiya Mazdoor Sangh (BMS), the Indian National Trade Union Congress (INTUC), the Hind Mazdoor Sabha (HMS), the All Indian Trade Union Congress (AITUC) and the Centre of Indian Trade Unions (CITU). The Hindu nationalist union BMS has no single strong basis for membership, but is represented in banking and insurance. INTUC's main members come from steel, mining, textiles, petroleum and chemical industries. HMS is mostly present in docks, ports and railways (Interview with ICFTU, 21 December 1999). CITU's and AITUC's bases are much more regionally oriented. Both are present in coal industries. AITUC is also present in metal and mining, while CITU represents workers in small-scale industries, mostly in West Bengal (Interview with ICFTU, 11 April 2000). Trade unions represent about 3 per cent of the working population in the country (Chandra, 1997: 46).

The lack of implementation of core labour standards might have been the reason for CTOs to favour a social clause, and to exploit the international pressure for a social clause in the GATT/WTO as an opportunity for improving labour standards at home. However, Indian CTOs have been strongly outspoken against a social clause. In the next section I explain why this is the case.

CTOs: Rejecting a social clause

In 1994, the position of the CTOs on the social clause issue was in the process of being formed. Confronting all CTOs alike was negative public opinion on a social clause. As an Indian newspaper wrote:

> In terms of purely short-term economism and populism it would be convenient for them [trade unions] to support the US position. In that sense, they now have a chance to show their government that they have the political maturity and the responsibility to shun such myopic considerations and build a national consensus on opposing the social clause that will in the long run hit the workers from the Third World by restricting trade from these countries and also constraining the growth of employment and wage levels. This will also enable the trade unions in India for example to effectively counter the campaign of the Government that they are guided solely by narrow sectional interests. (*Pioneer*, 8 April 1994)[6]

Only the INTUC was in favour of a social clause and seemed to fit this picture of a 'politically immature and irresponsible trade union', although HMS also approved the social clause, initially. The INTUC had been bombarding successive governments for years with letters trying to convince them to support a social clause. This CTO, aligned to the ICFTU, was torn between two sides. On the one hand, as a member of the ICFTU, the INTUC was expected to support the ICFTU's campaign for a social clause. On the other hand, the union was locked into a national pattern of influence mediation. Because the INTUC is closely related to the Congress Party (I), the ruling party until 1996, it was difficult for it to assume a stance against the national government on such a sensitive foreign policy matter.

In 1988, 1990 and 1994 the INTUC's General Secretary Gopeshwar asked the Minister for Commerce to support the ICFTU's call for a social clause in the GATT Uruguay Round (Gopeshwar, 1988, 1990, 1994). On all occasions the INTUC wrote its letters on the insistence of the ICFTU. By 1994, when the social clause debate was at its height in India, the INTUC was attacked in public for being a supporter of developed countries instead of India (*Pioneer*, 11 April 1994). In May 1994, the INTUC's president changed the position of the organization. From then on, the INTUC was against a social clause, thereby overruling the general secretary's position (*Patriot*, 1 March 1994). Even after the change of position had happened, the ICFTU kept faith that the INTUC would turn around. In November 1995, when the ICFTU recognized that the Indian trade union was not in full agreement with the ICFTU's position on a social clause, it saw 'a distinct change in its views towards the issue but a firm agreement will take some time' (ICFTU 1995c). However, this firm agreement never came. Not only did the INTUC continue to oppose a social clause, in March 1998 the organization even opposed the ILO Declaration (see also Chapter 7) (Government of India, 1998).[7]

While the INTUC was indecisive, other CTOs were quite consistent in their rejection of a social clause. All, including the INTUC, shared the same claims about a social clause. The first claim of the CTOs concentrated on the motives behind a social clause. Many CTO representatives equated a social clause with trade measures. An argument to support this claim was that once a social clause became a reality, trade sanctions would be too. There was no question in the minds of the trade unionists that the intentions of the developed countries were to safeguard their own industries: 'developed countries are using the so-called "social clause" as a weapon to deny us market access in their part of the world, and to prohibit the entry of our products into their markets' (CTOs Appeal, 1995).

Another argument in support of the claim emphasized the lack of credibility. The fact that the United States had a record of selectively using its trade laws against other nations predicted a similar treatment in case of a social clause (CITU, 1996: 33; Interview with HMS, 24 March 1998). As one union spokesman said: 'A social clause will only be used against those countries where the trade interests of the USA are not at stake. The USA does have trade relations with China, so the USA has a double standard' (Interview with INTUC, 4 December 1996).[8] The rejection of a social clause remained a matter of principle. Therefore, the unions made no suggestions concerning a possible WTO process that could precede the initiation of trade sanctions and make it as objective as possible.

With similar conviction the motives of the WTO were questioned (CEC, 1995: 19; Interview with AITUC, 25 November 1996): 'Both the discussions on investments and patents in the WTO have strengthened the impression that the WTO is not in the interest of the developing world. The WTO is there to safeguard capital' (Interview with HMS, 26 November 1998). Moreover, the same distrust befell the ICFTU (see, for example, HMS, n.d.: 34; BMS, 1996: 35):

> The ICFTU supported the demand because the organisation is dominated by developed countries and it wants to create the impression amongst the workers of the developed countries that their employment is suffering because of India's cheap labour. (Interview with AITUC, 25 November 1996)

The second claim made by the CTOs referred to the relationship between the level of social and economic development, and the universality of labour standards (AITUC's reply to questionnaire 1997). As a spokesman for the INTUC stated:

> INTUC has been in conflict within the ICFTU with the developed countries. They have another level of development. Instead of in 150 years, developing countries should change the conditions in a very short time. All unions in the world are against the exploitation of labour, but it is not feasible to ask developing countries to do in a short time what has taken developed countries 150 years. (Interview with INTUC, 4 December 1996)

The third claim made by the CTOs referred to the effectiveness of a social clause. Both the possible effects on the ILO and those on workers themselves were questioned (Interview with BMS, 4 December 1996). As one trade union leader stated:

> The ILO being a tripartite body . . . has to formulate some minimum labour standards for the member countries due to international trade union movement. By hijacking its functions, the imperialist countries – at the diktat of their transnationals – in fact want to completely neutralize the might of the workers and enable the transnationals to call the shots through the WTO. (CITU, 1996: 34)

Only HMS has argued that international enforcement of labour standards would be limited to the export sector, and therefore ineffective: 'At best, such policies [social clause] will shift the child labour from export industry to industry catering to domestic needs or other informal sector activities' (HMS, n.d.: 29).

The fourth claim concentrated on the issue of national sovereignty

(Interviews with AITUC, 25 November 1996; HMS, 24 March 1998). The way of expressing interest in national sovereignty differed according to the speaker, but the message remained the same. AITUC stated:

> You see, on some points employers and workers do not differ, because the main problem is with the multinational companies. The social clause is an attack on the country. We did unite with the local capitalists in fighting the imperialists and making demands. It is to save our economic independence. (Interview with AITUC, 25 November 1996)

Similarly, BMS claimed that: 'A social clause has no benefits for India. Omissions in the area of working conditions in India should not be connected to world trade, but should be dealt with by India' (Interview with BMS, 4 December 1996).[9]

Indian government: Discursive consistency

The Indian government supported similar claims to the unions against a social clause. The first claim related to the effectiveness of a social clause. It argued that India's persisting problems in the areas of child and forced labour would not be solved by linking the solution to trade sanctions:

> When it is only related to the exporting industry, how would it address problems like child labour? The problem would remain. . . . Take the carpet industry. Not all carpets are for export. There are a lot of carpets that are sold for the domestic market. And if you are going to impose sanctions on the carpets that are exported, it does not help anybody. It does not help the problem, it does not help the situation, so what are we talking about? (Interview with Ministry of Labour, 26 November 1996)

Other activities were considered to be more valuable:

> We have an international programme for the elimination of child labour under the ILO. It is only very recently that some other countries have joined us in that programme. In the beginning we kept saying: Why can there not be much more participation by countries instead of them making a noise about this, why countries can't come and share some of their resources? (Interview with Ministry of Labour, 26 November 1996)

Neo-liberal Discourse: India

> Child labour is not solvable unless you solve poverty. We need money, not sanctions. (Interview with Ministry of External Affairs, 27 November 1998)

It was also argued that the ILO would not survive if the element of trade sanctions was to be included (SLC, 1994: 41–5). By the same token, trade sanctions were not perceived to have a place in organizations such as the ILO:

> The argument saying that the ILO lacks deed has been given several times. That it does not have enforcement. But the very existence and survival of the ILO has been on the basis of consensus, within and among countries. It is developed as an institution to harmonize the wishes and aspirations with the views of the different players. . . . It has succeeded in setting standards and persuading the countries to adopt these standards and recognize the standards and try to the best of their ability to comply with the standards. The reason why it has succeeded is that there has been no force. The moment you talk about enforcement I am afraid that the whole superstructure of the ILO is liable to destruction. Actually it might break down as an organization once you talk about teeth and enforcement. (Interview with Ministry of Labour, 26 November 1996)

The second, economic, claim argued that the introduction of a social clause would add a trade barrier, instead of making world trade freer. In other words, the motives behind a social clause were questioned. The Indian government claimed that the move to study the relationship between trade and internationally recognized labour standards was:

> an attempt to introduce unilateral non-tariff protectionist barriers to the multilateral free trade regime that was emerging as a result of the GATT understanding, essentially triggered by recession and unemployment in the developed countries. (SLC, 1994: 11)

It was argued that:

> although labour costs make up only 10 per cent of the total production costs, we do view it as one of our comparative advantages. High wage countries are trying to countervail our low labour costs. (Interview with Ministry of External Affairs, 27 November 1998)

The third claim, combining economic and sovereignty claims, argued that the social clause issue was forced upon India in an undemocratic manner. It was felt that the specific Indian context was not taken into account and that India was being denied the making of its own laws:

> in a manner that is consistent with our own resources and capabilities and our own levels of development . . . as economic growth takes place with the expansion of trade . . . there is bound to be a corresponding emphasis on better quality of life, quality of working live. It is bound to follow, because if you have greater development, greater disposable income, then the question of giving a better deal to the workers is followed. But to say that you first give a better deal to the workers and then only you could grow is putting the cart before the horse. You cannot have that situation and that is why I specifically mention that the level of economic development of a country is very, very relevant. You cannot have the same kind of standards of working conditions that you have in the Western countries. (Interview with Ministry of Labour, 26 November 1996)

The fourth claim related to the exclusion claim. Several arguments were used to support this claim. It was argued that India was already engaged in a battle to keep additional issues out of the GATT/WTO. Investment and IPRs were particularly sensitive issues. Thus there was a general view that the WTO might become too encompassing. It was also argued that once a working group to study the social clause issue was allowed, it would only be a matter of time before it would become a real issue. Finally, there was the fear that a social clause would not be confined to the six Conventions:

> Payment of Minimum Wages could also eventually become an element of the social clause, though this was not explicitly discussed at the International Labour Conference . . . it is advisable to oppose it as a matter of principle, as subsequent expansion of the elements constituting the 'social clause' may be detrimental to our interests. (SLC, 1994: 43)

In addition, definition issues would become problematic, the Indian government argued: 'The United States uses a much broader definition of forced labour than India: every labourer under fifteen years of age is forced' (Interview with Ministry of External Affairs, 27 November 1998).

Developments at the national level

An opportunity for the Indian government to check the level of consensus between them and the CTOs and employers' organizations occurred in October 1994 during the 32nd session of the Standing Labour Committee (SLC). While a deviating position of the CTOs would not have convinced the government to depart from its chosen position to oppose a social clause, a consensus would give the government's position more legitimacy (Interview with Ministry of External Affairs, 27 November 1998). The tripartite SLC, which meets under the auspices of the Labour Ministry, devoted part of its meeting to a discussion of labour standards and international trade.

The government asked the partners in the SLC to support its opposition, since the issue would come up at various national and international occasions over the coming years. Therefore, it felt a need to 'forge an unambiguous and unified position on the subject' (SLC, 1994: 46). This did not fall on deaf ears. All present agreed to oppose a social clause. The resolution was accepted unanimously (*Hindustan Times*, 28 October 1994). However, the CTOs did repeat their demand that the Indian government should ratify the Conventions on collective bargaining and the right to organize (*Pioneer*, 31 October 1994).

The SLC meeting was followed by three decisions. First, India had to increase its pressure in the GATT to get more attention for the issue of freedom of movement. The aim was to ensure that other countries would absorb a larger part of the surplus of professionals in India (*Times of India*, 12 April 1994; *Telegraph*, 19 April 1994). Although the Uruguay Round was concluded with a commitment to facilitate the movement of natural persons, this area did not undergo significant liberalization (WTO, 1999d). Second, there was a decision to take a closer look at the problems related to child and forced labour. Third, the Commerce Ministry decided in August 1994 to establish a commission to study the protection of labour standards in the country. This commission, consisting of chairman Subramanian Swamy (Janata Party), S. L. Passey (member of the INTUC) and A. V. Ganesan (former Commerce Secretary) was given the assignment of studying the legal framework and the implementation of legislation related to exploitative labour practices (including prison labour, child labour and forced labour), freedom of association and the right to organize, practices of collective bargaining and non-discrimination in employment. The recommendations of the commission were supposed to take into account the issue of a social clause (Government of India, 1994). The power of the commission was limited; its recommendations were not binding, leaving the government free to ignore them (*Pioneer*, 3 February 1996).

In January 1996, the 1000-page report was ready and presented to the Prime Minister. One of the most remarkable conclusions was that the government was advised to seek international consensus on a social clause, since some core labour standards deserve to be enforced internationally. Instead of being defensive, the report argued that the government should take a more moderate position. India should ask the international community to grant funds to abolish practices such as child labour, and try to create a consensus. It also recommended that the government abolish child labour by the year 2010 (*Times of India*, 3 February 1996; *Pioneer*, 3 February 1996).

In general, the commission's report received a negative response, which may explain why it was not made public. The *Times of India* argued that while India's record of labour standards is better than that of most countries that oppose a social clause, this is not sufficient to support a social clause. A social clause is protectionist and will be used for selective and illegal ends, the paper argued. It further claimed that the social clause debate helped to obfuscate the role global inequality plays in generating inferior working conditions. Wages are low because of poverty and because of monopolization of world trade by TNCs. Workers need to be organized, but World Bank and IMF policies are making them only more vulnerable (*Times of India*, 8 February 1996). The legitimacy not only of the report, but also of the commission itself, was questioned. First, it had been the Commerce Ministry, and not the Labour Ministry, that had assigned the study, stimulating the belief that the establishment of the commission was a capitulation to international pressure (*Observer of Business and Politics*, 5 September 1994). Further undermining the little legitimacy the commission had left was the decision by its trade union member to dissociate himself from the conclusions (*Economic Times*, 27 December 1995). On 18 April 1996 the INTUC associate published an addendum to the commission's report. It expressed severe criticism on the report, mainly because it did not represent the interests of the different stakeholders concerning a social clause. The addendum argued that the trade unions collectively disapproved of a social clause, being guided by 'national considerations' instead of sectional or ideological ones. A social clause, he maintained, was protectionist and would 'increase the misery of the downtrodden', undermined the role of the ILO and contained an arbitrary selection of labour standards (core labour standards). Strangely enough, although the INTUC staff member regarded the selection of certain labour standards as core labour standards as arbitrary, he called upon the government to pay attention to exactly those labour standards that had been classified as core (Passey, 1996).

On the side of the ICFTU, hopes were high about the effects of the commission's report, as it supported the confederation's policy indirectly.

While the ICFTU was convinced that the recommendations of this high-level commission would be accepted (ICFTU, 1996c), the reverse was true. As a representative of the Ministry of External Affairs stated, 'whatever the Swamy Commission would have to say, the government's mind was made up' (Interview with Ministry of External Affairs, 27 November 1998).

Discursive similarities

From 1994 onwards, a strong anti-social clause coalition had emerged in India against a social clause. It was a coalition between workers, employers and the government, in action and in spirit: in action, because major international meetings, such as of the ILO, were jointly prepared; in spirit, because the claims used were to a large extent similar. The discursive nature of the coalition was steady and did not change over time. The high degree of similarity of the claims used by all groups suggests that they duplicated each other's claims, apparently agreeing on their approach to foreign intervention.

To a large extent, the claims of the coalition against a social clause were the same as the claims of the neo-liberals. Just as in the neo-liberal discourse, the opponents claimed that the sovereignty of India was compromised through a social clause. Just as the ineffectiveness claim argues, it was felt that not the WTO, but the ILO, was the place to discuss labour standards. It was also argued that international enforcement of labour standards would be ineffective as it was limited to the export sector. Most also pointed out that a social clause had a potential to be used arbitrarily and would damage India's trading position. This, in turn, would hurt the future credibility of the ILO. The claim that labour standards have a relative value argued that the stage of development matters for the introduction of basic standards. Such a claim coming from the mouth of the CTOs seems somewhat surprising, especially since most of the unions felt that a social clause forced Western labour standards upon them, while at the same time they argued that the proposed standards should be respected in India (CTOs Appeal, 1995; HMS, n.d.; BMS reply to questionaire, 1997; AITUC reply to questionnaire, 1997). As this argument concentrated on the principles, rather than on the measures to support the principles, it suggested an inherent contradiction, as if the same labour standards initiated domestically would have other effects than if they were initiated on an international level.

While it appears that the arguments of CTOs were not distinguishable from those of the other actors, this is not the case. The CTOs made a point of rejecting the neo-liberal policies of the WTO, and the WTO as a whole. In 1995, a meeting, which brought together different organizations to discuss a social clause, concluded that the CTOs rejection of a social clause 'is totally different from that of the government position since it involves the rejection of the WTO/GATT' (CEC, 1995: 19).[10]

The fact of the matter is that neither the employers' organizations nor the CTOs[11] have conducted any research on the effects of a social clause. Possible positive effects, such as the effects on India's trade rivals, were insufficiently studied. As one Indian newspaper wrote, not India, but China, Singapore and Hong Kong – India's trade rivals – had something to fear when it came to labour standards. The article concluded: 'Benign foreign pressure hurts our national pride. But it is false pride' (*Business Standard*, 15 April 1994).

The Indian context – low enforcement of core labour standards and a weak position in multilateral trade negotiations – provides enough reason to understand the position of the Indian government. However, trade unions could have adopted a different position because of the low enforcement of core labour standards. Yet the low enforcement on the side of the government seemed to mirror the lack of direct interest of the CTOs.

Why CTOs were against a social clause can be explained by pointing towards their members and interests. As described above, CTOs' membership is concentrated in the formal sector, where the enforcement of the core labour standards is the strongest. In other words, among their members CTOs may not find a strong interest in a social clause. While organizing informal sector workers is indeed a difficult task for trade unions (Datt, 1997), it is also hampered by CTOs' lack of interest. Child labour as an issue was only picked up by CTOs in the 1990s, partly because of the prospects of taking up projects under IPEC (ILO, 1996c: 49). Bonded labour is a sensitive issue to some CTOs. For example, the INTUC has argued that there is no discrimination in payment among men and women and that forced labour only exists in isolated cases. In fact, the INTUC still relied on a fifteen-year-old statement by Indira Gandhi that bonded labour no longer formed a problem (Reddy, 1998; Interview with INTUC, 26 March 1998). However, it is estimated that the number of children living in bondage is around fifteen million (Human Rights Watch, 1996), even though the government recognizes only about ten thousand (ILO, 1998e). In fact, the INTUC is not convinced that bonded labour has been eradicated. In 1994, when it started to participate in a trade union forum on child servitude, the CTO declared that 'The working children are the most exploited and a large number of them are almost bonded' (INTUC, 1994b).[12]

If the proportion of unorganized workers is increasing, as many have suggested (Masilamani, 1995: 77–8; Hensman, 1996: 1030; Chandra, 1997: 31; Datt, 1997: 12–13; Kumar, 1997: 292), one would expect the CTOs to undertake more efforts to organize the unorganized. Not only can neglecting the unorganized sector decrease their membership, as the unorganized sector is growing at the expense of the organized sector, it also increases regulatory competition between formal and informal sectors. This, and the argument that India's increasingly open economy suffers from cheap imports from other countries, such as Indonesia (Interview with HMS, 24 March 1998), might have created a more positive attitude towards a social clause.

That unions have not assumed a positive position on a social clause can be explained by their status. In fact, one may question whether the weak position of the CTOs would have allowed them to oppose the government on a foreign policy issue. Increasingly, unions face pressure from five factors.

First, new categories of workers are created, such as casual and trainee workers. These workers receive different payments from regular workers. In addition, many manufacturing enterprises have expanded employment in lower managerial positions. Often the skills of blue-collar workers are general enough to transfer to low white-collar workers. The result of this strategy is that control over the production process is taken away from the blue-collar workers. White-collar workers are less inclined to share the interests of the blue-collar workforce, since they are responsible for management. Also contributing to a fragmentation of the workforce are the practices management employed to gain control. These practices include an increase in workload and the 'farming out' of jobs to underpaid contract labourers. Even capital-intensive industries increasingly make use of this latter method (Ramaswamy, 1988: 3–9; 1997: 48; Breman, 1999: 429). In fact, the increasing socio-economic diversity of the workforce and the inability or unwillingness of unions to stand up for the growing unorganized sector are important factors lowering the popularity of trade unions (Tiwana, 1994: 745).

Second, industry is characterized by considerable labour saving automation. Although unions are often opposed to the replacement of people by machines, they also realize that the failure to do so might make an industry less competitive. This can lead to the lay-off of workers anyway. These trends do not contribute to a common interest of workers or a united trade union movement (Ramaswamy, 1988: 3–9).

Third, the liberalization policy has raised the aspirations of the working class for upward mobility. Some argue that, increasingly, money has become more important than rights (Bhatt et al., 1996: 56). This is decreasing the popularity of trade unions because they are perceived as blocking the road to peaceful cooperation between workers and employers. Workers who are more in favour of trying to negotiate better payments are unhappy with the political baggage of the federations. One of the reasons why BMS has increased its popularity over the past few years is that this union is reluctant to resort quickly to industrial action (Bhatt *et al.*, 1996: 57–9). That the ideological luggage of unions is more and more seen as a blockade is also illustrated by the growth of independent unions, particularly at plant levels (Sinha, 1994: 777). Just like the political unions, the independent unions have no real interest in the unorganized sector (Sharma, 1996: 55).

Fourth, the rise of enterprise unions is a threat in itself to the traditional unions. Enterprise unions focus on company issues and tend to neglect issues outside their area.

Fifth, because of these processes, the importance of trade unions for political parties is decreasing (Prasad, 1999).

That the power of workers in general and that of unions in particular has decreased since 1991 is illustrated by the fact that there has been a significant reduction of strikes, which does not stem from a substantial improvement in workers' conditions. The number of working days lost to strikes fell from 12.42 million in 1991 to 5.72 million in 1995, while those lost because of lock-outs rose from 14 million in 1991 to 15.72 million in 1995 (Bhatt *et al.*, 1996: 55; Ministry of Labour, 1996–7: 18). Particularly in the private sector, offensive lock-outs as a strategic weapon have increased; for example, to lay off workers in the absence of a clear exit policy (Sharma, 1996: 18, 61).

The decreasing power of trade unions is also evident in the view on collective bargaining agreements. Since the beginning of the 1990s, the small number of agreements have increasingly been seen as a method for the revival of unproductive industries rather than as a method for the improvement of the position of workers as such. The commitments employers and workers agree to may include wage agreements and employment security. However, these commitments increasingly include agreements on productivity and the flexibility of the labour force, cuts in salaries, the freezing of benefits and voluntarily suspension of trade union rights (Ramaswamy, 1992: 27–8; Venkata Ratnam, 1996: 351).

A pressure in itself is the loss of membership by the central union organizations. In 1987, registered unions had a total of 7,959,000 members. In 1990, membership had decreased to 7,020,000, while the number of unions had increased (Ministry of Labour, 1994–5). That these figures are disputed is illustrated by the claimed membership of the unions themselves. According to the thirteen trade unions with a claimed membership of one million or more, together they have a membership of 25 million (Prasad,

1999; for more details on membership see also *Business India*, 4–7 November 1996).

International Coalition Formation: The Intergovernmental Level

Just as at the national level, a process of coalition formation took place at the international level. India and other developing countries had suffered several defeats in the GATT with respect to the so-called new issues. If India wanted to prevent yet another issue becoming part of the GATT/WTO, it had to take a firm stand and try to raise support among the developing countries. The first opportunity presented itself at the beginning of 1994. During a meeting of the United Nations Economic and Social Commission of Asia and the Pacific (ESCAP), developing countries agreed that labour issues should not be linked to trade (*Pioneer*, 8 April 1994; *Tribune*, 13 April 1994). During a summit of the G-15 (the organization of seventeen developing countries that prepares input for other international meetings, such as those of the WTO and the G-7), concern was expressed about the inclusion of labour standards (SLC, 1994: 42; Interview with Indian Ministry of Labour, 26 November 1996). Meanwhile, the Indian government continued to repeat its rejection of a social clause at the international level. In an attempt to sustain the earlier formed Southern consensus[13] on the issue, the Fifth Conference of Labour Ministers of Non-Aligned and Other Developing Countries (NAM), held in Delhi in January 1995, devoted a part of its discussions to a social clause.[14]

The NAM reports are interesting because they attempt to analyse the labour standards issue more critically than either of the actors in India had done. In their analysis, it was pointed out that developing countries are increasingly exporters of manufactured goods, instead of raw materials. The growth of the overall output and the increased share of manufactured outputs are the result of technology transfer, capital flows and the transnationalization of production, in which companies prefer developing countries as the location for their production. An appeal from several Indian trade unions during the NAM conference made use of the same analysis. According to them a social clause was used to deny developing countries market access, and thus prohibit the entry of Indian products to developed countries' markets. The trade unions claimed that they would not accept a link (CTOs Appeal, 1995: 3). According to the NAM, developed countries were unreasonably concerned about the effects of translocation of production on their economies. It was argued that this fear of translocation on the basis of low labour standards is incorrect since: (a) about 50 per cent of foreign direct investment (FDI) in developing countries takes place in the mining industry, which is location-bounded; (b) the share of labour costs is rather low in the total of production costs; (c) therefore, a decision to invest abroad is based on other factors such as infrastructure; and (d) FDI is still concentrated in developed countries (NAM, 1995a: 1–11). Thus, the perception that problems of developed countries such as unemployment and increasing wage inequality can be written on the account of low wages in the developing countries was considered incorrect. Instead, the NAM document argued, developed countries have to look at technological changes if they want to find the reasons for job losses (NAM, 1995a: 12).

The counter-attack of the NAM emphasized a variety of claims. The first neo-liberal claim was an economic one, arguing that an upward harmonization of labour standards would undermine the liberalization of trade, which is based on comparative advantages and cost differences. Moreover, considering the present inequality between developing and developed countries, a social clause would further decrease the competitiveness of Third World products, create unemployment and therefore not improve labour conditions. Resource transfer, rather than trade sanctions, was expected to facilitate an improvement in labour standards. The second claim argued that if core labour standards are to be universal, it is wrong to approach them from an international trade perspective, since much of the production takes place outside the scope of trade. Although this claim made use of the universality claim rather than rejecting it, other parts of the NAM document suggest that the universality claim as such is not appreciated, as it does not take into account the levels of development.

The exclusion claim was also located in the neo-liberal tradition. Here the NAM argued that once the linkage between trade and labour standards was accepted, it would serve as a precedent for future proposals, including a wide range of labour standards. It was also argued that the earlier deals in the world trading regime, such as article XX(e) of the GATT on prison labour, have no meaning. In the fashion of the ineffectiveness claims, the NAM further argued that the process of standard setting would be jeopardized when brought under the umbrella of the international trading regime instead of under the ILO. The sovereignty claim was evoked in the document by the argument that assuring the compatibility of economic and social development is a task for national governments and not one for international organizations (NAM, 1995a: 14–17).

Although the NAM clearly rejected the link between trade and labour standards, it suggested some activities to eliminate some of the most pressing problems related to labour conditions. Among these were actions to eliminate gender discrimination in the workplace and the (progressive) elimination of child labour. However, NAM suggested that actions should be implemented taking the socio-economic and cultural characteristics of the respective countries into consideration. It also urged opposing any attempt to link ILO Conventions to international trade agreements. Instead, NAM recommended the strengthening, review and update of ILO standards. However, it argued to reserve the decision on whether and how to implement the standards for each country individually (NAM, 1995b, c).

The NAM meeting was a sign for the ICFTU to send a high-level delegation to Delhi, including ICFTU's General Secretary Bill Jordan, to lobby for a social clause. This lobby was directed not only towards the NAM countries, but also towards its own affiliates. During a 1995 meeting of the ICFTU's Asia and Pacific Regional Organization (APRO), the Indian affiliates made it clear that they were not in favour of workers' standards linked to trade (ICFTU/APRO, 1995a). However, despite the tension between the confederation and its Indian affiliates, a statement was adopted which called for a linkage between trade and labour standards (ICFTU/APRO, 1995b). Having passed the first barrier, the ICFTU delegation met with the Ministers of Commerce, External Affairs, Labour and Finance. That none of the ministers appeared to be responsive to the confederation's demands for a social clause (ICFTU/APRO, 1995a) was demonstrated by the results of the NAM meeting. To his credit, during a press conference Jordan referred to the doubts of the Indian affiliates that a social clause would serve the purpose of protecting workers' standards (ICFTU/APRO, 1995a). But he should not have taken the trouble. While the APRO issued its statement, emphasizing that a link between workers' standards and trade would not be intended to be protectionist, several CTOs (including ICFTU members INTUC and HMS) produced their own appeal to the NAM meeting, rejecting a social clause. Although demanding respect for ILO Conventions, this appeal stated that 'we notice that circles in developed countries are using the so-called "social clause" as a weapon to deny us market access' (CTOs Appeal, 1995).

Transnational Coalitions against Child Labour

While the perception that a social clause would not be in the interest of workers in Asian countries was confirmed during a meeting between Asian trade unionists in 1996 (South Asian Consultation on Social Clause/Labour Rights in Multilateral Trade Agreements, 1996), there were some dissenting voices, especially from the unorganized sector. This became apparent during a meeting organized by the Centre for Education and Communication (CEC) in 1995. Having been neglected by the CTOs and the government for many years, these representatives felt that in some cases more was to be gained by supporting Western governments than the Indian government. At the meeting, a spokesman for the fishworkers argued:

> On the one hand, it is clear that the real motivations of the developed countries are dubious, on the other hand, the failure of our government in protecting workers makes one wonder whether this is an opportunity to be exploited. (Kocherty, 1995: 9)

Feeding this perception was the feeling that the Indian government was not only unwilling to enforce labour laws, but in the future would also be less able to do so because of the increasing integration of India in the world economy. The flexibility of production units in terms of relocation and the decreasing levels of unionization demanded an international solution, and would call for exploring the usefulness of international mechanisms. As one argued, 'There is very little possibility of a purely internal struggle or mechanism that could solve the problem' (Chachi, 1995: 11).

Therefore it was urged that a 'social floor' for competition in the world market was needed to protect the standards of workers. Trade unions should use the opportunity that this international support gives them to bargain with the government:

> While the hypocrisy of the first world countries needs to be exposed . . . workers of the third world have to fight for inclusion of the social clause and not feel under any obligation to support their own ruling class in the name of national interest. (Swaminathan, 1995: 11)

Objections were also raised against the perception that India's comparative advantage should rely on cheap and exploited labour: 'The competitive edge that they tend to protect . . . is the miserable wage levels of the workers, the bad living and working conditions and the denial to them of basic human rights' (Gothoskar, 1995: 11).

Although these opinions were isolated, and were not reflected in the conclusions of the CEC meeting, they found response in the West. While most people in the West, either consumers or politicians, may not lose a minute of sleep worrying over the working conditions of a fisherman, no image has been stronger than that of small boys and girls, sitting for hours in the same position, weaving carpets or polishing gems, chained to their instruments. The emotional appeal of this image has provided a strong basis for transnational coalitions between Indian activists and Western activists and politicians.

Whereas trade unionists did not try to turn the pressure on the social clause debate to their advantage, with the sole exception of asking the government to ratify the core Conventions, child labour activists did link the social clause debate to their specific goals. From their side it was suggested that about 8–10 per cent of the child labourers working in the export sector could be helped by a social clause (Gathia, 1995: 13) or by a scheme that would provide tariff benefits for products produced without child labour (Satyarthi, 1995: 14). More than the formal sector representatives, these activists emphasized that the potential of a social clause would be not so much the instrument itself, but more a means to exercise pressure. In the same year that the social clause debate became important in India, Gathia of the Centre of Concern for Child Labour began to use the idea of a social clause in a media campaign. In a newspaper article of September 1994 he was quoted as saying that it has 'far-reaching consequences for the country's economy in the view of the US threat to ban imports from Third World Countries involving child labour' (*Patriot*, 16 September 1994). He added that the intended move of the United States 'to act in concert with the NAFTA would be a far more dangerous one for India as it would come from a trade bloc consisting of the US, Canada and Mexico. If NAFTA decided to impose the ban it would create a chain reaction' (*Patriot*, 16 September 1994). Just after the 1994 GATT Marrakesh meeting, Agnivesh of the Bandhua Mukti Mocha (Bonded Labour Liberation Front) also welcomed the idea of a social clause to help to eliminate child labour, even though he added that a social clause should be much more comprehensive, including issues like debt relief (*Tribune*, 18 April 1994). One year later, however, Agniveh accused the West of creating a bad situation for Indian exports by banning products made using child labour (*Times of India*, 18 June 1995).

Two events illustrated the great attention the child labour issue attracted. The first was foreign support for the child labour activist Kailash Satyarthi, and his involvement in the adaptation of the US Child Labour Deterrence Act of Senator Tom Harkin.[15] The second was the design of the Rugmark label for Indian export carpets, and the response to this initiative by the Indian government. Rugmark label is an initiative that certifies 'child labour free' carpets from India and Nepal. It includes a child labourer rehabilitation programme (ILRF, 1996).

In the early 1990s, US Senator Tom Harkin, a Democrat from Iowa, introduced for the first time the Child Labor Deterrence Act in the US Senate. The purpose of the Act was to stop the employment of children under the age of fifteen in the production of manufactured goods or mining products to be exported to the United States. While Harkin has failed as yet to get the Child Labor Deterrence Act 1993/4 adopted, the Act has been introduced several times in the US Congress. The text of the proposed Act has changed considerably, showing the involvement of Satyarthi.

After the Act was introduced a few times, Satyarthi met Harkin in Washington and discussed his criticism of the Act (ILRF, 1996: 8; Interview with SACCS, 24 November 1998). Satyarthi's main criticism was that the Act required the importer of a manufactured article to take reasonable steps to ensure, to the extent practicable, that an article is not a product of child labour (Child Labor Deterrence Act 1993). Satyarthi argued that the basis of the Act should be that a foreign industry identified as a user of child labour should be exempted from an import ban if it was able to produce a certificate that a particular article was not produced by child labour. Instead of the production of the evidence in the United States, Satyarthi saw a greater role for an inspection body in the countries concerned (SACCS, n.d.). As a response to the criticism, the Child Labor Deterrence Act 1994 changed considerably. The text stipulated that there should be a role for exporters and a certification agency that should include NGOs involved in child welfare (Child Labor Deterrence Act 1994). The proposal for the inspection body was similar to the initiative Satyarthi took with the inspection system of his brainchild, the Rugmark (ILRF, 1996).

Also in the first half of the 1990s, the US Department of Labor (DOL) accused India of not enforcing its child labour laws. DOL had initiated its research on child labour at the request of the US Congress Committee on Appropriations, which wanted to know which manufactured imports to the United States made use of child labour (*Observer of Business and Politics*, 22 September 1994). During a public hearing as a result of the report in 1994, Satyarthi testified on the use of child labour in Indian industry.

The attack on the Indian carpet industry that used child labour, through the Rugmark initiative and the Harkin Act, along with the debate on a social clause and the outrage about child labour in general, had started to put severe pressure on India. This resulted in renewed attention to the problem of child labour.[16] As Swamy wrote:

> There is now international pressure exerted on India, threatening her export prospects. The very prospect of the introduction of a social clause in trade has made the Government of India do some thinking on the possibility of eliminating the incidence of child labour. (Commission on International Labour Standards and Trade, 1996: 57)

In addition, the ILO started in 1992 the International Programme on the Elimination of Child Labour (IPEC), which also targeted child labour in India. The Indian government felt pressured by these initiatives, as illustrated by promotional material from the Ministry of External Affairs. It produced a pamphlet referring to Phil Collins's song 'Another Day in Paradise', and another, devoted to the promotion of the government's own carpet label, Kaleen, referring to the American dream. Under the heading: 'Meet Jalil Ahmed Ansari. Successful owner of a carpet manufacturing unit. And former "child labourer"', an Indian version of upward social mobility was portrayed.[17] The pamphlet suggested that those children who work in a family setting (which is 90 per cent of all working children) are not badly off, and that they can even acquire skills (Ministry of External Affairs, n.d.a).[18]

Through its Kaleen label the government hoped to frustrate the call for a social clause, arguing: 'You know that we realise the problem and are implementing and evolving lasting solutions. Support, advise, assist if possible, but do not disrupt through sanctions what is already being done!' (Ministry of External Affairs, n.d.a). Another illustration of the pressure felt by Indian politicians was a steady increase in the number of questions raised by Members of Parliament on child labour from 1992 onwards (ILO, 1997c: 23).

The foreign attention on the child labour problem resulted in an increase of government initiatives that 'outpaced all other initiatives against child labour in the country' (ILO, 1996c: 2). In 1994, the National Authority for the Elimination of Child Labour was created and about US$270 million was earmarked to eradicate child labour from hazardous industries by the year 2000, while previously no more than US$1.6 million has been devoted to this task annually (ILO, 1996c: 2–4). This initiative shows that the government was, and is, more concerned about children working in manufacturing and service sectors than about children who work with their families on the land. The latter group is the largest part of all child labourers (*Times of India*, 29 November 1994). Due to the foreign attention, an opportune moment existed for the Commission on International Labour Standards and Trade to criticize the government's efforts in the eradication of child labour. It recommended a budget increase to US$4.36 billion to eradicate all child labour (modestly estimated at 25 million children) by the year 2004 (*Times of India*, 14 June 1995). The Ministry of External Affairs (interviewed on 15 December 1998) expected that if this amount were needed the Commission's proposal could never be implemented.

Conclusion

This chapter showed that CTOs have concentrated on economic, sovereignty and effectiveness claims to argue against a social clause. The interests behind these expressed arguments seem clear – denial of economic advantages and the intervention in national affairs. In this context it is striking that only HMS argued that a social clause would not help to solve the problems related to child labour, despite the fact that this claim would be one of the most appealing claims contradicting the effectiveness of a social clause. Among the CTOs only HMS has attempted to broaden its members' understanding of the issue by publishing a booklet on the issue. One can therefore conclude that the social clause debate has not been taken very seriously by the CTOs in any other way than as a threat.

Besides these expressed interests, two other interests have potentially played a role in the opposition to a social clause by trade unions. First, the trade unions were too weak to contradict the government on such a sensitive foreign policy issue. Second, the CTOs were not strongly enough interested in organizing the unorganized to consider a more positive attitude towards a social clause.

If the lack of involvement with the unorganized workers explains part of the opposition of CTOs to a social clause, this seems to be short-sighted. One would expect the CTOs to be worried about the increasing proportion of unorganized workers. This proportion reduces union membership and increases the pressure on the formal sector to decrease regulation. Therefore all parties might be better off if the working conditions of the total population, instead of only of the organized part of the working population, improved. This fact and the associated one that trade unions feel that India's increasingly open economy suffers from cheap imports from other countries, such as Indonesia, could have created a more positive attitude towards a social clause.

The opposition of the Indian government has been primarily motivated by economic and political claims reflecting an international neo-liberal orientation with a strong sovereignty bias. To comprehend this orientation fully one has to understand that the labour standards discussion was not an isolated one. It took place at a time when the position of developing countries in international trade negotiations was under severe pressure from both national and international developments. Therefore, India's position, including that of the CTOs, can only be explained if one considers the way in which India has perceived its place in the international political-economic context.

I have shown that the effects of the foreign pressure were limited to the field of child labour. It seems that the pressure of the United States in Marrakesh, and the formulation of US trade laws to combat child labour, combined with the activities of Indian unorganized sector NGOs and the IPEC programme, have increased the trade unions' and the government's commitment to develop activities in the field of child labour. However, it remains to be seen whether one can speak of a sensitizing or substantive impact. Only when this is translated into concrete policies and budget allocations can it be considered a substantive impact. However, pamphlets such as those reproduced by the Ministry of External Affairs make one doubt that the extent of the problem is taken seriously. In addition, the huge differences between the estimates of the government and NGOs concerning the number of children living in bondage give reason to doubt whether the current uprising in activities is the result of a genuine change in perception or a way to ease foreign pressure.

These chapters on the United States and India have shown the differences between the national debates. These differences extend to the international level. For years, governments, trade unions and employers' organizations have discussed how international and regional bodies should respond to the social clause pressure. This is the subject of the next chapters.

Notes

1. I am indebted to Hensman (1996), whose views on the Indian social clause debate have influenced my agrument.
2. The NAM was established in 1961 as a forum to represent the interests of the developing world. Today it has 113 members (NAM, 1999). The Group of 77 (G-77) was established three years later after the conclusion of the first meeting of the United Nations Conference on Trade and Development (UNCTAD). The G-77, today with 133 members, helps developing countries to articulate and promote their collective economic interests and enhance their joint negotiating capacity on all major international economic issues in the United Nations system, and promotes economic and technical cooperation among developing countries (G-77, 1999).
3. When the Indian delegation agreed to accept the negotiations on services, the Indian parliament was in uproar, claiming that the delegation had sold India out (*Tribune*, 1 January 1997).
4. In fact, certain groups of public servants in India (depending on wages

and post) do not have the right to strike, cannot make joint representation, cannot openly criticize government policy, and cannot take part in politics and elections (*Pioneer*, 7 May 1992).

5. See Breman (1999) for a discussion of changes in agrarian bonded labour.
6. The *Pioneer* is the principal publication of the Communist Party of India.
7. The unwillingness of INTUC to support ICFTU's efforts on a social clause constrained the relationship between the two organizations. Gopeshwar, General Secretary of the INTUC, wrote to the ICFTU: 'There is an impression in the trade unions in developing countries that the ICFTU is Euro-centric. I wish that this silent feeling is not based on facts and is ill-conceived. The ICFTU draws its strength not only from the trade unions from developed countries but it is the democratic trade unions in developing countries that make the ICFTU an influential world body' (Gopeshwar, 1996).
8. This feeling was enforced not only by the US policy towards China, but also by an Indian newspaper reprinting a secret CIA document, which somehow got into the hands of the Cubans, alleging that most human rights violations in Cuba 'don't merit to be considered genuine', but useful for US interests (*Pioneer*, 18 April 1994).
9. While the consistency of views between the CTOs may not be surprising, the almost complete lack of differences with the employers' organizations (AIOE 1996, 47–8; Interviews with CII, 21 November 1996; ASSOCHAM, 21 November 1996; FICCI, 29 November 1996) and the government has puzzled some (Hensman, 1996).
10. On 20–22 March 1995, 80 representatives from the organized and unorganized sectors, and women, environmental, human rights and child labour organizations, came together to discuss the social clause and environmental standards in multilateral trade agreements (CEC, 1995: 1–2).
11. An exception is HMS, which published a paper including a broader perspective on the working of the WTO (HMS, n.d.).
12. The issue of the number of forced labourers in the country became part of a conflict between the ICFTU and INTUC. In 1998, the ICFTU sent a draft report on Indian labour standards to the INTUC's President. The parts of the report on forced/bonded labour, which were supposed to be used by country delegations to the WTO during the review of India's trade policy, were not appreciated by the INTUC because of the high estimates (Reddy, 1998; Interview with INTUC, 26 March 1998; ICFTU, 1998b).

13. As noted above, in March 1994 the G-15 summit expressed its concern about the protectionist nature of a social clause (Ghosh, 1995: 56).
14. During the previous NAM Conference of the Ministers of Labour, in 1990, the link between trade and labour standards was also rejected, on grounds of protectionist tendencies (NAM, 1995a: 18).
15. This support was, for example, illustrated in 1995 when he received the Robert F. Kennedy Human Rights Reward.
16. There are also other pressures inducing the Indian government to seriously address the issue of child labour. First of all, it is increasingly accepted that the role of human resources is important to industrial development. Therefore, skilled labour is emphasized. Secondly, it has become clear that there is a negative correlation between per capita income, infrastructure development, school enrolment ratio and female participation rates on the one hand and the incidence of child labour on the other (Castle *et al.*, 1997: 57).
17. The material is undated, but was probably produced around 1995.
18. However, as Weiner forcefully argues, no skills are acquired that could not be acquired at a later age. In addition, in the 'family-owned' workshops children are often involved in unregulated hazardous work (Weiner, 1996: 3009).

6 THE OECD STUDY ON TRADE AND LABOUR STANDARDS

As I have shown in Chapter 3, the OECD report on trade and labour standards is often cited as an authoritative source on the matter. Therefore, this study would not be complete without taking a look into this report.

In June 1994, the Ministers of the OECD gave the OECD Secretariat the mandate to study the link between trade and labour standards. The OECD's Trade Committee (TC) and its Employment, Labour and Social Affairs Committee (ELSA) conducted the study (OECD, 1995c: 2). The purpose of the study was: (a) to examine the observance of core labour standards in different OECD and non-OECD countries; (b) to present an analytical framework that assesses the links between labour standards, trade, investment patterns and economic development; and (c) to analyse possible mechanisms to enforce core labour standards, such as trade measures (OECD, 1994, 1996b: 22).

The final version of the report was published in 1996. It was expected by those involved that the report's conclusions would facilitate consensus building between OECD countries on the issue of labour standards. Such a consensus would help to focus the debate on a social clause at the WTO Singapore meeting that was planned to take place in December 1996. The fact that consensus building was at stake made the report important to proponents as well as opponents of a social clause. Naturally, among the former were the trade unions. Together with the member states and employers, they tried to influence the content of the several draft versions of the report that were distributed between 1994 and 1996.

The central argument of this chapter is that trade unions had little influence on the content of the OECD report. This was owing to their weak formal status as well as to the nature of the report, as explained below. Yet the results of the report did not frustrate all trade union interests, and in some respects were helpful to the trade unions' quest to keep a social clause on the international agenda.

This chapter analyses the nature and effects of the trade union viewpoints on the draft versions of the report. To facilitate an understanding of the organizational context in which this took place, the first section of this chapter looks at the structure of the OECD. This is followed by an analysis of the positions of the different actors in the debate. The main conclusions of the OECD report are presented, followed by an analysis of the interests and influence of trade unions on the evolution of the draft reports into the final report.

Organizational Features of the OECD

The OECD, established in 1961, currently organizes 29 member countries, predominantly from the developed world. It is the successor of the Organisation for European Economic Co-operation, which was established after the Second World War to manage US and Canadian aid under the Marshall Plan.

While OECD countries produce two-thirds of the world's goods and services, and most member countries are developed ones, the main criteria for being admitted to the organization is commitment to a market economy and a pluralist democracy. The most important purpose of this intergovernmental organization is to exchange information and to coordinate policies in different areas (OECD, 2000). It is therefore often seen as one of the largest international statistics offices. Even though the basis for cooperation of the member states is voluntary and decision-making takes place on the basis of consensus, the advice of the OECD is influential, as states believe that having compatible economic policies is beneficial for economic competition. The OECD maintains close ties with other international organizations, such as the WTO, IMF and World Bank. The ILO and the Commission of the EU are allowed to participate in OECD meetings and exchange information (Reinalda, 1999).

The OECD Secretariat in Paris stimulates the exchange of information and research results between the member states. It monitors developments in a number of areas, including technology, economy, agriculture and social issues. This work in turn facilitates the work of the Committees of the OECD, which aim to exchange information between country delegates in the same areas. The information exchanged can be used to improve economic and social policies on a national level, and may also serve as input for legal agreements between the OECD countries (OECD, 2000).

The highest decision-making power lies in the hands of the Council, formed by representatives of the member states. At the ministerial level, the Council meets once a year to determine the activities of the organization for the next year. Between the ministerial meetings, the ambassadors of the member states give general direction to the OECD activities (OECD, 2000).

The Trade Union Advisory Committee to the OECD (TUAC) is one of the public organizations consulted by the OECD Committees and by the Secretary-General before the annual ministerials. This consultation is not compulsory. Also once connected to the Marshall Plan, TUAC focuses on influencing the OECD and the G-7 economic summit and its employment conferences.[1] Forty-eight national affiliations, originating from 26 of the 29 OECD countries, are represented in the TUAC. In addition, international trade union organizations such as the International Confederation of Free Trade Unions (ICFTU) and the European Trade Union Confederation (ETUC) are represented through the TUAC. Together, these trade union organizations organize about 67 million workers (TUAC, n.d., 2000). While national trade union federations can voice their opinion on specific issues through the TUAC, they can also undertake action individually. The AFL-CIO, for example, has developed its own lobby activities to voice its own preferences. This federation meets on a regular basis with the US Trade Mission in Paris to exchange and, if possible, streamline, ideas (Interview with AFL-CIO Paris Office, 28 April 1997). Just like trade unions, employers' organizations have a consultative status at the OECD: the Business and Industry Advisory Committee to the OECD (BIAC).

During the discussion of the various drafts of the OECD report on trade and labour standards, TUAC and other trade unions stayed on top of the debate. Employers' organizations, and especially BIAC, were much less involved. The most likely reason for this situation is that the report's first (1994) draft was judged positively by BIAC, and therefore the organization did not feel the need to stay involved (Interview with United States Council for International Business, 19 June 1997). In addition, more than TUAC, BIAC was confronted with internal divisions over the subject. Two of its members, the Conseil National du Patronat Français and the Fédération des Entreprises de Belgique, were in favour, or at least could not support a total rejection of a social clause (BIAC, 1994; Interview with OECD, 30 April 1997).

Opposing Trade Unions' and Employers' Discourses

The positions of TUAC and BIAC on the question of how to deal with the relationship between trade, investments and labour standards in the OECD study were – with a few exceptions – diametrically opposed. TUAC perceived the study as an opportunity to demonstrate that the inclusion of a social clause in trade and investment regimes can be in the interests of both developed and developing countries. BIAC, on the other hand, wanted the study to show that there is hardly any link between labour standards and trade and investment regimes (BIAC, 1996: 2).

Support from the trade unions for the OECD study was mainly based on the reproduction of the universal human rights claim of the interventionist discourse. The labour standards considered by TUAC to form the core standards – Conventions 87, 98, 29, 100, 105, 111 and 138 – were perceived as human rights and as such aimed at the prevention of repression, exploitation and discrimination (TUAC, 1994).

During the discussion about the draft versions of the report, the trade unions involved brought forward other claims that sustained the introduction of a social clause. It was claimed that a social clause would increase the effectiveness of the trading system:

> At present there is a grave danger that for large numbers of workers the pressure of competition may lead to exploitation and the large potential benefits of trade liberalization will not or will only very slowly trickle down to workers. . . . Finding a workable multilateral system for resolving disputes about workers' rights and trade would create an anti-protectionist bulwark that would strengthen the role of the WTO and the ILO. (ICFTU, 1995b: 1)

Trade unions claimed that low labour standards were an element in attracting investment, providing the example of China, leading to a race to the bottom in which countries would try to underbid each other. Related to this, trade unions demanded throughout the preparation of the report that more attention should be paid to the role of EPZs. In addition, the trade unions wanted the study to conclude that the demand for unskilled labour (related to the level of employment) was negatively affected by trade. In this respect, they wanted to see the inclusion in the report of Wood's (1994) study, which sustained such a conclusion. Another argument in the economic claim insisted on classifying low labour standards as a form of social dumping or illegitimate export subsidy (ICFTU, 1995b: 4, 8; TUAC, 1995b).

BIAC, on the other hand, saw no reason to study the relationship between labour standards, trade and investment (BIAC, 1994). Its rejection was expressed through a neo-liberal discourse supported by six claims.

149

The first claim was an economic one. BIAC argued that the competitiveness of the South East Asian countries was not responsible for the high level of European unemployment.[2] Instead it was assumed that the restrictive legislative environment in the OECD countries was to blame. BIAC maintained that there is no proof that trade with non-OECD countries has a negative impact on employment, wages and/or labour standards. BIAC stipulated that to the extent that pressure on employment in OECD countries was the result of trade, intra-OECD trade should be appointed as the wrong-doer, as this trade is three times higher than trade with non-OECD countries. On the other hand, BIAC argued that wages in non-member countries had risen significantly in the four Asian tigers as a result of improved economic performance, suggesting that labour standards automatically follow economic growth. In same vein, BIAC argued that investments in non-member countries are not taking place at such a high rate as often suggested, and that the factual relocation of investment is improving labour standards in the non-member countries instead of degrading them. BIAC argued that sanctions would not improve the observance of labour standards but would have negative economic effects, while the improvement of labour standards would follow economic growth.

The second claim BIAC used was that there is no such thing as a universal labour standard: 'Even within those countries which embody these principles in their national legislation, there are frequently significant differences of opinion on how they should be interpreted and, certainly, enforced' (BIAC, 1994: 5). This is also illustrated by the fact that the core Conventions are not 'sufficiently' ratified (see, for ratification, the Appendix).

The third claim was that a social clause would contribute to an ineffective ILO. A departure from the ILO's voluntaristic nature would inhibit the ILO from functioning, and countries would start to leave the ILO if it joined hands with the WTO.

The fourth claim maintained that imposing detailed developed countries' labour standards on developing countries would be a serious breach of national sovereignty.

The fifth claim argued that the GATT and WTO do not provide precedents concerning the introduction of labour standards in trade agreements. This exclusion claim argued that the GATT/WTO article that allows the use of sanctions against countries using prison labour is not about objections against the inhumane nature of prison labour, but about the unfair comparative advantage resulting from trade in prison labour products. Therefore, there would be no basis to suggest that non-implemented labour standards constitute a breach of WTO rights.

While all the above claims are often cited in both the literature about trade and labour standards and the debates on the subject, the sixth claim of the BIAC is not. It was argued that the WTO lacks an adequate mechanism to deal with trade sanctions in the case of violation of labour standards. If a country fails to comply with labour standards, what financial value should be attached to this? Given the fact that core labour standards are difficult to define, determining injury would rely on subjective judgements. Moreover, if trade sanctions were enacted, the direct impact would be felt by companies rather than by governments, the latter being the main responsible party for adequate labour standards and their enforcement. Companies operating in specific sectors would be affected by sanctions, regardless of whether they had violated the standards. In addition, only exporting companies would be affected.

Two familiar discourses appear from this description of claims used by TUAC and BIAC. On the one hand, the claims used by the trade unions exemplify a strong connection to the interventionist discourse, using the classical claims of social dumping, race to the bottom, the universality of labour rights and the importance of a social clause in paving the way for free trade. On the other hand, BIAC's claims are strongly associated with the neo-liberal discourse, emphasizing the role of the economic recession in the West in calling for labour standards, the infringement of sovereignty, the consequences for the ILO if a social clause were introduced in the WTO and the lack of agreement on the universal nature of labour standards.

TUAC and BIAC, with their opposing positions, supported different groups of member states. There were strong differences of opinion among the OECD member states on the desirability of a report that would reproduce arguments for the inclusion of a working party on a social clause in the WTO. Divisions similar to those in the other international organizations occurred here: the United States, France and Belgium were the strongest proponents of a social clause, with the UK and New Zealand the strongest opponents (Interview with OECD, 30 April 1997).

Trade, Employment and Labour Standards: The OECD Report

In 1996, the OECD published its report on the relationship between trade, employment and labour standards. The rationale behind the study was explained as being twofold. First, it was argued that:

> The protracted rise in unemployment in many OECD countries has led some observers to look for external explanations, including claims of unfair

trade practices associated with competition from firms that allegedly base their comparative advantage on low labour standards. (OECD, 1995c: 9)

Second, it was argued that some labour rights are universal, and should be observed regardless of the level of economic development of countries. In short, the problem on which the report is based was about claims about economic protectionism and human rights claims (OECD 1996b, 21).

The report focused on the following labour standards as being core: (a) freedom of association and collective bargaining; (b) elimination of exploitative forms of child labour; (c) prohibition of forced labour; and (d) non-discrimination in employment (OECD, 1996b: 27). The decision to include these rights in the report was motivated by similar provisions integrated in labour and human rights regimes, such as the ILO Conventions, and by the fact that these rights provide framework conditions for other labour standards, i.e. they are enabling rights, serving as a condition to determine other rights/standards (OECD, 1996b: 26–8). The next sections discuss the main conclusions of the report.

Labour standards and economic efficiency

The first question to consider is whether free markets without labour standards are efficient. The main conclusions of the report were that the prohibition of forced labour, exploitative forms of child labour and discriminatory regulation are likely to improve the efficiency of market outcomes. Employment discrimination leads to a situation where labour is not allocated to the sectors where it obtains the highest rate of productivity. This is also the case for forced labour. In the case of child labour, inefficiency lies in the fact that children's education is undermined, which inhibits the accumulation of human capital. The efficiency effects of freedom of association and collective bargaining are perceived to be related to a number of factors, such as the extent to which wage distortions are stimulated between union members and non-members (OECD, 1996b: 80–2, 218–23).

As there was more information available on the implementation of freedom of association and collective bargaining legislation than on the implementation of the other labour standards, the study paid extra attention to the first two. The information available made it possible to link the level of implementation of core labour standards to several economic indicators, such as output and wages. It was concluded that there is probably a weak positive relationship between the degree of the observance of freedom of association and the level of per capita GDP. No correlation was found between freedom of association and growth in wages, implying that acceptance of such a standard would not necessarily increase wages (OECD, 1996b: 86–8).

Labour standards and trade

Three questions concerning the relationship between freedom of association and collective bargaining on the one hand and trade on the other were discussed. The first question was how a country's trade performance (measured by its share of exports in world trade) would be affected by its application of labour standards. It was concluded that there is no significant relationship between improved freedom of association and change in growth of total exports (OECD, 1996b: 92–6).

The second question discussed in the report was whether the observance of freedom of association and collective bargaining determined the comparative advantage (which relates to sectoral trade patterns) of a country. If there were a relationship, this would support the claim that the low labour standards in particular sectors create an unfair comparative advantage. The report concluded that there is no relationship between core labour standards and sectoral trade performance. Data show that similar export products from developing countries are priced at similar levels, even though the enforcement of freedom of association and collective bargaining differs. This means that comparative advantage is not, or only to a small extent, determined by low labour standards (OECD, 1996b: 101–2). An important reason for this relationship to be non-existent is misallocation of labour resources. In cases of forced labour and child labour, misallocation of labour resources resulting from the fact that workers cannot work in the places where they tend to be most productive is quite clear. In the case of freedom of association and collective bargaining, evidence of misallocation is more difficult to find, but still there. Without freedom of association and collective bargaining workers are more likely to be exploited, and this may lead to a situation of being underpaid and undereducated. This, in turn, may lead to a situation where workers are not able to refuse low-paid jobs or do not look for higher-paid jobs (OECD, 1996b: 218–23). The report also suggested that developing countries that improve their labour standards will not negatively affect their comparative advantage, and may even ensure improved economic performance. The failure to allocate labour to the sectors where it is most productive will be less frequent with higher labour standards (OECD, 1996b: 96–105).

A third question with respect to trade and labour standards asked whether there is a 'race to the bottom'. This means that some countries deliberately lower their standards to compete with low-standards countries. According to the study, economic data show that there is little relationship between freedom of association, collective bargaining and trade performance. Even if one takes into account the possible influence of labour standards on real wage growth, data still show that countries with high standards have smaller wage growth than do countries with low standards (OECD, 1996b: 90–2).[3]

These conclusions should take away the concerns of high-standards countries that low-standards countries gain export shares to the detriment of the former on the basis of differences in standards. They also undermine the perception that high core labour standards negatively affect economic performance. In fact, the report argued that there is more reason to think that the observance of core labour standards strengthens economic performance (OECD, 1996b: 105).

Trade, employment and wages

Another question concerned the relationship between trade and employment/wages. If one assumes that there is indeed a relationship between the level of core labour standards and wages and comparative advantage (the lower the standards, the lower the wages and the higher the comparative advantage), one can still question whether unemployment and wage inequality are the result of trade with developing countries. The OECD study, relying on secondary data, argued that the relationship between trade on the one hand and unemployment and wage inequality on the other is hardly visible on a macro level. However, as pointed out in Chapter 3, in some sectors, such as textiles, clothing, footwear and electronics, there is a stronger relationship. The OECD study pointed out that even though there is disagreement on the exact effect of trade on employment and wage equality, no disagreement exists on the effect of trade compared to that of other forces, such as technological development and institutional changes, which is thought to be much higher (OECD, 1996b: 124–30).

Labour standards and investment

The report presented evidence that foreign direct investment for the most part takes place between OECD countries. In these countries, the report argued, labour standards are generally respected. When FDI is directed to non-OECD countries, labour standards are not among the main factors determining the investment decision. However, even though labour standards might not be of crucial importance to investors, the fact that countries perceive them to be important suggests that they might suppress labour standards to attract FDI (OECD, 1996b: 113–24).

TUAC's Interests and the Evolution of Draft Texts

The OECD report of 1996 was the result of a two-year discussion between the OECD TC, ELSA and the OECD member states. Before the final report could be presented, several draft reports were circulated. During the drafting of the reports, the comments of BIAC and TUAC, and of other international organisations such as the ILO, were taken into account.

In this section, the claims and adjustments in the different versions of the reports are discussed. Successively, the relationship between labour standards and economic development, the selection of the standards and the evolution of discursive notions are analysed. Many other issues have evoked discussion, such as why countries do not observe labour standards and the way in which other organizations try to encourage compliance to trade and labour standards. Because the question on the relationship between economics and labour standards is the most crucial, since the debate has concentrated on this, I focus the discussion on this aspect. In addition, I focus only on the most important aspects of the relationship that appear in the comments of the trade unions. The material for this analysis is the drafts that were submitted and adjusted based on comments.

The relationship between labour standards and economic development

Labour standards and economic efficiency
Trade unions did not appreciate the questioning of the market efficiency enhancement of Conventions 87 and 98. While in the first draft of 1995 the relationship between core labour standards and economic efficiency was discussed under the heading 'Core labour standards as an instrument to improve economic efficiency' (OECD, 1995a: 21), in the following draft the relationship was posed as 'Do core labour standards improve the efficiency of

market outcomes?' (OECD, 1995b: 23). The question mark illustrated that the report tried to refute the allegations of being too biased towards the positive aspects of labour standards that the OECD probably had received. While in the first draft of 1995 the references to Conventions 87 and 98 were positive – they were seen as necessary instruments to counterbalance the market power of employers – in the second draft of 1995 these references were accompanied by the argument that the consequences of the two Conventions depended among other things on the level of collective bargaining. It was argued that they might have negative effects on an economy, as they increase economic costs (OECD, 1995b: 24). Despite protests from TUAC (1995a: 7–9), this argument remained in place. In the final report, references to the function of Conventions 87 and 98 to counterbalance the strong bargaining power of employers (the monopsony power of employers) *vis-à-vis* individual workers were replaced with much softer words, such as labour market imbalances (OECD, 1995b: 22–4; 1996b: 79).

Even though the language in the final report on the market efficiency of labour standards – compared to the first 1995 draft – has been weakened from the point of view of trade unions, the overall conclusion of the theoretical section on economic efficiency and core labour standards in the final report was more favourable to unions, compared with earlier drafts. The final report concluded that freedom of association and collective bargaining are likely to improve the efficiency of market outcomes (OECD, 1996b: 82). In the 1995 version the conclusion about Conventions 87 and 98 was: 'In sum ... ILO Conventions 87 and 98 can perhaps create a system of labour relations *consistent* with market efficiency' (OECD, 1995c: 25).

From the start TUAC had been very critical of this statement (TUAC, 1995a: 9). The United States proposed an adaptation of the conclusions on 15 February 1996 (US DOL, 1996). Instead of summarizing the theoretical conclusions without a reference to the positive efficiency effects of the two Conventions, on the insistence of the United States the final version included such references. It stated that: 'freedom of association and collective bargaining can produce positive efficiency effects; for instance, they can counteract the market power of employers, while also improving worker-management co-operation and information sharing' (OECD, 1996b: 82).

Labour standards and trade

The section on trade also underwent changes. The conclusion that there is no support for the claim that core labour standards play a significant role in a country's aggregated trade performance remained in force from the second

1995 draft to the final report. However, two other conclusions changed. While throughout the study the main conclusion has been that the relationship between labour standards and trade performance is weak, emphasis on this point shifted. The conclusion in the second 1995 draft emphasized that in the short run improvement of freedom of association is related to a loss of competitiveness. This was replaced in the final report with an emphasis that the observance of labour standards in the long run will probably strengthen the economic performance of all countries (OECD, 1995b: 40; 1996b: 104–5).

The second change is that the second 1995 draft report concluded: 'there is some evidence that core standards might have a bearing on sectoral trade patterns' (OECD, 1995b: 40). In the third draft of 1995 this was replaced by: 'there is little evidence to suggest a relationship between core labour standards and sectoral patterns of export performance' (OECD, 1995c: 37). The final report concluded: 'patterns of specialisation are mainly governed by the relative abundance of factors of production and technology differences' (OECD, 1996b: 105). In other words, the OECD concluded that there is no solid foundation to claim that there is a race to the bottom that translates low labour standards into export gains to the detriment of higher-standards countries. The denial of this relationship was criticized by the ICFTU, which commented: 'Overall it is regrettably true that there does exist "a race to the bottom" problem with freer trade in the absence of guarantees of labour standards' (ICFTU, 1995b: 8).

These remarks of the ICFTU and the OECD represented two sides of the same coin. Is it the theoretical economic relationship that should be defined (OECD), or is it the relationship that arises out of government or company practice (ICFTU)? While in the first drafts (1995) the OECD report emphasized the first definition, in its draft report of January 1996 (OECD, 1996c) there was a reference to EPZs, which remained there up and until the final report: 'There is, however, some evidence that, in a few countries, the denial of core standards has been deliberately used by governments with the aim of improving the trade performance of certain sectors or of attracting investment to EPZs' (OECD, 1996b: 105). While the reference to the 'race to the bottom' issue had been deleted, the reference that governments act as if competition on the basis of labour standards is advantageous was included.

Trade, employment and wages

The report claimed that there is barely a relationship between trade on the one hand, and unemployment and wage inequality on the other. This conclusion hardly changed through the drafts, although, probably on the insistence of the ICFTU (1995b: 8), the conclusions of Wood's (1994) study were used differently. The second 1995 draft put emphasis on Wood's conclusion that while the trade impact would be high, policies to reduce labour market rigidities rather than banning imports would be a good response (OECD, 1995b: 46). In the final version, however, this interpretation has been limited to the high impact of trade on wages, although it was accompanied by some criticism of Wood's methodology (OECD, 1996b: 125).

Labour standards and investment

In the final report, there was almost no recognition of the relationship between the decision to invest in a country and the level of labour standards. However, as said before, it was acknowledged that this knowledge did not necessarily affect the labour policies of non-OECD countries: 'some governments in non-OECD countries have restricted labour rights (especially in EPZs) in the belief that doing so would help attract inward FDI' (OECD, 1996b: 123). In the draft reports (see, for example, OECD, 1995b: 44), the role of governments was formulated not as a conclusion but as a possible argument. Presenting the role of governments in this way was a change that may well have occurred on the insistence of TUAC. During the discussions on the draft reports, TUAC claimed to provide nearly all information on EPZs and continuously emphasized the deliberate lowering of labour standards in EPZs to attract foreign investment (Interview with TUAC, 30 April 1997).

The discussion about the relationship between labour standards and investment took place in a special committee of the OECD, the Committee on International Investment and Multinational Enterprises (CIME). During consultations with CIME, TUAC emphasised the relationship between low labour standards, EPZs and investments (TUAC, 1995c). The part on the impact of TNCs on certain labour standards, such as freedom of association and collective bargaining, shifted from very positive (in the draft versions) to more moderate (in the final report). In the draft version, sentences appeared like: 'many of these affiliates [of TNCs] try as far as possible to apply labour standards similar to those they respect in the home country, including regular contact with trade unions' (OECD, 1995b: 45). It was exactly this sentence that caught the eye of the trade unions involved. TUAC argued that this may be true for some TNCs, but it is not the norm (TUAC, 1995a: 15). The final report presented this point. It argued that as the degree of unionization provides a proxy measure, 'The radically lower degree of unionization in EPZs in comparison with the domestic economy as a whole could suggest that MNEs do not contribute to the improvement of the practical situation of unions' (OECD, 1996b: 123).

Which standards?

In the first 1995 draft of the report (OECD, 1995a), core labour standards were defined as those that establish a framework under which working conditions could be determined. Core labour standards were distinguished from so-called 'promotional' labour standards, which are aimed at achieving certain outcomes, such as working hours, through compulsory government regulation. While working conditions, as regulated by the promotional standards, were thought to be dependent on economic development, core labour standards were viewed as an important condition for the free functioning of markets. The definition of core labour standards included references to ILO Conventions 87, 98, 138, 29 and 105. The grounds for selecting these five standards were the high number of ratifications and the fact that the ILO also referred to these standards as being part of the 'core'. Despite the reference to the ILO definition of core labour standards, the first 1995 draft report neglected to include Conventions 100 and 111 (on discrimination). The reason for this exclusion was the assumption that once unions organize themselves freely they will take care of the discrimination issue themselves (OECD, 1995a: 11–12).

As communication between the ICFTU and TUAC shows, the ICFTU argued that exclusion of Conventions 100 and 111 on discrimination is not based on sound considerations. For example, Convention 111 prohibits discrimination on different grounds from Convention 98 (which only prohibits anti-union discrimination) (ICFTU, 1995a). Even though different coverage of the Conventions did not directly contradict the OECD argumentation, which maintained that 'the most blatant cases of discrimination in the work place will be easier to prevent when workers can negotiate their working conditions freely' (OECD, 1995a: 12), the OECD responded to the ICFTU's criticism in its next draft version by including Convention 111 on discrimination (OECD, 1995b: 11–12). Up to and including the final report (OECD, 1996b), Convention 100 (on equal remuneration) was excluded, as 'the principles behind Convention 100 are embodied in Convention 111' (OECD, 1996b: 33). In a later draft, the authors of the report questioned whether equal remuneration should be seen as a human right (OECD, 1995b: 14), as advocated by TUAC (1995a).

Even though part of the discussion evolved around the inclusion of ILO Conventions, the drafts and final report only referred to these Conventions as a major source of international labour standards. However, the fact that the ILO Conventions were mentioned as the embodiment of the main features of the core standards was of importance to TUAC. According to

TUAC, countries such as the UK and New Zealand tried to use the discussion about core standards to show that they are not universal and need to be rewritten (Interview with TUAC, 30 April 1997). The UK argued that it was questionable whether the provisions of the ILO Conventions referred to universal human rights, as the interpretation of the Conventions differed between countries (McKinnon and Niven, 1996). By not basing the standards on the Conventions, the delegates of these countries implied that the specifics of standards would depend on circumstances.

The final report states: 'Despite some caveats and a less-than-universal ratification record, it can be asserted that, at present, Conventions 87, 98, 29, 105 and 111 are important references for monitoring observance of core labour standards' (OECD, 1996b: 36). This can be seen as a compromise acceptable to all parties concerned. While the report referred to the ILO Conventions merely as 'important references', at least the importance of the substance of the ILO core Conventions was recognized. The final report did omit Convention 138 as it dealt only with minimum age and not with exploitative forms of child labour.

These shifts in emphases between the drafts and the final OECD report are presented in Table 6.1.

Trade Unions' Interventions and Impacts

TUAC and other involved unions wanted an endorsement of a social clause by the WTO. To get this, the unions intervened in meetings and submitted comments on the OECD draft reports. At the top of their list was the need to gain recognition of the mutual relationship between trade and labour standards. As the OECD can influence the agenda setting of the WTO, the outcome of the OECD study was considered to be important by TUAC (Interview with TUAC, 30 April 1997).

Trade unions' interests and effects

Before reviewing the conclusions of the OECD report, it is worth reconsidering the interests of the trade unions on these questions. As has been illustrated by the use of discursive claims and by the comments of trade unions on the draft texts, the following six interests were voiced. First, some labour rights are universal rights. Second, the enforcement of these rights will increase the effectiveness of the economy. Third, low labour standards

Table 6.1 *Shifts between drafts and final report*

Draft(s)	Final report
Freedom of association and collective bargaining can create a system of labour relations consistent with market efficiency	Freedom of association and collective bargaining can also increase costs and their effects depend on level of collective bargaining; freedom of association and collective bargaining can have positive efficiency effects
Use of strong notions such as monopsony power of employers	Replaced by softer language: the absence of measures protecting workers' rights might aggravate imbalances of power in the labour market
Emphasis on: in the short-run improvement of freedom of association results in a loss of competitiveness	Emphasis on: in the long-run the observance of labour standards will probably strengthen the economic performance of all countries
There is some evidence that core standards might have a bearing on sectoral trade patterns	There is little evidence to suggest a relationship between core labour standards and sectoral patterns of export performance, but governments may act as if there is
Emphasis on Wood's conclusion that policies to reduce labour market rigidities are a good response to the impact of trade on employment	Emphasis on Wood's conclusion that trade has a high impact on wages and employment
The argument that some governments in non-OECD countries have restricted labour rights to attract inward FDI has no prominent place	This argument is in the final version part of the conclusion
TNCs try as much as possible to apply labour standards similar to those they respect in the home country	The radically low degree of unionization (as measure for the application of freedom of association) in EPZs suggests that TNCs do not contribute to the improvement of the practical situation of unions in non-OECD countries
Core labour standards referred to ILO Conventions 87, 98, 29 and 105	Convention 111 is also included

attract, or are assumed to attract, investment: 'The huge amount of foreign investment nowadays flowing into China is very clearly linked to that country's violation of virtually all the basic labour rights under consideration by the OECD' (ICFTU, 1995b: 1). Fourth, the trade unions had an interest in including and emphasizing reference to the negative effects of low labour standards on employment in developed countries. That is why they insisted on the inclusion of references to Wood's study. Fifth, trade unions wanted more attention given to the fact that TNCs do not always have similar labour standards in home and guest (non-OECD) countries. Sixth, trade unions wanted references to discursive notions of low labour standards such as social dumping or illegitimate export subsidy. The use of such notions would enhance the illegitimate nature of low labour standards from a trading system's point of view. This was important, as the trade unions wanted the report to be more positive about the possibilities of including labour standards in the WTO.

Some of these points found their way into the report, others not (see Table 6.2). The first interest was from the start included in the report. A reference to Convention 111 was included at a later stage, possibly due to the activities of the trade unions. While reference to Convention 100 was not included, all other relevant ILO core Conventions were referred to in the final version. The influence of the trade unions was therefore almost non-existent in this respect.

With respect to the second point, that the enforcement of the core Conventions will increase the effectiveness of the trading system, the text improved because the conclusions referred more positively to the efficiency effects of trade unions. This was probably the result of intervention by the US government. While it may well be true that this intervention was made on behalf of the AFL-CIO, no evidence was found to support this proposition.

The third point, the recognition that countries deliberately lower labour standards to attract investment and to stimulate trade advantages, has – with a small adaptation – been included. As I have shown, the final version of the report is compatible with those actors refuting the claim that low labour standards evoke trade advantages without denying the fact that countries may act as if lower labour standards attract investment. It was argued that while in reality low labour standards and attracting investment and trade performance may not have much bearing upon each other in the long term, the fact that governments think they do was crucial. On the insistence of trade unions, reference was made to the EPZs as indicative of this point. The attention on EPZs also allowed the conclusion that TNCs were not contributing to the improvement of the situation of trade unions in these areas of economic activity.

OECD Study on Trade and Labour Standards

Table 6.2 *The expression of trade union interests into sensitizing impacts, and the responsible actor*

Interest	Sensitizing impact	Intervention
Some labour standards are universal	Yes, all core ILO Conventions (except Conventions 100 and 138) have been recognized	Has been there from the start, with the exception of Convention 111, which may have been included on insistence of the trade unions
Enforcement will increase economic efficiency	Yes, final text is meeting trade unions' interests more than the first drafts	US government
Low labour standards attract investment and increase comparative advantage	Moderate: doubts about real effects, but acknowledgement that it plays a role in the minds of the decision-makers	Trade unions (by referring to EPZs)
Low labour standards in one country create unemployment in another	No: little impact was found, even though Wood's study was taken into account	Trade unions
TNCs do not apply the same labour standards in guest (non-OECD) countries as at home	Yes: this was noted with a reference to the low unionization level	Trade unions
Social dumping and illegitimate export subsidy	No: references to both notions have been included in a critical way; unions have stopped defining the inclusion as an interest because of strategic motivations	Not applicable
WTO as appropriate forum to link trade and labour standards	No: was rejected in the report	Not applicable

The fourth point, that low labour standards in developing countries have a negative effect on employment in developed countries, was not supported by the study. However, probably on the insistence of the trade unions, a reference to Wood's study (which argues the high impact of trade) was included. Therefore, the interest of trade unions in this respect was partly met.

The fifth point was to be more critical of the role of TNCs in applying labour standards in guest countries. This happened in the final report.

The sixth point of TUAC was to include a reference to notions such as social dumping and illegitimate export subsidy. The draft reports and the final report of the OECD were critical of the application of the notion of social dumping within the WTO trading regime (OECD, 1995b: 59–60; 1996b: 170–1). In its final report the OECD argued that the WTO definition of dumping does not allow for an application to social standards. One reason for this is that an essential element of the definition is actual price discrimination or a comparison of production costs to export price. As non-enforcement of labour standards does not involve actual costs, but only hypothetical costs, this part of the definition alone does not allow for dumping procedures to be applicable (OECD, 1996b: 170–1).

A similar reasoning was used for the notion of 'social subsidies'. The fact that some governments deliberately lower labour standards to increase their exports is seen by trade unions as a subsidy. The WTO defined a subsidy as a financial contribution, and abnormally low labour standards are not financial. The report argued that while one could also see a subsidy as income or price support, these two are difficult to apply to the issue of labour standards. In addition, if low labour standards are considered to be a subsidy, the subsidy itself needs to be granted only to specific industries, which is only the case with EPZs (OECD, 1996b: 172–3).

While the report also discussed the applicability of other measures within the WTO, it concluded that most of them were inappropriate, as the WTO was not seen as the right body for making a link between trade and labour standards. The reason for this is that the OECD's own analysis concluded that there is hardly any relationship between trade and labour standards, a point often made by developing countries. In addition, countries that trade more could be more affected than others; firms that do apply labour standards could be sanctioned too if they operate in the same sectors as those not applying labour standards. Moreover, the report raised the question, what would stimulate the use of sanctions: human rights or alleged domestic interests? Finally, sanctions could increase friction between countries (OECD, 1996b: 176).

To conclude, as both the OECD and the TUAC explained, the trade unions involved wanted references to low labour standards as a form of social dumping and subsidy included, but did not succeed and decided not to pursue these notions any longer, as they evoked very negative associations (Interviews with OECD, 30 April 1997; TUAC, 30 April 1997). It was felt that the negative associations would inhibit further meaningful discussion on the subject.

One of the purposes of the report has been to create a common viewpoint between the OECD countries, which could also be voiced within other international organizations, such as the WTO (Interview with OECD, 30 April 1997). Therefore, the report is important in terms of its sensitizing effects.

Probably the main sensitizing effect of the study has been the increased legitimacy given to the view that high labour standards are possible without negative economic effects. In fact, some of the effects may be positive. In addition, as Chapter 7 shows, the OECD report contributed to the legitimacy of the notion of fundamental labour standards. In fact, the OECD member states were able to agree on the definition of core labour standards, on the research results that differences in labour standards do not create unfair trade and on the fact that the ILO is the right forum to discuss the enforcement of labour standards. This created a common denominator that increased the acceptability of the OECD report. Of course, this also meant that the WTO was not seen as the right forum to discuss labour standards.

To increase support for the conclusions of the report, efforts were made to include non-member countries in the debate on trade and labour standards. After finishing the report, the OECD Council met in May 1996. Here, the members pledged to carry on working for the advancement of core labour standards around the world, welcoming the report on trade and labour standards. The Council wanted to stimulate members to engage in a dialogue with non-members about the conclusions of the report (OECD, 1996d).

This dialogue took place in October 1996. Over 180 participants from more than 40 countries came together to discuss the outcome of the report. The importance of this meeting was that it took place before the WTO Singapore meeting, and therefore could play a role in the process of developing common understandings. However, while everyone agreed that there was a problem, the exact nature of the problem was still under discussion. From the point of view of the trade unions, the effects of this meeting were limited. In terms of sensitizing effects, the participants were able to agree that some labour standards are fundamental. However, the non-OECD members did not want to discuss the relationship between trade and labour standards in the WTO (Anonymous, 1996). None of the non-OECD countries changed their opinion about the role of the WTO. Similarly, because some OECD members, such as the UK, refused to support a demand to include labour standards on the WTO agenda in Singapore, the OECD Council was unable to pursue this item (*Business Standard*, 23 May 1996). The OECD did, however, defend its study during the Singapore meeting. Probably in response to negative reactions to the report, the OECD argued:

> Armed with highly trained professional talent drawn from all corners of the OECD universe, it is the captive of no one. It has proved that time and again whether the task at hand relates to trade, the environment, the challenges of job creation, the appropriate allocation of tax revenues through transfer pricing guidelines or complicated and hotly debated issues such as the relationships, if any, between fair trade and labour practices. Any perception that the analytical work of the Secretariat is controlled or manipulated by a select group of rich countries is simply wrong. The credibility of the Secretariat's analytical scholarship speaks for itself! (WTO, 1996d)

In one way the report has had a substantive effect. The fact that the OECD has become increasingly interested in the issue of labour standards and trade facilitated some of the member states to link the accession of new member countries to their enforcement of labour standards. In 1996, South Korea wanted to join the OECD. As this country had been subject to complaints in the ILO relating to the observance of freedom of association, some OECD members insisted on making an improved observance of labour standards a condition for accession. South Korea became an OECD member, and a special procedure was designed to monitor developments in freedom of association in the country (Interview with OECD, 27 March 2000).

Explanation of trade unions' influence

The only significant influence of the trade unions on the report that I could establish is that the report has paid more attention to EPZs, even though TUAC found this reference too limited (Interview with TUAC, 30 April 1997). In addition, the inclusion of Convention 111 was probably due to the efforts of the trade unions. The limited success of the unions can be explained by the following factors.

The political process only allows unions to play an advisory role in OECD decision-making. This means that they are not an important power to be considered by the OECD staff. Related to this, the Committees dealing with the report wanted to produce a scientific report, and while they had to take into account comments of member states, they could disregard information of the trade unions if they considered that to be biased. Moreover, the discursive context in which the report was produced had a limited effect upon the conclusions. The discussion that led to the final report did not take place in an environment governed by a conviction about the importance of a specific historical opportunity (the fall of the Berlin Wall) or the increasing importance of human rights, as is the case with the ILO. The main idea behind the report was that the OECD should prepare a common standpoint, to be voiced at the WTO meetings. The fact that most OECD members were not willing to include labour standards in the WTO restricted the opportunities for trade unions to influence the contents of the study.

Thus far, this chapter has shown that even though trade unions have invested much energy in attempting to influence the outcome of the OECD report, they were not very successful. While some of their interventions found their way into the report, others did not (see Table 6.2). Nevertheless, while TUAC was not entirely happy with the conclusions of the report, it did consider the end version acceptable. For the AFL-CIO, however, the verdict about the report's conclusions was different:

> The OECD is dominated by neo-classically trained economists from all OECD countries. All begin the process by believing, and their models tell them, that workers' organizations and unions are merely an interference in the sufficient working of the market. Their paradigm does not allow a beneficial result of the study. Finally they decided: well, it is neutral. That is probably the best you could expect from these people. (Interview with AFL-CIO, 11 July 1996)

This negative attitude is not restricted to the report. The AFL-CIO was negative about the role of trade unions in the OECD as a whole:

> Unions have different interests. I think that we have to take this issue (because it is about worker empowerment) back to the shopfloor and back to people, and not spend our time and energy screwing around with the OECD. I do not think it useful . . . although you have to play along, you are not going to change their minds by the force of intellectual arguments because it is two ships passing in the night. You have to change that through political power and on-the-ground action. I think that it is a serious problem we have to confront because frequently on the international level, the federations and the ICFTU seem to satisfy themselves with playing the OECD, having meetings with the IMF once in a while, spending a lovely

three-and-a-half weeks in Geneva discussing the vagaries of the conventions. (Interview with AFL-CIO, 11 July 1996).[4]

The question is whether half-hearted support from the trade unions for the report's conclusions is justified. As Table 6.2 shows, even though the outcomes of the report are not always consistent with the expressed interests of the unions, they might be significant in potential.

Conclusion

The dominant interest of the trade unions discussed here was the inclusion of a social clause in the WTO. The report was not positive on this point. Some of the claims the trade unions wanted to have included in the report, because they believed that these would help to achieve more support for a social clause, were not incorporated (see Table 6.2). These mainly concerned references to the relationship between low labour standards, trade and unemployment, and references to low labour standards as a form of social dumping and as an illegal subsidy.

As shown in Chapter 3, trade unions are supporters of the interventionist position on trade and labour standards. However, one can argue that the fact that the report in some cases did support claims originating from the neo-liberal discourse may also be perceived as supportive of trade unions' dominant interest, the inclusion of a social clause in the WTO. When one looks at the outcome of the OECD study in terms of the two discourses presented in Chapter 3 the observations in Table 6.3 can be made.

Conclusions 1 to 3 support an interventionist discourse, and the trade unions' interest in getting labour standards included in the WTO. The observation that the observance of labour standards leads to improvement in economic efficiency, GDP and manufacturing output, but does not necessarily lead to an increase in wages, may help those promoting a social clause, as it may take away countries' fear of a loss of comparative advantage.

The fact that the study showed little relationship between freedom of association and collective bargaining and trade performance (conclusion 4) supports neither the interventionist discourse, which argues that by neglecting these standards countries gain unfair trade advantages, nor the neo-liberal discourse, which argues that differences in these standards result in fair trade advantages. While one can argue that the fact that there is little evidence that a country's comparative advantage is determined by the way it enforces its labour standards is in contrast with the claim of some trade

OECD STUDY ON TRADE AND LABOUR STANDARDS

Table 6.3 *The OECD report and competing views*

Conclusions	Support for neo-liberal discourse	Support for interventionist discourse	Support for trade unions
1. The prohibition of forced labour and of exploitative forms of child labour, and probably non-discrimination regulations, are an improvement for the efficiency of market outcomes	No	Yes	Yes
2. Probably a weak positive relationship between freedom of association and collective bargaining on the one hand, and growth in GDP on the other	No	Yes	Yes
3. No relationship between freedom of association and collective bargaining and wage increases	No	Yes	Yes
4. Little relationship between freedom of association and collective bargaining and trade performance	No	No	Moderate
5. Hardly any relationship between trade and unemployment and wage inequality	Yes	Moderate	Moderate
6. FDI flowing from OECD countries to non-OECD countries is not dependent on respect for labour standards, although governments think so	Yes	Yes	Moderate

unionists that low labour standards are responsible for unfair competition, the conclusion might also be in the trade unionists' interest, as it undermines the protectionist edge of the trade unionists' discourse. However, the fact that this conclusion denies the existence of a link between trade and labour standards undermines the legitimacy of a social clause in the WTO.

Conclusion 5 is mainly supportive of a neo-liberal discourse, and may also support trade union interests. Neo-liberals claim that it is not trade but inflexible legislation that is responsible for unemployment and wage inequality. This conclusion may be in the interests of trade unions as it takes away the protectionist edge of the social clause debate.

The OECD study points out that FDI flowing to developing countries is, for a large part, not dependent on low labour standards (conclusion 6). However, the fact that it is widely believed that FDI does depend on them provides some support for the neo-liberal claim that a social clause has a protectionist edge. It also provides some support for the claim that low labour standards are deliberately used as an export strategy. Similar to conclusions 4 and 5, this may be in the interest of trade unions. However, similar to conclusion 4, this conclusion weakens the case for the enforcement of labour standards through the WTO.

In sum, these observations illustrate that even claims supportive of the neo-liberal discourse might help trade unions to accomplish their goal. One of the main obstacles to the debate on a social clause has been the fear in developing countries of the possible impact of labour standards on their trade performance. Because the OECD audience did not include many of the countries fearing this impact but did include countries afraid of cheap imports, the ICFTU made the implicit claim that low labour standards in non-OECD countries cause a reduction in demand for low-skilled labour in OECD countries (ICFTU, 1995b: 4). The reasoning behind this was as follows. FDI flows to countries where labour standards are not protected. This happens because it affects the costs of production. Therefore, the ICFTU argued that low labour standards are an illegitimate export subsidy and a form of social dumping. By emphasizing Wood's study of the effects of trade on low-skilled labour, the relationship between low labour standards in non-OECD countries and unemployment in OECD countries was made. However, at the same time the unions claimed that higher labour standards do not necessarily lead to reduced competitiveness, as in many cases labour costs constitute only a minor element in total costs. In addition, the ICFTU argued that trade unions are responsible enough to refrain from making demands not in line with productivity, and that profits can be cut if higher labour standards have an effect on competitiveness (ICFTU, 1995b: 6–7). On other occasions, the Confederation often emphasized that minimum standards would help to ensure a kind of competition that facilitates social development instead of exploitation of workers: 'The primary beneficiaries would, in fact, be the developing countries wishing to ensure balanced social development and most vulnerable to cut throat competition on the basis of labour exploitation' (ICFTU, 1994d: 4). Although the two claims are not necessarily contradictory, there is a tension in the analysis. It is difficult to convince those who believe that social development will follow economic development, and therefore believe in the practice of increasing exports to the highest possible level, that there is merit in increasing the enforcement of labour standards that is believed to be bad for exports. It is even harder to make a convincing argument when such claims are made by interest groups that also emphasize the negative effects of cheap exports from developing countries for workers in developed countries. Therefore, in this respect, a study that concludes that there is hardly any relationship between exports from developing countries and unemployment and low wages in developed countries may be favourable for trade unions.

On the other hand, the fact that no strong relationship was established between trade, investment and labour standards leads to the conclusion that labour standards are not trade-related issues, as they have no transboundary effects. However, the fact that countries may behave as if there is indeed a relationship between low labour standards, investment decisions and trade performance creates a relationship.

The fact that the OECD report was able to point to some labour standards as being more fundamental than others increased the legitimacy of this group of standards in the ILO, as we will see in the next chapter. However, even though the report may have undermined the protectionist rationale for a social clause, this did not leave a lasting impression on the opponents of such clause.

Notes

1. The G-7 organizes the seven most industrialized economies in the world: Japan, the UK, France, the USA, Canada, Germany and Italy. Recently, Russia joined the conferences.
2. At that time (1994), none of the four Asian tigers was a member of the OECD. In 1996 Korea joined (OECD, 2000).
3. As shown later, the fact that there is no empirical relationship does not mean that governments do not act like there is one.

4. This was a staff member from the AFL-CIO headquarters speaking. When listening to staff members of the AFL-CIO Paris office, another sound can be heard. This office maintained that the work of the OECD is extremely important for the trade and labour standards issue. If the OECD found a connection between the two, the pressure on the WTO would only increase (AFL-CIO Paris Office, 17 November 1995).

7 Adjusting the ILO to Global Challenges: The Modest Result of the Laborious Debate on the Strengthening of the ILO

The International Labour Organization is dedicated to setting and promoting labour standards. One of its main principles is that this is done on a voluntary basis. This means that almost all Conventions of the ILO need to be ratified by the member states in order to evoke any action by the ILO. Since the ILO has no means other than technical assistance, exposure and persuasion, it is dependent on the ILO member states to enforce its Conventions.

An opportunity to put words into action occurred in 1994 when the ILO embarked on a debate to recapture its diminishing strength. At first, this debate was directed towards a joint action with the General Agreement of Tariffs and Trade (later succeeded by the WTO). In later phases, this debate shifted towards strengthening the ILO's supervisory mechanism.

This chapter looks at the efforts of the Workers' Group to influence this discussion in the period between 1994 and 1998. The Workers' Group is the body through which trade unions are organized in the ILO. The chapter assesses the changing interests and strategies of the Workers' Group, and their effects. In its final analysis, this chapter explains the successes and failures of the Workers' Group with the help of the framework presented in Chapter 2.

Historical Developments and Present Position

The ILO emerged out of the ashes of the First World War. The allied forces, gathering at the Paris Peace Conference, agreed to set up a labour commission, which was, on the proposal of the British government, extended to a new international organization, the ILO. The rationale behind the establishment of the ILO was the fear that the newly acquired peace could be followed by social unrest, and that revolutionary forces similar to those that had arisen in the Eastern part of Europe could spread to the Western world. The allied forces expected that international competition would diminish the possibilities for national regulation, which in turn would lead to a deterioration of the working conditions of workers. The Constitution of the ILO, drawn up in 1919 and amended several times after that, declared that any nation failing to adopt certain labour conditions would hamper other countries trying to improve such conditions inside their national borders. It subscribed to three principles viewed as fundamental to the Constitution, i.e. the promotion of social justice, the consolidation of international peace and the diminishing of international competition. The Constitution claimed that labour should not be seen as a commodity, that workers should be protected and that people should have the right of association for lawful purposes. The last claim materialized in the ILO through its unique tripartite structure. From the very beginning, each member state was represented in the two main bodies of the ILO, the International Labour Conference and the Governing Body, by two government delegates, one worker and one employer delegate (Cox, 1973: 102–3; Boonstra, 1996: 11–14).

In 1944, an important amendment was made to the Constitution. The Second World War had shown the consequences of disrespect for human rights. Therefore, the Declaration of Philadelphia included a specific reference to human rights related to labour issues: 'All human beings, irrespective of race, creed or sex, have the right to pursue both their material well-being and their spiritual development in conditions of freedom and dignity, of economic security and equal opportunity.' The Declaration gave the member states certain new obligations, such as the obligation to guarantee freedom of expression. Besides references to civil liberties, the Declaration also broadened the ILO's scope by expressing that it is the responsibility of the ILO to examine fiscal and economic policies in the light of these human rights, thereby accepting that these policies have social implications (Boonstra, 1996: 14–15).

The 1944 amendment was part of the ILO's strategy to increase its influence in the post-war environment. With the collapse of the League of Nations and the establishment of the Bretton Woods institutions (the World Bank, the International Monetary Fund and the International Trade Organization) under the United Nations system, the ILO wanted to ensure its place among these institutions dealing with social and economic questions (Wilkinson, 1999a: 3–4).

The ITO contained a provision to cooperate with the ILO. Chapter 2 of the ITO's 'Havana Charter' stipulated that the achievement of full employment through free trade should take into account 'fair labour standards'. Therefore, collaboration between the ILO and the ITO was foreseen. The ITO, however, never came into existence. Another opportunity to link the regulation of the trade system to labour standards was provided by the establishment of the WTO. As I have shown in previous chapters, this opportunity was not realized in any other way than a WTO commitment to the standard-setting work of the ILO. With this commitment, the WTO members adhered to the neo-liberal argument that through the liberalization of world trade, labour conditions will improve naturally (Wilkinson, 1999a: 7–22).

Today, the ILO is considered to be in a weak position. Two contributions try to explain this weakness. Wilkinson (1999a) points out that there is a decreasing threat of social unrest in the Western world, making the ILO less needed. In addition, the ILO has no place in the system of global governance (i.e. the cooperation between the Bretton Woods institutions). While the discussions on a social clause in the WTO provided opportunities for the ILO to secure a place in this system of global governance, neither ILO and WTO officials, nor the major supporter of a social clause, the United States, were willing to push the issue to the limit. In this respect, Wilkinson refers to a survey conducted among ILO officials, which showed that there was great uneasiness among these officials in departing from the ILO emphasis on voluntarism and persuasion in favour of a sanction-based approach (Wilkinson, 1999a: 25–33). Despite the US insistence on the social clause, before the Singapore meeting US and WTO officials made it clear that the political mood inhibited a delay in the ratification of the Uruguay Round deal on behalf of the workers' rights issue (ICFTU, 1994e: 2).

In another contribution, Reinalda (1998: 59–61) maintains that the ILO has been weakened. He argues that because of the diminishing of East–West tensions, the traditional basis for an alliance between Western nations, employers and workers against the former Eastern Bloc has been taken away. Moreover, developing countries have started to question the universality of standards and human rights, and the rate of ratification of Conventions has slowed down. In addition, the ILO is confronted with external competition from other UN organizations and the G-7 that have organized conferences on issues within the mandate of the ILO without even consulting the organization, which shows a decreased legitimacy of the ILO.

However, it should be noted that the trends in ratification have been changed. In May 1995, a campaign to promote the ILO's fundamental human rights Conventions was initiated. In March 1998, this effort resulted in 82 new ratifications, while the number of countries that had ratified all seven core Conventions increased from 23 to 35 (ILO Press Release, 27 March 1998). With this campaign, the stagnation, or even fall, in the rate of ratification of Conventions, as pointed out by Reinalda (1998, 59), had actually been reversed.

There is no dispute that the ILO has not been able to force the other global governance institutions to take it into account as a relevant institution. However, in this chapter I argue that the strength, or weakness, of the ILO should be assessed not only by the functioning of the organization itself, but also by the way in which it is able to legitimize its goals. One of these goals is to ensure respect for labour standards. One of the ways to achieve this is to facilitate a consensus on the importance of a package of selected labour rights that can serve as a vehicle to promote the idea that labour rights need to be respected and promoted, and do not come naturally from economic development. This chapter argues that the ILO has made some progress in this field, and that trade unions have played a role in this progress.

Organization and Function of the ILO

Before turning to developments in the recent history of the ILO, I first describe its internal structure (Cox, 1973: 114–26; Boonstra, 1996: 24–42; ILO, 1999). As mentioned above, the ILO is a tripartite organization, in which states, employers and workers are represented in the various bodies.

The *International Labour Conference* (ILC) is the legislative body of the ILO. Its main tasks are to design (in committee) and adopt (in plenary) international labour standards in the form of Conventions and Recommendations. The Conference also passes resolutions that provide guidelines for the ILO's general policy and future activities. Meeting once a year, it consists of four representatives from each member state: two from the government, one from the employers and one from the workers. These representatives are organized in several groups: different groups of states, the Employers' Group, and the Workers' Group. The voting ratio of these groups is 2:1:1. Workers and employers are represented through their own groups. Since the breakdown of the Eastern bloc, these groups have been dominated by the ICFTU and the International Organization of Employers (IOE).

Since the 1960s, regional caucusing has been a mode of operation of the government delegates in the ILO. Examples are the Group of 77 (developing countries), the IMEC group (Industrial Market Economy Countries) and the European Union. In the past there has also been a socialist voting bloc.

These caucuses try to coordinate their voting behaviour through informal consultations.

The *Conference Committees*, permanent and non-permanent, are appointed by the Conference to deal with specific subjects, such as finances, the adoption of Conventions and the study of country reports on the implementation of the Conventions. The main permanent committees are the Committee of Experts, which studies the annual reports of governments on the application of standards, and the Committee on the Application of Conventions and Recommendations, which examines the reports of the aforementioned committee and selects the most urgent cases for discussion.

The *International Labour Office* is the permanent secretariat of the ILO. It distributes information, assists governments in preparing the country reports, processes country reports and prepares the agenda of the Conference under supervision of the Governing Body. The *Director-General* (DG) is responsible for the work of the International Labour Office.

The *Governing Body* (GB) is the executive body of the International Labour Office. Meeting three times a year, it takes decisions on ILO policy, decides on the agenda of the International Labour Conference, adopts the draft Programme and Budget of the Organization for submission to the Conference, and elects the DG. It is composed of 56 titular members (again with a voting ratio of 2:1:1). Ten of the government seats are permanently held by 'States of Chief Industrial Importance', which are Brazil, China, France, Germany, India, Italy, Japan, the Russian Federation, the United Kingdom and the United States. The GB has several committees, among which are the Committee on Freedom of Association and the Working Party on the Social Dimensions of the Liberalization of International Trade (SDL).

The three instruments of the ILO are Conventions, Recommendations and Resolutions. The Conventions create legal obligations once ratified. Since 1919, the ILO has created 182 Conventions. Countries are obliged to inform the DG about the measures taken in accordance with their ratification. Both law and practice are considered. Recommendations cannot be ratified, but serve as guidance to the development of policy, legislation and practice. Often a Recommendation is a complement to a Convention, and in that case suggests how to implement a Convention. Resolutions can deal with the internal activities of the ILO, such as the initiation of a new institution, and are binding. They can also deal with a specific member state, to expose injustice, such as apartheid in South Africa. These kinds of Resolutions do not impose legal obligations. The implementation of Resolutions is supervised by the DG, who reports to the ILC.

Phase 1: Discursive Clashes and the Institutionalization of the Social Clause Debate

The issue of the social clause is not new within the ILO. In the 1970s and in the early 1990s, the social clause was subject to debate in the ILO, but no consensus could be reached (Hansenne, 1993). However, with the establishment in June 1994 of the Working Party on the Social Dimensions of the Liberalization of International Trade it was the first time that this issue materialized in the institutional context. The working party was the direct consequence of two interrelated developments. First, within the GATT the United States predominantly exercised pressure to include a reference to labour standards in the final Declaration of the Uruguay Round. Such a provision would have altered the autonomous role of the ILO with respect to the monitoring of standards implementation.

Second, in 1994, the (then) DG of the ILO, Michel Hansenne, published a report to celebrate the 75th anniversary of the ILO. Addressing the social clause issue in his report was a response to what was generally felt by the critics to be an indirect attack on the autonomy of the ILO. Hansenne believed that since the fall of the Berlin Wall, earlier tensions between delegates to the ILO had diminished, and disagreement concerning the universality of standards had also decreased. Combined with the globalization of the economy and the proliferation of social problems, Hansenne maintained, this should inspire an evaluation of the ILO (Hansenne, 1994: 7–23).

Of the many activities suggested by the ILO's DG to address the needs of a changing world, his proposals concerning respect for standards are most relevant to this chapter. One of the problems that the ILO is facing is a lack of means, other than persuasion and technical assistance, to enforce the application of its standards. None the less, Hansenne rejected the idea of the application of sanctions to member countries that do not comply with the ratified Conventions (social clause). According to him:

> At first glance this idea might seem enticing. It has, however, been repeatedly discarded since the ILO's earliest days for pragmatic reasons that are still valid today: in addition to the difficulty of implementing sanctions, the mere prospect of sanctions is capable of discouraging ratification, or even membership in the Organization. (Hansenne, 1994: 52)

According to Hansenne, the ILO should not advocate restrictions to trade or a compulsory equalization of social costs. To do so would be at odds with the ILO's premise that free trade should be stimulated and differences in costs have the potential to spur economic development. In addition, the ILO has no mandate to regulate international trade. Moreover, the compulsory equalization of social costs is not a task of the ILO, since the ILO opts for cooperation and persuasion, and not force (Hansenne, 1994: 58).

As an alternative to a social clause, Hansenne proposed a two-way street: states should examine the possibility of ratifying ILO standards and apply these to the extent that their situation and means allow. However, certain standards, the so-called basic or core labour standards, should be respected regardless of the level of economic development. These core labour standards are seen as a precondition to exercise other rights, and they are conditional for an optimally functioning labour market (Hansenne, 1996: 5). Hansenne suggested in his 1994 report that it should be examined whether the same procedure could be applied to these standards as for the Convention on Freedom of Association (CFA), i.e. making the respect for these rights a condition for ILO membership, regardless of ratification (Hansenne, 1994: 52–6, 59).

In return for respect for core labour standards, countries (read developed countries) should respond by removing their unilaterally imposed trade barriers, since social progress depends on economic development, and economic development depends on liberalized world markets. At the same time, countries that have to carry the costs of social development should be supported by the ILO in terms of technical and financial assistance. In addition, the collaboration between the WTO and the ILO should be strengthened to see if there is a source for financing the costs of adjustment (Hansenne, 1994: 59–62; 1996: 7).[1]

Although it does not look as if Hansenne envisaged a hidden sanction system, i.e. deliberately linking the violation of standards to a justified use of a unilateral sanctioning system, he did use the threat of unilateral trade barriers, together with the known pressure of the United States in the WTO, as a stick to stimulate those countries that are not taking the ILO Conventions too seriously to do so in the future. In fact, Hansenne seemed determined to pre-empt the call for a social clause by the ILO by presenting alternatives. He called for an international labour Convention, in which there is an agreement that 'States would undertake to abstain from applying unilateral trade restrictions . . . in exchange for a greater commitment by their trading partners to strive towards the social progress expected from Members of the Organization' (Hansenne, 1994: 62–3).

Hansenne's report can be conceived as the first step towards a definition of the problem facing the ILO. However, it also marked a split in the definition of the problem under debate. Some of the representatives at the ILO defined the problem as related to the erosion of social protection and the loss of jobs under globalization partly as a result of the declining powers of the national state and partly as a result of the desire to remain competitive. For others, the real problem was the threat underlying the debate. The pressure to place social problems related to globalization on the international agenda implied that some ILO delegates were forced to deal with an issue they did not want to deal with: trade-enforceable labour standards.

Discursive conflicts

Responses to Hansenne's report in June 1994 during the ILC and GB meetings illustrated the strong disagreement among the ILO delegates on the issue of whether labour standards should be linked to multilateral trade sanctions. In fact, the ILO delegates were for the largest part divided into two coalitions along the lines suggested in Chapter 3: an interventionist and a neo-liberal discourse coalition. In addition, a large group, mainly consisting of government representatives, remained undecided, either because they called for more research or because they supported greater attention for the social dimension of trade liberalization, but were unsure about the sanction mechanism.

The lobby efforts of the Workers' Group, which represents the trade unions in the ILO, were initially directed towards gaining, or keeping, the support of the United States, Mexico, Brazil, India and Northern African countries for a social clause. In addition, the targeted allies in Europe were Germany, France and the UK. Finally, the support of the Employers' Group was considered to be helpful (Interview with ICFTU, 24 February 1997). Table 7.1 shows, in 1994, which interests coalitions were supported by the representatives of which states and groups.

Table 7.1 *Discourse coalitions in Phase 1*

Interventionist discourse coalition	Neo-liberal discourse coalition	Undecided
USA	India	Germany
France	Majority of Employers' Group	
Majority of Workers' Group	Mexico	
	UK	
	Egypt	

The interventionist discourse coalition emerging in the ILO in June 1994 emphasized the necessity of international intervention, in the absence of strong enforcement mechanisms for the ILO, to help workers to acquire the benefits of economic development. This perspective was characterized by four arguments (ILO, 1994a). The first was that trade liberalization and social progress should be achieved simultaneously, and in order to achieve this the intervention of governments is needed. The minimum step towards social progress would be to acknowledge that there are certain rights that cannot be denied to anyone. These rights are considered to be universal, and therefore underdevelopment should not be regarded as a pretext to deny workers such rights. The rights frequently mentioned were freedom of association, freedom to organize and bargain collectively and freedom from forced and child labour. Some (mainly members of the Workers' Group) also referred to other standards, such as equal remuneration and non-discrimination in employment.[2] Second, the interventionist coalition stressed that since denying these rights perverts the rationale of free trade, labour standards can no longer be regarded as strictly internal affairs. Third, it pointed out that the multilateral nature of a social clause would end the contemporary variety of unilateral trade measures. In fact, the WTO was regarded as the most appropriate forum to deal with setting up a link between trade and labour standards. Fourth, it emphasized that the quest for a linkage should not be considered protectionist. Sanctions would only be used as a last resort after all other solutions had failed. A social clause would not be aimed at denying developing countries their competitive advantage, and there would be no call for a global minimum wage. In short, the interventionist discourse made use of the international sovereignty claim, in combination with neo-institutional ideas about the relationship between economic and social development. It also emphasized the universality of certain labour standards.

The interventionist discourse was challenged by the neo-liberal discourse coalition, which shared the view that a social clause has to be avoided (ILO, 1994a). Vigorously supporting this neo-liberal discourse was the majority of the employers, supported by a resolution of the government delegations of Indonesia, Malaysia, the Philippines, Singapore and Thailand. Most of the contra-linkage coalition actors were tied together by a perspective highlighting the following arguments. First of all, instead of a mutually enforcing relationship the neo-liberal discourse coalition stressed a rather one-sided relationship between economic development and social progress. Economic growth was seen as a condition for social development, including the observance of (core) labour standards. One aspect of this reasoning is that child labour is the result of poverty, and would disappear with the alleviation of poverty. Second, it emphasized that the existence of a link between trade and labour standards was a protectionist act. Such a link would negatively affect the economic progress of developing countries, because it impedes the comparative advantage of developing countries. The neo-liberal discourse highlighted the positive instead of the negative effects of global liberalization. Third, it emphasized that the mere discussion of a trade link would threaten any further ratification of ILO Conventions. Fourth, this coalition argued that a link between labour rights and trade is not within the mandate of the ILO. Fifth, rigid labour policies were seen as the cause of economic problems (including unemployment) among industrialized countries. The neo-liberals expressed the fear that once basic labour standards were linked to trade sanctions, other labour standards would follow. Sixth, there was a strong tendency within this discourse to the idea that revision would encourage more countries to ratify the Conventions. In this respect, a reference was often made to Convention 138, the Minimum Age Convention, since the details included in this Convention inhibit many ILO members from ratifying it.[3] In addition, many representatives that did not support a link called for more technical assistance from the ILO and questioned the universal application of standards as practised by the ILO. They attributed the low ratification rate of Conventions to insufficient consideration for differences in development. They therefore proposed to re-examine the ILO's standards policy, which soon became one of the prominent issues.

All these arguments stem from a neo-liberal analysis. The idea is that labour standards will create an economic slow-down. The reason is that they interfere with the comparative advantage of nations. It is this advantage that is the condition for social development. Protectionist sentiments are the driving force behind the link. Basically it is argued that not economic growth, but the lack of economic growth, is responsible for social underdevelopment. The ILO should not interfere with the liberalization of trade, as this liberalization itself will stimulate social development. In addition, the ILO standards should be brought up to date, because their content is the reason for the lack of ratification.

The stalemate between the two discourses remained in place during the period 1994–8. Although in general terms it resembled a conflict between the North and the South, the dividing lines were not that clear. For example, the Employers' Group was an excellent example of unity between developing and developed countries on this subject: leaving aside two or three exceptions it opposed a link between trade and labour standards (ILO, 1994a: 6/16–6/17).

Containing conflict within the ILO

Despite the irreconcilable positions of the neo-liberals and the interventionists, and with two definitions of the problem under discussion, the ILC and GB meetings in June 1994 resulted in two major decisions. First of all, core labour standards were defined. The 1994 ILC adopted a resolution which stipulated that institutions and structures need to be reviewed to ensure their relevance to a changing environment, and included a reference to fundamental rights in the form of the ILO Conventions 87, 98, 100, 29, 105 and 111 (see Appendix). The original text of this resolution, submitted by some European government delegations, the United States and Chile, did not include this specific reference to Conventions. However, another (non-adopted) resolution submitted by workers' delegates did make such reference to these specific Conventions and to Convention 138 (minimum age) (ILO, 1994a: 1/2–1/6; 1994b, 3–4). This suggests that part of the workers' delegates' resolution was included in the final adopted resolution. The final resolution was supported by some of the most persistent violators of these Conventions, who were trying to prevent even less favourable intervention, i.e. the involvement of the WTO in the issue of labour standards (Interview with ICFTU, 24 February 1997).

The reference to core or fundamental labour Conventions is remarkable since in previous years discussions on the social clause failed to come up with a definition of fundamental labour rights (Blanchard, 1988: 6; ILO, 1996d). Even Hansenne refrained in his own report for the 75th anniversary from referring to specific Conventions (Hansenne, 1994). The ICFTU itself had defined core labour standards in earlier years, and prior to the 1994 ILC, the Confederation met the DG to re-express its support for the definition of a set of core Conventions (ICFTU, 1994d).

The second major decision was the establishment of the SDL to discuss the social dimensions of the liberalization of international trade. After some protest the proposal to set up this working party, which had come from the DG, was accepted. The Workers' Group's vice chairman proposed to open the working party to all members, which also was accepted (GB, 1994a: 2; 1994d: II/5; 1994e: 2). Although during the 1994 ILC it was pointed out that the decision to create a working party in no way entailed a decision to accept a social clause, Indian, Egyptian and Indonesian governments were still afraid of the political consequences of a working party, and pleaded at least for the broadening of the term international trade to globalization, since international trade was not considered to be a specific mandate of the ILO. All opponents of a working party were overruled and it was decided that it would have its first session in November 1994 (GB, 1994c).

The first meetings of the SDL party took place in November 1994, during the GB meeting. Membership of the SDL is the same as membership of the GB, which means that it is open to all members of the Workers' Group, the Employers' Group and the Government Group. Despite extensive discussions within the SDL, the standoff between the two discourse coalitions remained largely the same. This meant that the total number of participants taking a pro-linkage stand was heavily outnumbered by the discourse coalition against and by actors that remained indecisive.

Because the overwhelming majority of members of the SDL appeared not to favour a link between trade and labour standards, actors expressing the interventionist discourse coalition were pushed on to the defence. To keep the SDL alive (many had proposed its elimination), the Workers' Group had to agree not to pursue a study of a link between trade and labour standards. Instead, it was agreed that the purpose of the working group had to be redefined. The Workers' Group emphasized, however, that it expected that the recognition of the fundamental nature of the six standards, something most participants had agreed to, should be accompanied by specific measures (GB, 1994c: 62). What these specific measures looked like became the next topic of debate.

Phase 2: Strengthening the ILO

Now that the social clause was no longer on the agenda, and the strengthening of the ILO became an issue, the bloc of the IMEC group (roughly representing the OECD countries), South Africa, Egypt, Mexico, Nigeria, Argentina, Brazil, Chile, Peru, Colombia and Pakistan and the Asia-Pacific group were seen by the Workers' Group as important actors that could make or break further progress on the strengthening of the ILO supervisory procedures (Interview with ICFTU, 23 April 1998).

During the SDL meetings the revision and strengthening of standards and the supervision mechanism became prominent. They were offered as alternatives to the link between trade and labour standards. During the discussions in the SDL some opponents of a link between labour standards and trade suggested the revision of standards as an alternative. In addition, many opponents emphasized the need for technical assistance by the ILO to comply with standards. Thereby they emphasized that it was not a lack of political will that was responsible for non-ratification, but a lack of technical possibilities. Indeed, between 1991 and 1996 the annual budget of the ILO for technical cooperation had decreased significantly (ILO, 1997b). On the other hand, the Workers' Group, including the unions that were otherwise against a social clause, preferred a strengthening of the ILO supervisory procedure more than a revision of standards (Interview with ILO staff member, 8 July 1997). This was because it was felt that a revision would imply that less time would be available for the adoption of standards (Interview with ICFTU, 11 July 1997), and a revision would have the danger of a weakening of the standards, rather than a strengthening of them.

The idea that technical assistance, rather than force, is needed to make ratification, and subsequent implementation, possible fits well into the neo-liberal argument. Intervention should be kept to a minimum, and voluntarism kept to a maximum. Intensifying the possibilities for observing the standards, on the other hand, agrees with the interventionist line of argument.

Not all the work related to revision and strengthening could be done by the SDL itself, and thus it was 'subcontracted' to other committees. For example, it was agreed upon that the *Committee on Employment and Social Policy* should undertake research with respect to the issue of child labour, and that the *Committee on Legal Issues and International Labour Standards* (LILS) should promote the core labour standards. In May 1995, the LILS undertook a campaign to promote the ILO's fundamental human rights Conventions, or core labour standards. In March 1998, this effort had resulted in 82 new ratifications, while the number of countries that had ratified all seven core Conventions increased from 23 to 35 (ILO Press Release, 27 March 1998). With this campaign, the stagnation, or even fall, in the rate of ratification of Conventions, as pointed out by Reinalda (1998: 59), had actually been reversed.

The very fact that these labour issues could be dealt with in other settings than the working party led the Indian government to suggest eliminating the SDL. The main reason for this was that India considered the context in which some SDL members wanted to set the discussion in the working party, namely the liberalization of trade, as too narrow. It also feared that the Workers' Group would again bring up the link between trade and labour standards (GB, 1995a: 5–7). Although India's opinion was shared by some other governments, it was decided that the SDL should concern itself with an open-ended debate, study the developments of other international organizations working in the field of the liberalization of trade, be a contact point for these organizations and look at the progress in other ILO bodies with respect to fundamental human rights and child labour. More specifically, it was decided that a questionnaire should be distributed to all three constituents of the member states with respect to the developments in and impact on globalization and liberalization of trade, looking at the effects of FDI on economic growth and labour standards. It was also agreed that an examination of the OECD report on the social clause (once ready) should take place. In addition, an initiative unfolded to research the positive economic effects of implementing core labour standards in developing countries (ILO, 1996b: 2/2, 32; GB, 1996a, 1997d).

Strengthening the ILO supervisory mechanism: Applying the CFA procedure

The strengthening of the ILO's supervisory mechanisms in relation to the core Conventions turned out to be one of the most controversial issues during the November 1995 GB meeting and in the years to come (GB, 1995b, 1996a, b, c). The main point of discussion was whether the existing supervisory mechanisms of the ILO were sufficient to stimulate the application of the core Conventions, or whether new mechanisms were needed. With respect to new mechanisms, the Workers' Group proposed applying a procedure analogous to that of the CFA to cover other Conventions. This procedure would put obligations on non-ratifying

Table 7.2 *Positions on applying the CFA procedure*

Interventionist discourse coalition	Neo-liberal discourse coalition	Moderately in favour
USA	Pakistan	Germany
France	Employers' Group	Canada
Workers' Group	Asia-Pacific Group	Chile
Finland	UK	Argentina
	Italy	
	China	
	Bangladesh	
	India	
	Russian Federation	
	Malaysia	
	Spain	
	Brazil	

Note: this table only includes those representatives who made a statement published in GB (1996c).

countries and provide a complaint procedure. At that time a decision could not be taken because the legal grounds for extending the CFA procedure were unclear, as many opponents pointed out (GB, 1995b: IV/2–9).[4] Nevertheless, this proposal did give rise to a new debate between the 'old' coalitions, as Table 7.2 shows.

Table 7.2 does not reveal many surprises. As expected, those who believe that intervention is needed to secure certain standards for workers are more sensitive to an instrument that secures such standards *regardless of ratification*. The Workers' Group was strongly in favour of the creation of a supervisory procedure for Conventions 29, 105, 100 and 111 along the lines of the CFA procedure (Interview with ICFTU, 11 July 1997). The main arguments to do so were: (a) that it would send a strong signal to the WTO, which was about to meet in December 1996 in Singapore and was to decide on the formal start of a debate on the inclusion of labour rights; and (b) that it would be an effective way to apply these prominent ILO principles, thereby enhancing the ILO's credibility. The Workers' Group received the support of France, Finland and the United States.

Table 7.2 also shows that there was a group of countries that was unsure about the application of the CFA procedure, but nevertheless sympathized with strengthening the existing supervision procedure and wanted a further discussion on the creation of new machinery.

Apart from the impact of the Social Summit, it is interesting to note that the International Labour Office pointed out that the OECD study on trade and labour standards had facilitated the recognition of fundamental rights too (ILO, 1998d). As shown in Chapter 6, this study selected freedom of association and collective bargaining, the elimination of exploitative forms of child labour (i.e. bonded labour and forms that are considered to be unhealthy or unsafe), prohibition of slavery and compulsory labour, and non-discrimination in employment as core labour standards (OECD, 1996b: 26–8). The fact that in other settings the definition of a specific group of labour standards was achieved increased the legitimacy of this group of standards in the ILO.

Other countries whose support the Workers' Group considered to be indispensable in order to be successful were having serious doubts about the extension of the CFA procedure: Brazil, the Asia-Pacific Group and many of the IMEC countries opposed the application of the CFA to the mentioned Conventions, or were at least doubtful. Not surprisingly, the Employers' Group was also against this proposal.

The arguments of the representatives against the application of the CFA procedure to other standards were based on efficiency, legal and historical grounds. They were not based on political grounds, which was in fact the main issue. With respect to efficiency, many opponents suggested that labour standards should be promoted through technical assistance. In this way, obstacles that inhibit members ratifying and applying these standards could be overcome. In addition, some pointed out that applying a CFA procedure would inhibit further ratification of the Conventions. In the opinion of some of the opponents, the legal basis was still rather weak, since the Vienna Convention on the Law of Treaties, which is also applicable to the ILO Conventions, only creates obligations for members that have ratified Conventions. Moreover, many opponents pointed out that the CFA procedure was unique and developed in a specific historical context, and could not be duplicated (GB, 1996c: 5–20).

No conclusion was reached other than to continue the discussion the following year. This was especially disappointing for the Workers' Group and the United States, since the WTO Singapore meeting was about to start. If even an institution such as the ILO could not reach consensus on the strengthening of core standards, even without economic sanctions, the WTO members would certainly not be able to do so. However, the ILO discussion showed that the definition of fundamental standards was widely accepted, which provided at least a foundation to proceed from.

At the December 1996 WTO Singapore Conference, the link between labour standards and trade was hotly disputed and very delicate, partly because of the withdrawal of the invitation to the ILO's DG to address the Conference. The WTO members agreed to suspend any discussions on the labour standards–trade issue, re-emphasizing the ILO as the competent body to deal with labour standards (see Chapter 1).

Alternative mechanisms

When the WTO discussed the issue of labour standards, it identified the ILO as the most suitable forum to debate such standards. This must have pleased the ILO's DG Hansenne. He rightly pointed out after the conclusion of the Singapore Conference that the ball was in the court of the ILO (Hansenne, 1997: 1). The Singapore decision left room only for continuing discussions on how to improve the strength of the ILO itself. The aim of the neo-liberal discourse coalition was to end the social clause discussion once and for all. With the immediate threat of an established relationship between trade and labour standards gone, the opponents started to consider some sort of regulation that would address the concerns of those who advocated a social clause.

Anticipating the WTO outcome, the Employers' Group proposed to adopt a Declaration of Fundamental Principles in November 1996. This proposal was not entirely new, as Hansenne had made a similar proposal in 1994. This Declaration would provide a basis for additional action within the supervisory system, and could even be incorporated into the Constitution. Such a Declaration would embody the essence of the core Conventions and of the principles of the Constitution, including the Declaration of Philadelphia (ICFTU, 1997d).

With the ILO regaining the initiative, and without the threat of a WTO-related social clause, it was obvious to the Workers' Group that they would have a difficult time getting their proposal concerning the application of the CFA accepted. Therefore, the Workers' Group embarked on informal consultations with the Employers' Group prior to the GB meeting of March 1997, in search of common ground on the matters of a Declaration and follow-up mechanisms (ICFTU, 1997a, b). The first informal meetings between the two groups took place on 10 and 11 February 1997. In these meetings, the Employers' Group made clear that it had no intention whatsoever of adopting a new supervisory mechanism. Instead, it argued for a Declaration on principles, rather than on the Conventions themselves. This stance was taken despite the fact that the ILO Office had said that there was enough legal basis to consider new ILO work without a Declaration (GB, 1996b). However, recognizing that a debate on legal aspects would be pointless, the Workers' Group agreed to a Declaration based on principles, even though it doubted its necessity and recognized the possible danger to the core rights Conventions. The compromise the Workers' Group proposed was a new role for the Committee of Experts in supervising non-ratifying countries with respect to their application of the core rights Conventions, or, alternatively, the principles therein. Through this mechanism, trade unions as well as employers would have the opportunity to present complaints against governments that did not observe fundamental rights. It was clear, however, that the Employers' Group would not support a complaint-based procedure.

During the March 1997 GB meeting the Workers' Group formally agreed to study the possibilities of a Declaration to clarify the content of the principles (the essence of the core Conventions), provided that it would not set aside the Conventions themselves. However, the difference between the groups with respect to the follow-up mechanisms had not been resolved. The workers emphasized complaints, the employers agreed to representations.[5]

Nevertheless, the employers seemed to become more sensitive to the workers' concerns. In November 1996, the Employers' Group spoke of the involvement of: 'reports from member States, and observations from employers' and workers' organizations', while in March 1997 it spoke of 'reporting, observations and representations from employers' and workers' organizations and governments', thus emphasizing a greater role for non-governmental representatives. However, it still could not agree on how to deal with complaints (GB, 1997a: 8, 5; 1997b: 6). Both groups did agree that a follow-up mechanism would apply to countries that had not ratified (some of) the core Conventions. Rather than setting aside the existing mechanisms for members that have ratified Conventions and the specific CFA procedure, this mechanism required an annual report of all non-ratifying states on the core Conventions.

From the government side, the Asia-Pacific countries were not happy about the proposal to expand the ILO's supervisory machinery. Again, they pointed out that the proposal 'did not address the real problems of ratification and application of the standards, and contradicted the promotional role of the ILO; they could even hinder further ratifications' (GB, 1997b: 9). Pakistan mentioned the possibility of a Declaration, which would speak out against arbitrary and unilateral actions and protectionist campaigns, and would provide for a complaint procedure in the case of unilateral trade measures. Such a complaint procedure would of course be very different from the one the Workers' Group had in mind. India explicitly stated that the CFA procedure should not be extended to other Conventions. In general, proposals that disregarded the ratification of Conventions were considered unacceptable. On 11 March 1998, a tripartite consultation was held in India, including the major central trade unions, the employers' organizations and government officials. During this consultation, the Indian government repeated that it would only accept a Declaration that reaffirmed a political commitment to the promotion of core labour standards and respected the specific national circumstances and the level of socio-economic development. In addition, a Declaration should reconfirm that the ILO is the only international body competent to set and monitor labour standards, which should not be binding or undermine the principles of voluntarism and should regard technical assistance as the cornerstone of efforts to promote core labour standards. Perhaps surprisingly, the trade unions present at this consultation were even more cautious than the Indian government (see also Chapter 5). Some referred to the hidden agenda of the Declaration, which was to bring about a link between trade and labour standards; for example, in the form of social labelling (Government of India, 1998).

Many Latin American governments held similar views to those of the Asia-Pacific. The Brazilian government supported the statements made by the other Latin American countries, but also mentioned more explicitly keeping an open mind towards a Declaration. At the same time it indicated that it would be against a complaint procedure. Brazil also did not want an erosion of the distinction between ratifying and non-ratifying countries. Other developing countries, such as Argentina, supported the possibility of a Declaration, but they also opted in favour of the existing supervisory machinery, and not a complaint procedure. Most developed countries agreed to discuss all possibilities after the International Labour Conference in June 1997 (GB, 1997b: 5–22).

Declaration (1998)

The discussion on the Declaration showed that while everyone agreed that the ILO had to adapt to its changing environment, there was no agreement on what this adaptation should mean. On the one hand, there were those who saw the internationalization of the economy as threatening labour. On the other hand, there were those who had, quite successfully, shifted the discussion from 'threats' to an emphasis on technical difficulties and outdated Conventions. The only common ground between the two groups was the notion of core labour standards. But without a well formulated consensus on the nature of the problem related to core labour standards, a decision on the way to strengthen the ILO mechanism with respect to these core standards could only be weak. The Workers' Group of course envisaged a Declaration with strong enforceability, and urged a more substantial evaluation of the implementation of the rights subscribed in the Declaration.

To end this controversy, the Office of the ILO published a document to be considered at the 1998 Conference, explaining the debate that had taken place thus far and clarifying the remaining issues (ILO, 1998d). Two issues, brought forward by the representatives that had reservations towards a Declaration, dominated. The first was whether a Declaration is legally binding and the second was whether it forms the basis of protectionist measures.

According to the Office document, a Declaration does not add further obligations to those that already exist under the Constitution and under constitutional practice. When they became a member of the ILO, states had already committed themselves to the Constitution, which refers to the seven core standards (including minimum age). Because a Declaration is based on the essence of the Conventions, no member will be subjected to specific provisions of Conventions that it has not ratified (the exception being the Freedom of Association Convention). The follow-up mechanism in the form of annual reports from non-ratifying countries does not entail new obligations, since it was decided in 1995 to extend the system of four-yearly reports under article 19(e) of the Constitution for the Discrimination Convention to the six other Conventions concerning fundamental rights. For the purpose of a Declaration, the only changes that would be made were those concerning the frequency and the procedure.

With respect to the question of whether a Declaration would form a legal basis for countries to adopt trade measures against countries violating (one of) the core Conventions, the answer was again negative. However, there was discussion on whether to emphasize this in a Declaration. This showed that although a Declaration would not create a legal basis, it could indeed have a political basis. As one of the Indian central trade unions mentioned in March 1998, 'no useful purpose would be served by the proposed Declaration unless it has a hidden agenda which would not be in the interest of developing countries such as India' (Government of India, 1998). And, indeed, one could maintain that the importance of the Declaration is found in its 'hidden agenda'. The fact that, among others, the Workers' Group opposed the text that 'no ILO Member may rely on this Declaration to adopt trade measures that are of a protectionist nature or measures that would call into question the comparative advantage of other countries' suggests that the significance of the Declaration is political and reaches beyond the ILO.

In 1998, the Declaration was finally adopted, with no votes against, and 43 abstentions. The Declaration stipulates that:

> all Members, even if they have not ratified the Conventions in question, have an obligation arising from the very fact of membership in the Organization, to respect, to promote and to realize, in good faith and in accordance with the Constitution, the principles concerning the fundamental rights which are the subject of those Conventions, namely: (a) freedom of association and the effective recognition of the right to collective bargaining; (b) the elimination of all forms of forced or compulsory labour; (c) the effective abolition of child labour; and (d) the elimination of discrimination in respect of employment and occupation. (ILO, 1998c)

Its follow-up mechanism consists of the same procedure under article 19(e) as adopted earlier, with the understanding that the frequency of reporting would be increased, accompanied by a Global Report. No additional complaint procedure has found its way into the Declaration. Workers' and employers' organizations are allowed to comment on the reports.

Hardly anyone seemed to agree fully with the text of the Declaration. In fact, with the exception of the acceptance of fundamental principles, no change in the discursive position had taken place. Many developing countries, such as India and Egypt, continued to express their fear of protectionism, and emphasized the promotion and observance of fundamental principles and rights at work in the context of the specific national circumstances and the level of socio-economic development. On the other hand, the United States left the door open to cooperation with other international organisations, such as the WTO (ILO, 1998f).

Assessment of Influence

Defining impacts

In this section, I answer the question of to what extent the debate in the ILO has served the interests of the Workers' Group. The impacts that may correspond with the interests of the Workers' Group are: (a) the acceptance of discussion of the social clause; (b) the establishment of the SDL; (c) the definition of core labour standards; (d) the increased ratification of Conventions resulting from the campaign of the DG, since the definition of core labour standards and the threat of WTO action facilitated the campaign; and (e) a Declaration that refers to core labour standards. On the other hand, there are two impacts that did not correspond to the interests of the Workers' Group: (f) there was no call for a WTO social clause; and (g) there was no support for a strong supervisory system that would give the Declaration teeth. Table 7.3 summarizes these interests and the subsequent impacts.

Agreement to discuss the social clause and the acceptance of core labour standards can be classified as a sensitizing (or discursive) impact, accompanied by institutionalization of these matters in the form of the SDL (substantive impact). The increased ratification is also a substantive impact. The fact that a reference to core labour standards found its way into the Declaration can be considered a sensitizing impact.

Table 7.3 *Interests and impacts*

Interests	Substantive impacts	Sensitizing impacts
Placing the social clause on the ILO agenda and getting core labour standards accepted	Yes: establishment of SDL, temporarily a focus on the social clause (a, b)	Yes: definition of core labour standards (c)
Influencing the WTO	No: the WTO has not taken up the social clause (f)	Yes: the WTO has made a reference in its Singapore Declaration to core labour standards (c)
Increasing the respect for ILO standards	Yes: ratification increased (d)	Yes: Declaration referring to core labour standards (c, e)
New ILO supervisory mechanism for core labour standards with strong enforceability	No: no strong new mechanism was developed (g)	

Explanation: Impacts, successes and failures

The question is: to what extent has the Workers' Group had any influence on the impacts of the debate corresponding to their interests. To establish a relationship between interests, actions and impacts, the following conditions should be fulfilled: the interest of the Workers' Group needs to be expressed (see Table 7.3); the Workers' Group needs to have access to the process leading to the impacts; there is a short time lag between the expressed interests (goals) and the impacts; and the impacts and interests are similar (Arts, 1998: 78).[6] With respect to the time lag, there seems to be no problem stating that there is a clear period in which the interests were expressed and the impacts materialized. In order to achieve its goals, the Workers' Group, which is dominated by the ICFTU, had access to the other decision-makers, or actors with influence, in a variety of ways (see Table 7.4).

The access issue does not seem to pose a problem in the case of the ILO. The emphasis of the activities of the Workers' Group was on formal participation in the relevant bodies within the ILO. These bodies were the ILC, the GB and the related committees (including the SDL). The Workers' Group is part of the decision-making mechanism. Votes in the GB and in the

Table 7.4 *Characteristics of collective action*

Strategy of direct influence (internal and external modes)	Formal	Informal
Non-public: lobby	Involvement in ILC and GB (including committees) discussions	Meetings with the DG and other ILO delegates
		Meetings outside the ILO with other interested parties

ILC are cast in a ratio of 2:1:1 by the states, employers and workers, respectively. However, in all bodies, preference is given to creating consensus instead of majority voting, which is allowed as long as the decision does not require a two-thirds majority. ILC and GB committees allow equal representation, as well as consensus voting (Interview with ILO, 9 August 1999).

In addition, the Group participated in outside conferences, such as one organized by the Quaker UN Office in November 1994. At this conference, meant as an informal attempt to help to achieve consensus on the social clause issue, members of the Workers' and Employers' Groups, together with staff from the ILO secretariat, the US Trade Office and the GATT, attended (ICFTU, 1994e). Another way in which the Workers' Group tried to achieve its goals was through informal meetings with the DG, Hansenne, and with opponents and proponents of the social clause. With the DG, informal meetings took place to convince him to speak out in favour of a social clause when addressing meetings outside the ILO, such as during EU meetings (ICFTU, 1994d). Informal meetings have taken place between the ICFTU, national trade unions and certain trade representatives – for example, from the United States and India – often just to exchange views (Interviews with US Mission, 24 February 1997; ICFTU, 27 March 1997; Permanent Mission of India to the Office of the United Nations, 17 July 1997). Several meetings occurred with Ruggiero, at that time the head of the WTO. Finally, an important attempt to reconcile views on the strengthening of the ILO supervisory mechanism took place in meetings in 1997 between the Workers' and Employers' Groups (ICFTU, 1997d).

It is, however, hard to arrive at solid conclusions with respect to the effectiveness of the informal activities of the Workers' Group. The ILO's DG might have been affected by the ICFTU's proposals, but it was not possible to determine whether this was so. The effects of the Quakers' conference proved not to be very successful in breaking the stand-off between pro- and anti-social clause parties. However, it helped the pro-social clause parties to gain more insight into the possibilities (ICFTU, 1994e; Interview with ICFTU, 27 March 1997). The effects of meetings with regional bodies or specific ministries in various countries have been assessed in Chapters 4 and 5. The impact of meetings with Ruggiero are also difficult to assess, as the GATT/WTO head may have had the ability to influence the agenda setting of the WTO, but it is up to the government representatives to make final decisions. At one of the meetings with Ruggiero that took place before the Singapore meeting, the ICFTU was informed that the Singapore Declaration would refer to labour standards, but that there would be no follow-up. This was exactly what happened (Interview with ICFTU, 24 February 1997). In terms of lobbying these meetings may therefore not have been very successful, but in terms of gathering strategic information they may well have been.

The effects of the meetings with the Employers' Group are among the clearest in terms of assessing impacts. As we have seen, it was not so much the Workers' Group that was able to get its point across; instead, it was the Employers' Group that proved to be able to make the Workers' Group accept its conditions concerning the Declaration. Overall, it can be concluded that these informal actions have not been very effective in terms of convincing opponents to change their views, since, during three years of debate in the ILO, no major shifts have taken place in the discourse coalitions.

Compared to the effectiveness of the informal activities, it is less difficult to arrive at conclusions concerning the formal participation of the Workers' Group within the ILO bodies. Here it is possible to trace back the influence of the Workers' Group on the progress of discussions. Through the ILO's Workers' Group, the trade unions occupy a strong position because of their voting rights in the ILC, the GB and related committees. The political process further shows that there is a pattern of voting behaviour related to caucus. The Workers' Group and the Employers' Group both try to maintain unity among their members, while the government representatives tend to vote according to the blocs they form: Asia-Pacific countries, non-aligned countries, IMEC and to a lesser extent the EU. The problem that the social clause and related debates illustrate is the tendency by actors to take North–South positions, with the South more unified against any changes in favour of strengthening the ILO. As Arts (1998) has shown, this is one of the factors that keep non-governmental organizations from becoming influential. The informal rule that no attempts to form coalitions will be made between individual employers' organizations and workers' organizations has not limited the influence of the Workers' Group: not obeying this rule would have gained it the support of two or three employers, but at the same time would have cost it the support of some of the workers.

All interests of the Workers' Group were very concrete, i.e. the ILO had the power to meet the demands they made. However, most of the interests translated into positive impacts cannot be considered a result solely of the Workers' Group. While it may have had an impact on the definition of core labour standards because of the ICFTU's long-term campaign on the matter, most of the positive impacts were the result of the report that the DG wrote in 1994 (Hansenne, 1994).

The debate that took place in the ILO shows that it was not the level of concreteness but the level of excessiveness of the separate proposals supported by the interventionist discourse coalition that was decisive for the successes or failures. The demand to send a strong message to the WTO with respect to a social clause was too ambitious. As a consequence, this demand clearly lacked support, not only among the employers and the governments but also among the trade unions themselves. The same was true for the development of a strong supervisory mechanism. On the other hand, demands that were perceived as relatively costless by those that did not support a social clause, such as the demand to select core labour standards, did yield successes. It can be concluded that the specific combination of the different demands accounted for the success. The more extreme demands were threatening enough to provide space to get the more moderate demands accepted.

Being part of the interventionist discourse coalition made unions more successful. The translation of the demands of the Workers' Group into positive outcomes, with the help of the DG and the coalition partners, was also facilitated by changes in the context. There was some fear among the ILO member states opposing a social clause that the GATT/WTO regime would respond to the pressure exercised by the United States. This, in turn, facilitated the approach taken by the DG in 1994. In addition, the OECD report and the Social Summit both helped to gain acceptance for the notion of core labour standards by referring to them and by pointing out the absence of a negative relationship between economic growth and social development.

The idea raised in Chapter 2 that the lack of common interests of the international trade union movement seriously hampers their impact, because it limits a strong attitude towards international issues, was not confirmed by the developments that took place in the ILO. Some unions from developing countries did view the emphasis on international solidarity as nothing more

197

than a hollow phrase disguising the Northern unions' desire to export domestic problems like low wages and unemployment. Therefore, these unions tended to identify more with their governments than with fellow foreign unions. This was illustrated by the example of India. These kinds of differences between unions were not always reflected by the ILO debates. As said, a large majority of the unions represented at the ILO are allied to the ICFTU, and the support of the ICFTU for the various issues raised by the Workers' Group may pre-empt deviating statements by unions. With a weak national and international position, unions must weigh the costs against the gains of internal division. With the exception of two occasions, unions with deviating viewpoints kept quiet, even though they clearly did not agree with the Workers' Group.

Conclusion: Discursive Strongholds, Change and Outside Effects

The case study of the ILO depicts the difficult environment in which trade unions operate. Not only were they confronted with a presentation of the social clause debate along North–South lines, they also found the same kind of contradictions within their own rank and file. The extent to which they have seen their demands being translated into positive impacts has mainly been dependent on three facts. The first is that the characteristics of the ILO's political process – the tripartite mechanism – allows trade unions to be involved in the decision-making process. The second is the support of other actors involved in the decision-making process, such as certain government representatives and at times the DG. The third is the favourable context, provided by the establishment of the WTO, the subsequent discussions in this forum on trade-related labour standards and the acceptance by other forums of the notion of core labour standards.

In the end, however, it is the *interpretation* of this context that really matters. I have distinguished two central discourses, the interventionist and the neo-liberal. These two discourses were supported throughout the four years of debate in the ILO by roughly the same coalitions. Neither the commitment made during the Social Summit nor the results of the OECD study have left impressions on the neo-liberal coalition other than acceptance of the notion of core labour standards. In other words, it has been sensitized towards accepting the idea that some labour standards are more fundamental than others. Through the Declaration this neo-liberal coalition has accepted that differences in economic development should not be used to challenge the universality of these fundamental standards.

However, the core of the argumentation by both coalitions has not changed, and the discussions in other forums have not influenced the way the neo-liberal coalition views the relationship between trade and labour standards. The result of the ILO debate has therefore been a compromise that cannot be assessed as being unequivocally in the interests of the majority of the Workers' Group. As this chapter has shown, the Workers' Group accepted the Declaration based on the essence rather than on the Conventions only on the condition that it would be accompanied by a new supervisory mechanism; for example, in the form of a complaint procedure. However, the group was then stuck with a Declaration it did not want in the first place, and a weak supervisory procedure that will contain hardly any additional obligations to the established ones supported by ILO members. While the Declaration is applicable regardless of ratification, the role of the Workers' Group is limited to providing an opinion. The Declaration also specifically stipulates that labour standards should not be used for protectionist purposes. Since there is no agreement on when an act can be considered protectionist, the odds are that every move towards an international enforcement of labour standards will be called protectionist.

What is the significance of this Declaration? I represented the ILO as being marginalized by internal and external developments. It seems that the Declaration has not really fortified the ILO's position. The fact that there are no substantial obligations other than those the member countries had already committed to in the ILO Constitution shows that the Declaration is nothing more than a reaffirmation.

There are, however, two aspects that make the Declaration useful for trade unions, because they have strengthened the essence of the ILO, which is to ensure respect for labour rights. First of all, it applies to all ILO member states, even if they have not ratified the core Conventions. Second, the snag in the Declaration is that it may be a step towards increasing the legitimacy of a social clause. This was clearly seen and feared by its opponents. Through the acceptance of these fundamental standards as universal, and through a follow-up mechanism that at least may increase the transparency of the application of these standards in various countries, workers may have strengthened the legitimacy of their quest for the observance of labour standards. In the future, the acceptance of universal standards could provide a basis within other organizations for the pursuit of trade-enforceable labour standards. It could be argued that the debates in the ILO, together with those in the OECD and during the Social Summit, have paved the way for the inclusion of labour standards in the trade policy reviews of the WTO.

Notes

1. Hansenne continued to put the strengthening of ILO Conventions on the agenda. However, in a 1996 speech in which he discussed the Singapore Meeting of the WTO, he no longer referred to the financial commitment the WTO could have in supporting the adjustment that countries have to make. He did, however, continue to emphasize the threat of unilateral trade action that could be taken by developed countries. He stated that if no international agreement were reached on how to deal with social problems related to the internationalization of trade, unilateral actions by powerful nations or trading blocs would be hard to avoid (Hansenne, 1996: 7–9). Hansenne also pointed out, to the dismay of the Workers' Group, that the discussion in the ILO on mandatory trade sanctions linked to labour standards had reached a dead end, and that new ways needed to be explored to strengthen the ILO.
2. At that time, these standards referred to the following Conventions: Forced Labour Convention (29), the Freedom of Association and Protection of the Right to Organize Convention (87), the Right to Organize and Collective Bargaining Convention (98), the Equal Remuneration Convention (100), the Abolition of Forced Labour Convention (105), the Discrimination (Employment and Occupation) Convention (111) and the Minimum Age Convention (138). In June 1999, a new Convention on child labour was adopted.
3. Convention 138 of the ILO states that no children below a certain age should be involved in work or employment. By this definition, all countries allow a certain degree of child labour. In June 1999, a new Convention (182) was adopted. This one covers practices such as slavery, drugs trafficking and prostitution (ILO, 1999; White, 1999).
4. The legal issue was resolved with the submission of the LILS report in November 1996, which concluded that there is indeed a constitutional basis to extend the CFA procedure to other Conventions regarding discrimination and forced labour. These standards, together with the freedom of association, are referred to, directly or indirectly, in the Constitution and the Declaration of Philadelphia, which makes it legally possible to supervise the application of these standards in countries that have not ratified the Conventions related to them (GB, 1996b: 6–7).
5. In a case of representation, the most serious decision the GB can make is to publicize the case. In case of complaints, a Commission of Inquiry may be established, and in case the report of the Commission is not

accepted it can be brought before the International Court of Justice (Bartolomei de la Cruz et al., 1996: 89–97).

6. The fifth condition, i.e. that decision-making remained in the same hands during the period studied, is not considered. I assume that the representatives are bound by the objectives of their governments or members. Generally speaking, these objectives seemed to have remained the same. Only in the case of Germany was a change in position noticed.

8 Trade Unions and Global Governance: Summary and Conclusions

This book illustrates the increasing concern about the international labour standards issue. At national levels and in international organizations, policies have been developed to address this concern. However important these developments have been, they have not led to a new regime on labour standards and trade that would make labour standards trade-enforceable (a social clause). The two organizations from which such a regime might have emerged – the ILO and the WTO – chose not to do so. Within the WTO, labour standards have not become a part of its policy, despite the fact that they are sometimes included in the trade policy reviews. The ILO has chosen not to promote the enforcement of core labour standards by means of trade sanctions.

There are three reasons why a new regime has not been developed. First, the majority of countries view the principles of the two regimes as incompatible. While the principles underlying the trading regime increasingly include trade-related non-tariff issues, most actors do not see labour rights as being related to trade. Second, even if the level of observance of labour rights is related to trade, many question whether trade sanctions are the best way to address the violations of these rights. Connected to this is the third reason: there is no agreement on the problem under discussion. While some feel that the trading system is under pressure from social problems resulting from the nature of that system, others feel that the dominant pressure on the trading system is the attempt to introduce limits to trade, based on either social considerations or economic self-interest. This is seen as an act of protectionism.

The lack of a single definition has not hampered the adjustment of policy to the social concerns, as the pressure to deal with them is real. In India, more attention is being paid to the problem of child labour. In the United States, labour standards have become a real part of foreign and development policies. The OECD has incorporated labour standards into its new-member accession policy. In the ILO, the discussion has led to new consideration of the core labour standards.

Even though these policy initiatives do not constitute a new regime, they cannot be considered isolated cases. The discussions in these separate forums had an impact on each other. In addition, other international organizations – such as the IMF – have increasingly been confronted with questions concerning labour standards. Moreover, the adoption of the Copenhagen Social Summit Declaration has emphasized the importance of labour rights. All these initiatives have contributed to an increased international consideration for labour standards.

The social clause issue has become a controversial topic in debates about economic liberalization. This is the result of greater concern about increasing economic competition and its consequences for workers. There are reasons for trade unions to be concerned. In the 1980s, FDI grew more than four times faster than world GNP. In the same period, the growth of trade in services exceeded for the first time the growth of trade in manufacturing products. While the United States, Japan and Germany still account for the majority of the world's total manufacturing output, between the 1950s and the mid-1990s developing countries increased their share of manufacturing output by a factor of four. For the United States this meant a decline of its relative share of world manufacturing output from 40 per cent in 1963 to 27 per cent in 1994. During the same period, Japan's output rose from 5.5 to 21 per cent. In addition, exports from developing countries have grown considerably during the past twenty years.

Many trade unionists believe that intensified global competition will result in a 'race to the bottom', i.e. a worldwide lowering of standards and wages. In addition, trade unionists (especially those from the North) are concerned that competition will lead to a shift of industrial activities and investments from countries with high standards to those with low standards, which in turn will lead to unemployment and increased wage inequality in countries with higher standards. This will then affect the level of organization of unions. In addition, trade unionists fear the rise of the informal sector. Finally, they worry that global competition will limit the ability of the state to protect workers.

While there is no disagreement on the question of whether global competition needs to be regulated, the nature and coverage of such regulation is subject to debate. The ICFTU considers the regulation of core labour standards at the international level essential in order to give workers a fair share of the returns from their labour. The notion of core labour standards generally refers to the principles embodied in ILO Conventions 87 (on the freedom of association and protection of the right to organize), 98 (on the right to organize and collective bargaining), 100 (on equal remuneration), 111 (on discrimination in employment and occupation), 138 (on minimum age), 29 (on forced labour), 105 (on the abolition of forced labour) and 182 (on the abolition of the worst forms of child labour); see Appendix. If necessary and if all other means become exhausted, the Confederation argues, these core labour standards should be enforced by means of trade sanctions, preferably enacted at the level of the WTO.

The opportunity for such a demand to be made was certainly there. While for a long time negotiations within the framework of the GATT were confined to reducing trade barriers, domestic policies – such as subsidies and technical barriers – have become increasingly important since the Tokyo Round negotiations (1973–9). Since the Uruguay Round of the GATT started in 1986, many non-tariff issues (such as intellectual property rights and services) have been included.

The ICFTU argues that respect for core labour standards stimulates balanced economic growth. By eliminating the exploitation of workers, competition would be focused on improving productivity rather than on decreasing wages and working conditions. In this way, a social clause would contribute to constructive competition because a minimum floor would reward good employment practices. On the other hand, the ICFTU argues that a social clause would not stimulate protectionism or hurt the comparative advantage of certain countries, because a social clause containing the core labour standards would not support a global minimum wage but would enable workers to choose their own working conditions.

The ICFTU and other trade union organizations have launched a campaign to get a social clause included in the WTO. However, the opposition to such a clause is strong, even among trade unions. As shown in Chapter 3, opponents believe that a social clause would stimulate protectionism and infringe national sovereignty. In addition, these opponents claim that it would be an ineffective instrument with which to address violations of labour standards and such economic issues as unemployment, and even question the universal nature of the core labour standards themselves.

This opposition to a social clause was voiced in many international forums, such as the WTO, the OECD and the ILO. Except for the WTO, which does not allow trade union representation, trade union organizations have been actively involved in these bodies to get the social clause on the agenda.

I have analysed the influence of trade unions on the social clause debate within the OECD and the ILO. The OECD entered into the debate with a study of the relationship between trade and labour standards. The ILO – as the prime international body dealing with labour standards – had an intrinsic involvement in the debate. The extensive debates on a social clause within these bodies should be viewed as preparations for the positions taken within WTO meetings.

The ICFTU was studied, as it is the single largest confederation and as such acts as a representative of the unions' views at the international level. It dominates both the Workers' Group in the ILO and the Trade Union Advisory Committee to the OECD.

Unions in India and the United States were selected for two reasons: first, policy decisions about a social clause are also made on the national level; second, these two countries and their unions represent contradictary views on a social clause. In India, the international pressure for a social clause provoked an alliance between national trade union federations and successive governments *against* the international enforcement of labour standards. In the United States, an alliance emerged between the AFL-CIO and the successive governments *supporting* a social clause.

The key questions of my thesis are: (a) how have selected unions attempted to influence the debate on the inclusion of minimum labour standards in the WTO agreement; (b) what accounts for their success or lack of success; (c) what conclusions with respect to the effective behaviour of trade unions in the construction of international policy can be drawn from these experiences? The following sections summarize and analyse the results of this study. First, I address the demands of the trade unions as related to the general outcomes of the discussions in the separate settings. These outcomes are not necessarily the effects of the demands made by the trade unions. Therefore, the next section considers to what extent the outcomes are a result of the demands of the trade unions. Subsequently, the factors that have accounted for the influence of trade unions will be explained. In the final section the larger implications of this research are discussed.

Trade Unions' Interests and the Debate on International Labour Standards

Each union study looked at the sensitizing and substantive impacts of the debate on a social clause. Sensitizing impacts are those that have changed perceptions of consequential actors (i.e. those actors whose actions are taken into account by other actors) in such a way that issues are included on the agenda. Substantive impacts are the outcomes in terms of changes in policies. In addition, a distinction between expressed and potential interests was made. The former are those voiced at different times and in different contexts, and are shaped by institutions. Potential interests are equally plausible alternatives.

The influence of the AFL-CIO and aligned unions on the debates and legislation related to trade and labour standards was the subject of the first national union study (Chapter 4). I defined the following five impacts of debates related to a social clause. First, in the 1980s the GSP, which allows for duty-free imports from developing countries, was up for renewal. The Federation did not want this system to be renewed because it feared competition. The AFL-CIO and aligned unions demanded that if the GSP was to be renewed, it should include a provision on labour standards. Such a provision would make it possible to block the import of products made by workers labouring below certain minimum standards. The GSP was renewed and included labour standards. This led to the exclusion of some countries from the GSP. I defined this as a moderately positive substantive impact. From the perspective of trade unions, the debate on the renewal of the GSP has had a positive sensitizing impact because it clearly defined a set of minimum labour standards. However, it also had a negative sensitizing impact, as it created ill feelings among the potential targets (i.e. developing countries), which affected the social clause debate in the WTO.

Second, in the 1990s negotiations on the NAFTA started. The AFL-CIO resisted NAFTA because it feared the impact of this agreement on jobs in the United States. The Federation demanded a renegotiation of the agreement to ensure the inclusion of labour standards. In 1994 NAFTA came into force and included a side agreement on a limited number of labour standards that were defined on the basis of national laws. I have argued that these impacts of the NAFTA discussion should be viewed as moderately positive substantive impacts.

Third, in 1988 the Trade and Omnibus Act was enacted. The AFL-CIO wanted this Act to give the US President the authority to include labour standards in the GATT Uruguay Round. In addition, it demanded that Section 301 of this Act should define non-compliance with certain labour standards as an unfair trade practice. This would create the potential to punish countries for non-compliance. The Trade Act 1988 included both demands. However, the substantive impact of the Act was limited, as trade unions failed to petition countries under the Act. In addition, because the adherence to labour standards was conditioned on the level of economic development of the potentially targeted country, this outcome should be considered as moderately positive in terms of its sensitizing impact.

SUMMARY AND CONCLUSIONS

Fourth, trade unions wanted the US government to demand the establishment of a working party on workers' rights in the GATT/WTO. In 1994 the Uruguay Round Agreements Act, which approved and implemented the Uruguay Round trade agreement, was adopted. Section 1.31 of this Act directed the US President to seek the establishment of a working party in the WTO on workers' rights. Although this was a substantive impact, it had only a moderately positive sensitizing impact, as it was not a high priority among the US negotiators.

Fifth, in 1994 President Clinton's fast-track authority expired. Fast-track legislation gives the President the authority to negotiate a trade agreement that cannot be amended by the US Congress. Congress is expected to decide on the negotiating objectives in advance and to vote for or against an agreement. Trade unions did not want a renewal of fast-track authority as they were not satisfied with previous progress of the United States on including workers' rights in the GATT negotiations. Fast-track authority was not renewed. This should be viewed, from the perspective of trade unions, as a positive substantive impact.

The second national union study (Chapter 5) analysed the influence of trade unions on the labour standards debate in India. There was absolute agreement between trade unions, employers' organizations and the government that a social clause should be rejected. The argument was that trade unions not only rejected a social clause, unlike some representatives of the unorganized sector, but also failed to take advantage of the pressure on the Indian government created by the social clause debate to press for demands for the promotion of domestic labour standards. This conclusion implied that Indian trade unions have not been an influential actor concerning the position of India at the international level. This was not their objective.

I explained that there are three factors behind this uncritical rejection of a social clause. First, Indian trade unions have been governed by their distrust of the international community, including foreign trade unions. Second, the trade unions have a weak domestic political position. Third, they were not sufficiently interested in groups that could potentially benefit from a social clause (e.g. unprotected workers) to take a positive attitude towards a social clause.

Chapter 6 considered the demands of the TUAC concerning the drafting of the OECD report on trade and labour standards. The impacts were mainly discussed in terms of sensitizing effects. The following impacts were revealed. First, besides the references to all core Conventions, TUAC wanted to see Conventions 100 and 111 included. The first was incorporated, the second was not. Second, TUAC wanted to see a positive relationship established between the enforcement of core Conventions and economic efficiency. The final report complies with this more than previous ones. Third, TUAC wanted to include a reference to the fact that some countries deliberately lower their labour standards in order to attract investments. The final report is more sensitive to this point than earlier drafts. Fourth, TUAC requested more consideration for the negative consequences of trade for wage levels and employment. Again, the final report is slightly more considerate towards this point than earlier drafts. Two suggestions for moderating the report were rejected: the report did not consider low labour standards as a form of social dumping or as an illegitimate export subsidy, and did not portray the WTO as the appropriate forum for stimulating the observance of labour standards.

The second international union study of the ILO (Chapter 7) illustrated the diversity of trade unions' positions on a social clause. Indian trade unions appeared to be breaking ranks by speaking out against a social clause. I concluded that the impacts of the social clause debate in the ILO corresponded with three interests of the majority of the members of the Workers' Group. The interests expressed were: (a) a discussion of a social clause in the ILO that would eventually lead to a positive attitude of the organization towards such a clause; (b) the definition of core Conventions, the obligations of which should be respected regardless of the level of economic development; and (c) a Declaration on core labour standards combined with a strong supervisory mechanism with which to enforce respect for core labour standards. Two sensitizing impacts were the agreement to discuss the social clause and the acceptance of the notion of core labour standards. Two substantive effects of the ILO debate were the increased ratification of Conventions resulting from the campaign of the Director-General and the acceptance of the Declaration on Fundamental Principles and Rights at Work, which addresses core labour standards. The Declaration stipulates that all members of the ILO – even those that have not ratified the core Conventions – are obliged to respect, promote and realize the rights embodied in the Conventions. On the other hand, there were two results that did not correspond with the interests of the Workers' Group: there was no positive position achieved on a social clause, and there was no support for a strong supervisory mechanism that would give the Declaration meaning.

The Compatibility between Demands and Outcomes

The sensitizing and substantive impacts of the debates sometimes corresponded with the expressed interests of trade unions. In the case of the

SUMMARY AND CONCLUSIONS

United States, I concluded that trade unions have been mainly influential in getting labour standards included in the GSP and the NAFTA (even though this was a weak side agreement). In addition, defining the lack of labour standards as an unfair practice in Section 301 of the Trade Act 1988 can also be considered a result of the influence of trade unions. Finally, trade unions have played an important role in arresting fast-track legislation covering the Uruguay Round and the insertion of the objective to establish a working party in the WTO under the Uruguay Round Agreements Act. In the case of India, I concluded that the demands of trade unions did not differ significantly from those of the other actors. Therefore, no separate influence could be established.

The other levels of analysis were equally revealing. Trade unions influenced some of the adjustments in the OECD report, especially concerning the remarks about the relationship between labour standards and investment, and between labour standards and unemployment. Within the ILO, trade unions have influenced the definition of core labour standards, which enabled the design of the Declaration on Fundamental Principles and Rights at Work and increased ratification of the Conventions related to the core labour standards.

How Can These Effects Be Explained?

Besides establishing the relationship between the demands and successes of trade unions, I have tried to explain the relationship. The importance of the different factors in explaining the relationship is now discussed along the lines of six assumptions, i.e. the compatibility, the moderation, the accessibility, the power resources, the internal unity and the double pressure assumptions (see Table 2.2).

The compatibility assumption

This assumption maintains that the greater the compatibility between the goals of trade union actors and the perception of other consequential actors (such as policy-makers) of the discursive context, the higher the probability of success. I have analysed the discursive context in which the debates on a social clause took place. I explained that the discursive context concerns the way in which consequential actors perceive the larger political power relations and global economic developments. In addition, the discursive context includes the perception of the nature and compatibility of the existing trade, labour and human rights' regimes.

In one of the four studies (the United States), the dominant perception of the context facilitated the debate on labour standards and trade, and was partly responsible for a positive outcome as far as the interests of trade unions were concerned. The US debate on a social clause took place in the period during which the 'fair trade discourse' gained dominance, and was facilitated by this. The discourse was founded on the economic claim that the 'playing field' of trade relations needed to be levelled in such a way that countries would be enabled to compete without foul play, such as deliberately lowering labour standards or limiting market access. This fair trade discourse resulted from the increasing trade deficit and helped to contain the social conflict that had arisen over trade.

This discourse paved the road for greater government intervention in trade-related areas. However, this commonly accepted interpretation of the economic position of the United States did not mean that there were no differences of opinion with respect to the measures with which to combat this trade deficit. While some used the fair trade discourse as a way to justify threats and actions against foreign countries aimed at protecting US industry, others wanted to employ this discourse to force foreign countries to increase their liberalization efforts.

The AFL-CIO and affiliated unions – especially those representing workers in the automobile industry and the textile industry – were increasingly fearful of liberalization and imputed the trade deficit largely to an insufficient response by the US trade policy community. An effective policy, the AFL-CIO argued, needed to include workers' rights provisions.

The trade unions found support for this demand in the Democratic Party. With the administration in the hands of the Republicans in the 1980s, trade policy and appropriate trade measures to combat the trade deficit had become part of the electoral battle. The influential Democrat Gephardt and other Democratic members of Congress, such as Pease, supported many of the demands of the trade unions. This pressure on the Republicans resulted in greater attention being paid to workers' rights. The Republicans – afraid that the call for workers' rights in unilateral legislation would only increase protectionism – agreed to pursue the issue in the GATT. In the 1990s, when the Democrats came into office, workers' rights stayed on the political agenda. It is noteworthy that while the fair trade discourse remained important, another, partly compatible, discourse emerged: the sovereignty discourse. This discourse expressed the fear of foreign intervention in US domestic policies, and found support among both Republicans and

SUMMARY AND CONCLUSIONS

Democrats. The emergence of this discourse inhibited the extension of fast-track legislation.

In India, the dominant interpretation of the context was compatible with the interests of trade unions, although there was no significant change in policy. The trade unions, respective governments and business organizations opposed the inclusion of a social clause in the Uruguay Round. While the three groups disagreed on many matters, they did agree that the ILO regime was incompatible with the GATT/WTO trade regime and that a social clause would hamper India's development. India found support for this perception in many other developing countries. The major force behind the coalition of developing countries was the perception that many international trade arrangements were biased towards the interests of developed countries. A counter-hegemonic coalition of developing countries had arisen in which India took a leading role. However, the basis for this coalition was very weak owing to the increasing differentiation of the levels of development between developing countries. The rise of the newly industrializing countries in particular weakened the perception of common interests among developing countries.

During the Uruguay Round negotiations, the coalition of developing countries rejected the inclusion of such new non-tariff issues as services, intellectual property rights and labour standards. The coalition argued that the GATT was not the appropriate forum for discussing these matters as they were considered to be national matters and unrelated to trade. In fact, the inclusion of such issues would constitute a barrier to trade rather than make it more free. While the coalition of developing countries was forced to accept many of the newly introduced issues and was not able to keep a united front in its opposition, most countries continued to oppose the inclusion of labour standards, and with success. The claims that tied together the coalition against a social clause were the following. It was argued that an upward harmonization of labour standards would undermine the liberalization of trade, which is based on comparative advantages and cost differences. Moreover, considering the present inequality between developing and developed countries, a social clause would further decrease the competitiveness of Third World products, create unemployment and therefore worsen labour conditions. Resource transfer, rather than trade sanctions, was expected to facilitate an improvement in labour standards. By the same token, it was argued that the ILO was not the appropriate forum for discussing trade sanctions, as this labour rights regime could only survive because of its emphasis on voluntarism.

I have argued that the coalition that emerged among developing countries and in India was in itself one of neo-liberal signature. This seems rather odd, as India cannot be considered a strong supporter of neo-liberal politics. However, one must appreciate the difference between how countries regulate their domestic policies and the claims they use to defend their position on a social clause.

While most of the claims the trade unions used were part of the neo-liberal discourse, they also made use of claims inconsistent with that discourse. The trade unions were critical of the GATT/WTO trade regime and of the increasing power of transnational companies. However, their rejection of a social clause was compatible with the neo-liberal discourse of the government.

As argued in Chapter 7, the dominant discourse of voluntarism was being challenged by the social clause discussion, and this positively affected the outcome of the demands of trade unions. The perceived threat of the decreasing importance of the ILO if the GATT should decide to take workers' rights under its wing, combined with social problems resulting from increased economic competition and the opportunities arising from the dissolution of the Eastern bloc, stimulated the then Director-General of the ILO, Hansenne, to put the social clause discussion high on the agenda of the 1994 International Labour Conference. The fact that this issue came to dominate many of the meetings within the ILO led to the consolidation of the notion of core labour standards and a number of initiatives, such as a campaign to increase ratification of the core Conventions and the adoption of the Declaration on Fundamental Principles and Rights at Work.

The study of the OECD report on labour standards and trade showed that there was no dominant perception being challenged. Instead, the report was the result of an extensive process of redrafting and commenting on the content of the draft versions of the report. I argued that while the outcome of the report did not reflect all the expressed interests of trade unions, in the long run their interests might be served, as the report's conclusions denied the relationship between unemployment in the North and low labour standards in the South. In addition, it downplayed the importance of low labour standards for economic efficiency.

In sum, there seems to be a strong relationship between the discursive context and the successes of trade unions. In the case where trade unions were least successful (the OECD), there was no dominant discursive context that facilitated the demands of trade unions.

The moderation assumption

This assumption argues that the more concrete and moderate the demands, the higher the probability of success. It is related to the previous one because the compatibility assumption creates the boundaries for the acceptance of demands. This means that it is very unlikely that demands – however concrete and moderate – will be accepted if they do not fit into the dominant perception of the context. However, within these limits it will be possible to make both modest and far-reaching demands.

It appears that the studies both sustain and reject this assumption. It is evident that demanding concrete measures related to adjustments within the limits of decisions already taken is a successful strategy. With the exception of India, this was illustrated by all cases.

While it is true that more moderate demands are easier to fulfil, the studies of the United States and the ILO also illustrated that if the opposition to far-reaching demands is strong, there might be attempts to accommodate these demands by offering concessions. This seems to be the case when far-reaching demands can count on some support from influential allies, or when the discursive context is such that the opposition is forced to deal with the subject matter of the far-reaching demands. This was most clearly shown in the case of the NAFTA. The request for the negotiations to be terminated was not granted, but resulted in a side agreement. In the case of the social clause discussion in the ILO, the demand to support trade-enforceable labour standards led to the Declaration. Even though neither outcome addressed the initial demands of the trade unions involved, both took into account the interests of trade unions developed during the policy processes.

In sum, although the element of concreteness of this assumption was confirmed, the element of moderation was not.

The accessibility assumption

This assumption maintains that the greater the access to and the greater the differences among policy-making actors, the higher the probability of success. In all cases trade unions had formal and informal access to the decision-making process. The extent of this access did of course differ.

The AFL-CIO has access through testimonies before the Ways and Means Committee and the Finance Committee, and through the two advisory committees it sat on. However, this formal access was not very productive in terms of exercising influence. There are several reasons for this. First, the two Congressional Committees are dominated by free-traders. Subsequently, there are hardly any differences in opinion to be exploited. Second, the advisory committee dominated by trade union representatives is not very influential, and in the advisory committee dominated by business, trade unions have no influence. In terms of informal access, the AFL-CIO has been more influential. It was shown that the position of the representative who was the strongest supporter of trade unions – the Democrat Pease – was influenced by his concerns for his constituents, among whom were a relatively large number of trade unionists. Therefore, the actions undertaken by Pease and the trade unions should be seen as a legitimate response to the concerns of US workers. By maintaining informal contacts with Democratic Congressmen, trade unions were able to exploit the differences between the Democrats and the Republicans on trade policy.

Chapter 6 showed that the formal non-compulsory consultation status of the trade unions in the OECD allowed them to influence the content of the OECD report on labour standards. Another way to access the discussion was through the trade missions of the individual countries. It was shown that the AFL-CIO met on a regular basis with the US Trade Mission to exchange and streamline ideas. This may have helped to translate the ideas of the AFL-CIO into the report on trade and labour standards.

The fact that the ILO is a tripartite body means that the trade unions, through the Workers' Group, are part of the decision-making machinery. However, in order to achieve positive outcomes, the Workers' Group needed the support of the Employers' Group or governments. With respect to the support for a social clause, the Workers' Group formed a coalition with the United States and France. A similar coalition existed with respect to the application of a freedom of association procedure to increase respect for core labour standards. While neither demand materialized into policy, both have helped to create consensus on related matters. In particular, the threat of a social clause enabled the reaffirmation of the core labour standards.

In sum, there appears to be reason to think that formal access to policy-makers is not a necessary condition for exercising influence; nor is it sufficient. The study of the OECD shows that formal access facilitates influence but is not sufficient to be influential. In the study of the United States, it was not the formal access but the ability to obtain influential allies that facilitated trade union successes. In the study of the ILO, formal access was of enormous importance given the fact that it allowed unions to be part of the decision-making machinery. In addition, as states have more voting rights, coalition-making is an essential part of the political process. Therefore, it can be assumed that the greater the informal access is to the decision-making actors, the higher the probability of success.

The power resources assumption

This assumption maintains that the greater the power resources, the higher the probability of success. Power resources are the ability of trade unions to: (a) use material resources; (b) create coalitions with other NGOs; and (c) generate such qualities as legitimacy, trust and credibility in order to convince others to accept their arguments. Here, trust is defined as the quality of being reliable and responsible. Credibility is defined as the quality of being believable and is therefore closely related to trust. Trust is related to the overall perception of an actor, while credibility is connected to the specific actions of an actor. Behaviour that elicits trust or credibility should be perceived by the target of that behaviour as relatively costly for the sender and as provided voluntarily. Legitimacy is defined as the correctness of an issue according to the opinions of most people.

The fact that the AFL-CIO provides the Democrats with finances means that its interests should be taken into account. In addition, the AFL-CIO secures votes for the Democratic Party, and as such is a reliable ally. However, as explained in Chapter 4, the fact that the Federation has an interest in a wide variety of issues necessarily means that not all demands will be granted. This is what happened in the NAFTA case. The NAFTA debate also illustrated that trade unions found allies among other non-governmental groups. This, however, did not change the course of the debate significantly, implying that these allies were not influential enough.

In India, the part played by trade unions in the process of the social clause debate was limited. Here the trade unions are poor and have lost much of their legitimacy in the eyes of the workers and thus in those of the policy-makers. If the trade unions had opted to demand that the government take a positive position towards a social clause the impact would have been limited.

Within the international organizations, material resources played a lesser role. Financial resources play a role to the extent that they make it possible for trade unions to maintain international offices. Membership plays no important role at the international level. In the ILO and the OECD, selected trade unions have a formal position, regardless of the absolute number of workers they represent.

In general it can be argued that the ability to generate trust was not a quality of the ICFTU in the cases studied. The main reason why trade unions in the social clause debate had difficulties generating trust is that they are interest groups, which almost by definition inhibits this. As stated, behaviour that normally generates trust should be perceived by the target of that behaviour as relatively costly to the sender and as provided voluntarily. The fact that trade unions seemed to have a unilateral interest when they demanded a social clause meant that information provided by this group was looked upon with distrust. This, combined with the highly political nature of the debate and the lack of consensus concerning the economic issues dominating it, means that trade unions were not viewed as a reliable source.

Nevertheless, the argument could be made that the trustworthiness of the trade unions' proposals might have increased had the ICFTU and related organizations been able to convince governments that a social clause would be in the interests of all. In theory, because many governments believe that their comparative advantage is derived from low labour standards, it will be virtually impossible to convince them that a social clause would be in their interest. In practice, it proved to be impossible. Many governments continued to view the social clause issue as an expression of protectionism. This perception was strengthened by the feelings that a country such as the United States appeared to use labour rights to protect its own industries. The ICFTU was well aware of this. In 1990 the Confederation had warned the AFL-CIO that the inclusion of unilateral labour rights in the GSP had created ill feelings among the governments of developing countries, and asked the Americans to reconsider US unilateral actions.

The power resources assumption maintains that the greater the power resources, the higher the probability of success. This assumption should be adjusted and split into four separate assumptions. The first of these is that material resources play a much larger role in exercising influence at the national level than at the international level. The second is that interest groups will not be able to exert influence based on their trustworthiness. The third is that if the material resources in terms of membership on the national level are important, the legitimacy of proposals may increase. On the basis of this research, the fourth assumption on the role of coalitions with other NGOs cannot be adjusted, as the material did not provide sufficient information in this respect.

The internal unity assumption

This assumption maintains that the stronger the common interests of trade union members, the higher the probability of success. In other words, the lack of unity within the international trade union movement on a social clause inhibited its ability to be influential. There are two reasons for this. The first is that unions opposing a social clause did not pressure their respective governments to take a positive stand on a social clause, and the second is that the lack of unity is thought to undermine the legitimacy of a social clause.

The first reason is undoubtedly true. Trade unions in India did not pressure the government to support a social clause. However, in this specific case, even if they had this would not have had much result because of their weak position. The second reason again concerns the issue of legitimacy. While the ICFTU tried to increase the legitimacy of the social clause by emphasizing that it was also supported by trade unions in developing countries, in reality there were trade union organizations that opposed a social clause not only within the ICFTU, but also in public. On a number of occasions (for example, during the Singapore meeting of the WTO and in the ILO), some unions spoke out against a social clause. This was very damaging in the eyes of the ICFTU. It undermined the Confederation's efforts to emphasize the lack of protectionist intent, for which it believed it needed at least the support of the developing countries' unions. However, while unity is undoubtedly better than diversity in this matter, no evidence was found that the disunity evoked strong reactions among governments.

On one occasion I found deviating interests among unions inside a country. In the case of the United States, there were differences between the AFL-CIO and aligned unions with respect to the rejection of the GSP, but this was more in terms of the strength of this rejection than anything else. This example, however, is more illustrative of strategically motivated considerations than of differences in core values.

The limited role for unity found in this study is partly explained by the selection of cases. Only the ILO provided an opportunity to look at this issue, as opposing trade unions are represented there. Therefore, the assumption should not be adjusted. In fact, the role of unity is an interesting research subject in itself.

The double pressure assumption

The last assumption maintains that the combination of international and national strategies increases the chances of success. In general, the combination of national and international strategies is important for success, as the international trade union organizations are able to concentrate their efforts on international issues, something that national trade unions are not capable of doing. International trade union organizations have the knowledge and the contacts to influence policy-making at the international level. The study of the United States illustrated the value of this assumption. The

AFL-CIO has contributed to the inclusion of labour standards as a negotiating objective in trade agreements and coordinated its strategy with the trade missions. This resulted in US negotiators taking a positive position on a social clause – albeit at times kicking and screaming while in that position.

However, the powerful position of the United States has been both an advantage and a disadvantage. On the positive side, it was very important in putting a social clause on the agenda of many international organizations and secured US support at the international level. The main drawback was that it was the United States. Suffering from a large trade deficit and not known for hesitating to interfere in the domestic affairs of other countries, the United States did not help the realization of a social clause.

Summary

In sum, this study leads to the following conclusions. First, the dominant interpretation of the larger context is an important condition for effective behaviour. If the dominant interpretation of policy-makers and the public at large is compatible with the specific demands of trade unions, there is a higher chance that the demands will be translated into successes. The extent to which trade unions are able to influence the dominant perception is an interesting research topic in itself.

Second, formal access to policy-making is not always necessary and is seldom sufficient. Instead, the ability to create stable informal contacts is important, especially in cases where there are differences between policy-makers that can be exploited.

Third, within the national context, membership and financial resources are important. Internationally, finances create the condition for unions to operate individually or jointly. However, both membership and finances matter less in the international context.

Fourth, the ability to present credible and concrete proposals for solving the problems addressed by trade unions is important in both national and international contexts. However, far-reaching demands do not necessarily limit overall impact, as the opposition to these demands will be more willing to make compromises.

Fifth, unity among trade union organizations is important as it enables simultaneous efforts on the national and international levels to exercise influence. Although legitimacy derived from unity may not be very important in terms of influencing policy-making, the lack of unity on such a politically sensitive matter as a social clause does not contribute to the internal strength of the international trade union movement.

The Larger Implications

The ICFTU's campaign on a social clause has contributed to putting the international labour standards issue on to the political agenda. However, in order for the labour standards issue to remain on national and international agendas and to produce positive effects, continued pressure is needed. A large part of this pressure should come from such trade union organizations as the ICFTU. It is, however, questionable whether this pressure should continue to come in the form of a social clause in the way currently campaigned for.

It is undoubtedly true that the demand for a social clause has evoked enough fear among employers and governments for them to take labour standards in a global context more seriously. It is probably true that without such a strong demand, the policy initiatives in the individual forums would not have taken place. However, as I have shown, some trade union organizations and governments of developing countries are reluctant to support this demand, because they do not trust the expressed view of the ICFTU that a social clause would be in the interests of all. Instead, they believe that trade unions in the North want to protect the old industries.

This has led to increased animosity within the international trade union movement. Even though this lack of uniform interest has not seriously decreased the legitimacy of the social clause demand as perceived by policy-makers, it has certainly not increased it. Furthermore, the ICFTU has to rely heavily on the US government's support in promoting a social clause. This has produced ill feelings, as the United States is not seen as an impartial actor.

If the campaign on a social clause is sustained, the ICFTU will probably continue to encounter distrust on the part of developing countries and among its own membership. Trust can be built only when trade unions in the North disassociate themselves from protectionist sentiments associated with the social clause debate. The adoption of a minimum floor for labour standards is an aim that should be sustained from a human rights perspective, not from one that generates feelings of protectionism. The protectionist position the AFL-CIO took in the national debate on the NAFTA may have encouraged national coalition-building, but at the same time undermined international coalition formation.

While the ICFTU can help to expunge the feelings of distrust, trade unions that oppose a social clause (e.g. those in India) should evaluate their own position. The pressure of the social clause debate has created an opportunity to strengthen workers' rights, and thus also the position of trade unions and workers in the informal sector. Even though the established unions are confronted with political and economic difficulties, this does not relieve them from looking beyond the interests of their own membership and taking into account the interests of the informal sector workers. Not only are they obliged to do so, it is also necessary. In the long term, the decreasing membership of trade unions will result in a weakening of national and international positions they acquired.

In sum, the Confederation has not been able to convince all its member unions and the majority of governments that trade sanctions are an option, and that financial support to implement labour standards is in fact an integral part of its campaign. Thus far, the social clause debate has been about trade sanctions, not labour rights.

The ICFTU should ask itself whether it has the ability to weaken the current distrust. If it cannot, the best strategy seems to be to reconsider its demand to make labour standards – even as only a last option – trade enforceable. An exception could be made for forced labour, as making this an illegal practice in the WTO will probably not encounter much opposition. A more sustainable campaign should have a dual goal: it should focus on achieving economic development by persuading financial institutions to implement, for example, debt relief, as well as on the improvement of human rights. Such a campaign should also include a demand for a positive social clause, one focusing on increased market access for countries that respect core labour standards.

The pressure for such a strategy is there. Within the WTO the issue has become somewhat stale, as shown by the statement of Moore, the organization's Director-General:

> I have never seen a contradiction between trade and labour because I don't believe one exists. Open economies, imperfect as they are have delivered more jobs, opportunities and security to more people than alternatives. Countries that have embraced openness and freedom have increased the real incomes of their workers, which in turn has raised labour standards and reduced poverty. Countries that remain closed, remain poorer, underdeveloped, cut off from the world of rights and freedoms . . . This is why I find the bitterness and divisiveness of the current trade and labour debate so destructive and confusing. It is destructive because it is in many

ways a false debate. It is destructive because it obscures the underlying consensus that exists about the social problems all countries face in this interconnected world, and the need for shared solutions. (Moore, 1999)

The opportunity for such a strategy is there, as the institutional tiredness is mirrored by the increasing activities of civil society organizations. During the 1999 WTO summit in Seattle, tens of thousands took to the streets to protest against the international trading community's lack of responsiveness to social problems. However diverse the interests represented, they cannot be ignored. The recent protests provide an opportunity for the international trade union movement to intensify its ties with other civil society organizations in order to keep international financial organizations under pressure to come up with a financial solution to social problems. Those organizations that do not represent sectoral interests, but more universal interests such as a clean environment or human rights, should more than ever be viewed as potential allies. The social challenge to trade is to make labour standards an international public good, with rewards for those countries that meet the challenge.

Appendix: ILO Core Conventions and Their Rate of Ratification

Convention 29: Forced Labour (1930)

The essence of this Convention is that members must undertake steps to suppress the use of forced or compulsory labour. Forced or compulsory labour is defined as 'all work or service, which is exacted from any person under the menace of any penalty and, for which the said person has not offered himself voluntarily' (Article 2). Numerous exceptions are made, such as for prison labour, provided that 'the said person is not hired to or placed at the disposal of private individuals, companies or associations' (Article 2).

Ratified by 153 countries.[1]

Convention 87: Freedom of Association and Protection of the Right to Organize (1948)

The core of this Convention is that workers and employers shall have the right to establish and join organizations of their own choosing without previous authorization. No public authorities shall interfere in a way that would restrict this right or impede the lawful exercise thereof. States should also undertake the necessary steps to ensure that workers and employers may freely exercise the right to organize.

Ratified by 130 countries.

---

1. The ratification rate was determined in August 2000. The total number of possible ratifications is 175.

Appendix: ILO Core Conventions

Convention 98: The Application of the Principles of the Right to Organize and to Bargain Collectively (1951)

This Convention stipulates that workers shall enjoy adequate protection against acts of anti-union discrimination with respect to their employment. Employers are not allowed to make the employment of a worker subject to the condition that he or she shall not join a union or shall relinquish trade union membership. In addition, it is not allowed to dismiss or otherwise prejudice a worker resulting from union membership or because of participation in union activities outside working hours or, with the consent of the employer, within working hours. Acts that are designed to promote the establishment of workers' organizations under the domination of employers or employers' organizations, or to support workers' organizations by financial or other means, with the object of placing such organizations under the control of employers or employers' organizations, are also not allowed. It further stipulates that, where necessary, the development and utilization of machinery for voluntary negotiation between employers or employers' organizations and workers' organizations should be encouraged.

Important exceptions are that this Convention only applies to the armed forces and the police if national laws or regulations do not prohibit this, and that this Convention does not deal with the position of public servants engaged in the administration of the state.

Ratified by 146 countries.

Convention 100: Equal Remuneration (1951)

In this Convention, members are urged to apply the principle of equal remuneration in their policies. Remuneration includes 'the ordinary, basic or minimum wage or salary and any additional emoluments whatsoever payable directly or indirectly, whether in cash or in kind, by the employer to the worker and arising out of the worker's employment' (Article 1). Equal remuneration 'refers to rates of remuneration established without discrimination based on sex' (Article 1). The Convention does not apply to differential rates of remuneration between workers that correspond to differences as determined by objective appraisal in work.

Ratified by 147 countries.

APPENDIX: ILO CORE CONVENTIONS

Convention 105: Abolition of Forced Labour (1957)

Member states have obliged themselves to suppress and not make use of any form of forced or compulsory labour for purposes of political coercion or education or as a punishment for holding or expressing political views or views ideologically opposed to the established political, social or economic system. In addition, the use of forced or compulsory labour is not allowed as a method of mobilizing and using labour for purposes of economic development, as a means of labour discipline, as a punishment for having participated in strikes or as a means of discrimination.

Ratified by 145 countries.

Convention 111: Discrimination (Employment and Occupation) (1958)

Discrimination referred to in this Convention includes 'any distinction, exclusion or preference made on the basis of race, colour sex, religion, political opinion, national extraction or social origin, which has the effect of nullifying or impairing equality of opportunity or treatment in employment or occupation' (Article 1). It further stipulates that any distinction, exclusion or preference with respect to a particular job based on the inherent requirements thereof shall not be considered to be discrimination. Members are supposed to pursue a national policy designed to promote equality of opportunity and treatment with respect to employment and occupation.

Ratified by 143 countries.

Convention 138: Minimum Age (1973)

According to this Convention, each member should pursue a national policy designed to ensure the effective abolition of child labour. In addition, policies should be designed to increase the minimum age for admission to employment to a level consistent with the fullest physical and mental development of children. The minimum age this Convention refers to is not less than the age of completion of compulsory schooling and, in any case, shall not be less than fifteen years. A minimum age of eighteen years applies to work that by its nature or the circumstances in which it is carried out is likely to jeopardize the health, safety or morals of children. This Convention includes numerous exceptions. For example, less economically developed members may apply a minimum age of fourteen years or may limit the scope of the application of this Convention.

Ratified by 97 countries.

Convention 182: Worst Forms of Child Labour Convention (1999)

Under this Convention, members are obliged to take 'immediate and effective measures to secure the prohibition and elimination of the worst forms of child labour' (Article 1). Persons under eighteen years of age are considered to be children. The term 'worst forms' applies to all forms of slavery, to the use, procuring or offering of a child for prostitution and pornography, to the use, procuring or offering of a child for illicit activities and to work which is likely to harm the health, safety or morals of children.

Ratified by 33 countries.

Note

The information in this Appendix is taken from www.ilo.org (visited on 2 August 2000).

Bibliography

ACTPN (1991), *A Report to the US Congress Concerning the President's Request for the Extension of Fast-Track Procedures Implementing Legislation for Trade Agreements*. Washington, DC: USTR Archives.
—— (1994), *A Report to the President, the Congress, and the United States Trade Representative Concerning the Uruguay Round of Negotiations on the General Agreement on Tariffs and Trade*. Washington, DC: USTR Archives.
ACTU (1994), *Letter of Martin Ferguson to Ramanujam*, 30 May. Brussels: ICFTU Archives.
AFL-CIO (1990a), *Memorandum*, 7 September. Washington, DC: AFL-CIO Archives.
—— (1990b), *Memorandum*, 3 October. Washington, DC: AFL-CIO Archives.
—— (1994), 'Kirkland Notes "Small Step" on Worker Rights in GATT', Press release, 7 April.
—— (1995), *Executive Council Report, New York Convention*, 23–26 October. Washington, DC: AFL-CIO.
—— (1996), 'Republicans Try to Silence the Voice of Working Families', Press release, 9 October: http://www.aflcio.org/publ/pr10092.htm (visited November 1999).
—— (1997a), *The Exploitation of Prison Labor*: http://www.aflcio.org/publ/estatements/may1997/exploita.htm (visited November 1999).
—— (1997b), *Executive Council Report, Pittsburg Convention*, 22–25 September. Washington, DC: AFL-CIO.
—— (1999), *Executive Council Report. Los Angeles Convention*, 11–13 October. Washington, DC: AFL-CIO.
—— (n.d.), *Special Report: Two Years of Progress for Working Families*: http://www.aflcio.org/convention96/sr06_recognizing.htm (visited November 1999).
AIOE (1996), 'Indian Employers on Social Clause', in FES/IIRA, *Social Clause*

in Trade. *Trade Unions' Perspective.* New Delhi: Friedrich Ebert Stiftung/ Indian Industrial Relations Association, pp. 47–53.

American Academy of Paediatrics (1995), 'The Hazards of Child Labor. Policy Statement', *Paediatrics*, 95(2), 311–13: http://www.aap.org/policy/00661.h (visited October 1999).

Amsden, Alice H. (1994), 'Macro-sweating Policies and Labour Standards', in Werner Sengenberger and Duncan Campbell (eds), *International Labour Standards and Economic Interdependence. Essays in Commemoration of the 75th Anniversary of the International Labour Organization and the 50th Anniversary of the Declaration of Philadelphia.* Geneva: International Institute for Labour Studies, pp. 185–93.

Anderson, Mark A. (1987), *Memorandum to Secretary-Treasurer Thomas R. Donahue*, 11 May. Washington, DC: AFL-CIO Archives.

—— (1989), *Remarks on Worker Rights*, 16 May, National Association of Manufacturers. Washington, DC: AFL-CIO Archives.

—— (1995a), *Statement on Behalf of the Labor Advisory Committee for Trade Negotiations and Trade Policy to the United States Trade Representative on Negotiations with Chile on Accession to the NAFTA*, 28 April. Washington, DC: AFL-CIO Archives.

—— (1995b), *Submitted Statement to the Committee on Ways and Means, Subcommittee on Trade, US House of Representatives on the Generalized System of Preference*, 27 February. Washington, DC: AFL-CIO Archives.

Arts, Bas (1998), *The Political Influence of Global NGOs. Case Studies on the Climate and Biodiversity Conventions.* Utrecht: International Books.

Baldwin, Robert E. (1993), 'Changes in the Global Trading System: A Response to Shifts in National Economic Power', in Dominick Salvatore (ed.), *Protectionism and World Welfare.* Cambridge: Cambridge University Press, pp. 81–96.

Banuri, Tariq (1990), 'Comments on Fields', in Stephen A. Herzenberg and Jorge F. Perez-Lopez (eds), *Labor Standards and Development in the Global Economy.* Washington, DC: US Department of Labor, pp. 51–61.

Barnes, Ian and Paula M. Barnes (1995), *The Enlarged European Union.* London: Longman.

Bartolomei de la Cruz, Hector, Geraldo von Potobsky and Lee Swepston (1996), *The International Labour Organization. The International Standards System and Basic Human Rights.* Boulder, CO: Westview Press.

Bendick, M. Jr (1998), *Discrimination against Racial/Ethnic Minorities in Access to Employment in the United States: Empirical Findings from Situation Testing*: http://www.ilo.org/public/english/90travail/migrant/paper/usempir/index.html (visited November 1999).

Benería, Lourdes (1995), 'Response: The Dynamics of Globalization', *International Labor and Working-Class History*, 47 (Spring), 45–51.

Berveling, Jaco (1994), *Het Stempel op de Besluitvorming. Macht, invloed en besluitvorming op twee Amsterdamse beleidsterreinen*. Amsterdam: Thesis Publishers Amsterdam.

Bhagwati, Jagdish (1994), 'Policy Perspectives and Future Directions: A View from Academia', in US Department of Labor, *International Labor Standards and Global Economic Integration: Proceedings of a Symposium* (July 1994). Washington, DC: US Department of Labor, Bureau of International Labor Affairs, pp. 57–61.

Bhatt, Mayank, Devina Dutt, Thothathri Raman and Sudipt Dutta (1996), 'Trade Unions: Losing Clout?', *Business India*, 4–7 November, 54–60.

BIAC (1994), *Linking Labour Standards with International Commerce. Discussion Note*. Paris: Business and Industry Advisory Committee to the OECD.

—— (1996), *BIAC Comments on the OECD Paper 'Trade and Labour Standards'. Com/Deelsa/TD(96)8 (REV 1)*. Paris: Business and Industry Advisory Committee to the OECD.

Blanchard, Francis (1988), *Address by Mr Francis Blanchard, Director-General of the International Labor Office*. Washington, DC, 27 April.

BMS (1996), 'Indian Trade Unions on Social Clause', in FES/IIRA, *Social Clause in Trade. Trade Unions' Perspective*. New Delhi: Friedrich Ebert Stiftung/Indian Industrial Relations Association, pp. 33–6.

Bogaerts, Geert-Jan (1996a), 'VS Dreigen Handelsakkoord over Telecom op te Blazen', *De Volkskrant*, 12 December, 2.

—— (1996b), 'Miss Snelvuur Helpt in Achterkamer', *De Volkskrant*, 13 December, 2.

Bolle, Mary Jane (1996), *Workers Rights Provisions and Trade Policy: Should They Be Linked?* Washington, DC: Congressional Research Service.

Boonstra, Klara (1996), *The ILO and the Netherlands. Different Views Concerning Government Influence on the Relationship between Workers and Employers*. Leiden: Stichting NJCM-Boekerij.

Brandtner, Barbara and Allan Rosas (1998), 'Human Rights and External Relations of the European Community: An Analysis of Doctrine and Practice', *European Journal of International Law*, 9(3), 468–90.

—— (1999), 'Trade Preferences and Human Rights', in Philip Alston, Mara Bustelo and James Heenan (eds), *The EU and Human Rights*. Oxford: Oxford University Press, pp. 699–722.

Breman, Jan (1999), 'The Study of Industrial Labour in Post-colonial India. The Informal Sector: A Concluding Review', *Contributions to Indian Sociology*, 33(1/2), 407–31.

Bibliography

Brittan, Leon (1994a), *Social Issues and EU External Economic Relations: The Options*. Brussels: Communication to the Commission by Sir Leon Brittan, Sec(94)303/1.

—— (1994b), *Social Issues and EU External Economic Relations: The Options. Workers' Rights: Key Questions*. Brussels: Communication to the Commission by Sir Leon Brittan, Sec(94)303/4.

—— (1994c), *Improving Social Rights Worldwide: The European Union's Contribution*. Brussels: Speech before the European Parliament, 29 March 1994.

Brock, William (1987), *Letter to Dan Rostenkowski*, 23 March. Washington, DC: AFL-CIO Archives.

Brown, George E. (1994), *Letter to Mark Anderson*, 21 April. Washington, DC: AFL-CIO Archives.

Bywater, William H. (1994), *Prepared Statement for the Committee on Labor and Human Resources, United States Senate*, 3 November. Washington, DC: US Government Printing Office.

Caire, Guy (1994), 'Labour Standards and International Trade', in Werner Sengenberger and Duncan Campbell (eds), *International Labour Standards and Economic Interdependence. Essays in Commemoration of the 75th Anniversary of the International Labour Organization and the 50th Anniversary of the Declaration of Philadelphia*. Geneva: International Institute for Labour Studies, pp. 297–317.

Campbell, Duncan and Werner Sengenberger (1994), 'International Labour Standards and Economic Interdependence: The Problem of Renovating the Social Pact', in Werner Sengenberger and Duncan Campbell (eds), *International Labour Standards and Economic Interdependence. Essays in Commemoration of the 75th Anniversary of the International Labour Organization and the 50th Anniversary of the Declaration of Philadelphia*. Geneva: International Institute for Labour Studies, pp. 381–94.

Cantor, Joseph (1997), *Business and Labor Spending in US Elections. Washington DC: Congressional Research Service Report 97-973*: http://www.senate.gov/~dpc/crs/reports/pdf/97-973.pdf (visited September 2000).

Cappuyns, Elisabeth (1998), 'Linking Labour Standards and Trade Sanctions: An Analysis of Their Current Relationship', *Columbia Journal of Transnational Law*, 36, 659–86.

Castle, Robert, D.P. Chaudhri, Chris Nyland and Trang Nguyen (1997), 'Labour Clauses, the World Trade Organisation and Child Labour in India', *Indian Journal of Labour Economics*, 40(1), 51–65.

CEC (1995), *Outright Rejection or Strategic Use? Perspectives from Various Sectors in India on the Linkage of Labour Standards, Environmental Standards and Human*

Rights Standards with International Trade. New Delhi: CEC Report of the Proceedings of the National Consultation on Social Clause in Multilateral Trade Agreements, 20–22 March.

Chachi, Amrita (1995), Cited in 'Part Four: The Unorganised Sector', in CEC, *Outright Rejection or Strategic Use? Perspectives from Various Sectors in India on the Linkage of Labour Standards, Environmental Standards and Human Rights Standards with International Trade.* New Delhi: CEC Report of the Proceedings of the National Consultation on Social Clause in Multilateral Trade Agreements, 20–22 March.

Chandra, Navin (1997), 'The Organizing Question and the Unorganized Labour', in Ruddar Datt (ed.), *Organizing the Unorganized Workers.* New Delhi: Vikas Publishing House, pp. 31–47.

Charnovitz, Steve (1987), 'The Influence of International Labour Standards on the World Trading Regime: A Historical Overview', *International Labour Review*, 126(5), 565–84.

—— (1992), 'Environmental and Labour Standards in Trade', *World Economy*, 15(3), 335–56.

—— (1994), 'The World Trade Organization and Social Issues', *Journal of World Trade*, 28(5), 17–33.

—— (1995), 'Promoting Higher Labour Standards', *Washington Quarterly*, 18(3), 167–90.

Christern, Max (1996), 'WTO-Top Scoort in Slotfase', *NRC Handelsblad*, 14 December, 16.

CITU (1996), 'Indian Trade Unions on Social Clause', in FES/IIRA, *Social Clause in Trade. Trade Unions' Perspective.* New Delhi: Friedrich Ebert Stiftung/Indian Industrial Relations Association, pp. 33–5.

Clapham, Andrew (1999), 'Where Is the EU's Human Rights Common Foreign Policy, and How Is It Manifested in Multilateral Fora?', in Philip Alston, Mara Bustelo and James Heenan (eds), *The EU and Human Rights.* Oxford: Oxford University Press, pp. 627–83.

Clinton, Bill (1992), *Expanding Trade and Creating American Jobs.* Remarks by Governor Bill Clinton at the North Carolina State University, Raleigh, 4 October.

Cobb, Joe (1994), 'The Issue of US Sovereignty under the New GATT Agreement', in *The Hearing before the Subcommittee on Trade, House Ways and Means Committee, March 13, 1996, on the Implementation of the Uruguay Round Agreement and the World Trade Organization*, pp. 31–5.

Commission on International Labour Standards and Trade (1996), *Part I – Child Labour.* New Delhi: Ministry of Commerce, unpublished.

Committee on Ways and Means (1986), 'Correspondence Pease and Yeutter,

Bibliography

January/February 1986, 99th Congress, Hearing of the Committee (House of Representatives), 20 February 1986', in *Trade Policy Agenda and Outlook for 1986*. Washington, DC: US Government Printing Office.

Congressional Quarterly Almanac, Volume XL (1984). Washington, DC.

Constitution of India (1990). Allahabad: Allahabad Law Agency.

Cowie, Jefferson R. (1994), *The Search for a Transnational Labor Discourse for a North American Economy: A Critical Review of US Labor's Campaign against NAFTA*. Duke University of North Carolina, Working paper no. 13.

Cox, Robert W. (1973), 'ILO: Limited Monarchy', in Robert W. Cox and Harold K. Jacobson, *The Anatomy of Influence. Decision Making in International Organization*. New Haven, CT: Yale University Press.

CTOs Appeal (1995), *An Appeal from the Central Trade Union Organisations of India to the Fifth Conference of Labour Ministers of Non-aligned and Other Developing Countries*, New Delhi, 19–23 January.

CTU (1994), *Memo on the 69th APRO-ICFTU Executive Board Meeting*, 23–24 August, Seoul, Korea.

Dark, Taylor E. (1999), *The Unions and the Democrats. An Enduring Alliance*. Ithaca, NY: Cornell University Press.

Datt, Ruddar (1997), 'Introduction', in Ruddar Datt (ed.), *Organising the Unorganised Workers*. New Delhi: Vikas Publishing House, pp. 1–28.

Davala, Sarath (1994), 'Labour in the Unorganised Sector: Issues and Concerns', in Sarath Davala (ed.), *Unprotected Labour in India: Issues and Concerns*. New Delhi: Friedrich Ebert Stiftung, pp. 1–17.

De Castro, Juan A. (1995), *Trade and Labour Standards. Using the Wrong Instrument for the Right Cause*. Geneva: UNCTAD discussion paper no. 99.

De Groep van Lissabon (1994), *Grenzen aan de Concurrentie*. Brussels: Vupress.

Decision on the Establishment of the Preparatory Committee for the World Trade Organization (1994): http://www.oas.org (visited June 1999).

Destler, I. M. (1992), *American Trade Politics*. Washington, DC: Institute for International Economics.

Dhar, Biswajit (1997), 'Setting the Agenda', *Business Standard*, 2 January.

Dicken, Peter (1998), *Global Shift. Transforming the World Economy*. London: Sage.

DLR (1994), 'European Commissioner Warns of Protectionism Arising from Mixing Trade with Labor Standards', *DLR News*, 12, A-2/A-3 (published by the Bureau of National Affairs, Washington, DC).

—— (1996), 'EC Proposes Forming Working Group on Labor at World Trade Organization', *DLR News*, 143, A-13/A-14 (published by the Bureau of National Affairs, Washington, DC).

Donahue, Thomas (1986), *Letter to US Ambassador Clayton Yeutter*, 8 July.

Washington, DC: AFL-CIO Archives.

—— (1989), *Letter to US Ambassador Carla Hills*, 8 August. Washington, DC: AFL-CIO Archives.

—— (1990a), *Letter to William C. Doherty*, 3 August. Washington, DC: AFL-CIO Archives.

—— (1990b), *Letter to US Ambassador Carla Hills*, 3 April. Washington, DC: AFL-CIO Archives.

—— (1990c), *Letter to US Ambassador Carla Hills*, 13 September. Washington, DC: AFL-CIO Archives.

—— (1990d), *Letter to Deputy US Trade Representative Julius Katz*, 31 October. Washington, DC: AFL-CIO Archives.

—— (1991), *Statement of Thomas R. Donahue before the Committee on Finance, United States Senate, on the Proposed US–Mexico Free Trade Negotiations*, 6 February. Washington, DC: AFL-CIO Archives.

—— (1993), *Statement Before the Senate Labor and Human Resources Committee on the North American Free Trade Agreement*, 13 October. Washington, DC: AFL-CIO Archives.

—— (1994a), *Statement before the Senate Commerce, Science, and Transportation Committee on the Uruguay Round Implementation Legislation*, 14 October. Washington, DC: AFL-CIO Archives.

—— (1994b), *Letter to Labor Secretary Reich*, 21 August. Washington, DC: AFL-CIO Archives.

Dorman, Peter (1995), *Policies to Promote International Labour Rights: An Analytical Review*. Lansing: Michigan State University.

Ebbinghaus, Bernard and Jelle Visser (1994), *Barriers and Pathways to 'Borderless' Solidarity. Organized Labour and European Integration*. Reader ACCESS Course 1994–5. Amsterdam: University of Amsterdam.

Edgren, Gus (1979), 'Fair Labour Standards and Trade Liberalisation', *International Labour Review*, 118(5), 523–35.

Emmerij, Louis (1994), 'Contemporary Challenges for Labour Standards Resulting from Globalization', in Werner Sengenberger and Duncan Campbell (eds), *International Labour Standards and Economic Interdependence. Essays in Commemoration of the 75th Anniversary of the International Labour Organization and the 50th Anniversary of the Declaration of Philadelphia*. Geneva: International Institute for Labour Studies, pp. 319–28.

EP (1999), 'Resolution on the Communication from the Commission to the Council on the Trading System and Internationally Recognised Standards (Com(96)0402-C4-0488/96)', in *Minutes of the European Parliament*, 13 January (provisional edition), A4-0423/98.

Esty, Daniel (1994), *Greening the GATT: Trade, Environment and the Future*.

Washington, DC: Institute for International Economics.

'EU (EU/GSP): Council Adopts Regulation Granting Additional Customs Reductions for Countries Respecting Certain Social and Environmental Standards (Especially Child Labour and Tropical Timber)', *Europe*, 7233 (27 May 1998), 8.

'EU (EU/Trade): Positive Reactions from the Trade Unions and Criticism from the Third Countries Concerned and European Importers to the New Social and Environmental Clauses in the EU GSP', *Europe*, 7233 (2/3 June 1998), 15.

EU (1999), *India: General Features of Trade Policy*. Market Access Sectoral and Trade Barriers Database, EU: http://mkaccdb.eu.int/mkdb/chksel.pl (visited 20 October 1999).

Fairbrother, P. and Yates, C. (eds) (forthcoming) *Union Organizing and Renewal*. London: Continuum.

Feis, Herbert (1994), 'International Labour Legislation in the Light of Economic Theory', in Werner Sengenberger and Duncan Campbell (eds), *International Labour Standards and Economic Interdependence. Essays in Commemoration of the 75th Anniversary of the International Labour Organization and the 50th Anniversary of the Declaration of Philadelphia*. Geneva: International Institute for Labour Studies, pp. 29–55.

FIAN (1995), *The Social Clause: No Help for Human Rights*. Herne: German Section of the International Human Rights Organisation-FIAN.

Fields, Gary S. (1990), 'Labor Standards, Economic Development, and International Trade', in Stephen A. Herzenberg and Jorge F. Perez-Lopez (eds), *Labor Standards and Development in the Global Economy*. Washington, DC: US Department of Labor, pp. 19–34.

Freeman, Richard B. (1994), 'A Hard-headed Look at Labour Standards', in Werner Sengenberger and Duncan Campbell (eds), *International Labour Standards and Economic Interdependence. Essays in Commemoration of the 75th Anniversary of the International Labour Organization and the 50th Anniversary of the Declaration of Philadelphia*. Geneva: International Institute for Labour Studies, pp. 79–92.

—— (1996), *Trade and Labour Standards. A Review of the Issues*. Paris: OECD.

G-77 (1999), *What Is G-77?*: http://www.g.77.org/geninfo/whatis77.htm (visited November 1999).

GAO (1997), *North American Free Trade Agreement: Impacts and Implementation*. Testimony, 09/11/97, GAO/T-NSIAD-97-256: http://www.gpo.gov (visited November 1999).

—— (1998a), *Child Labor in Agriculture. Changes Needed to Better Protect Health and Educational Opportunities*: http://www.gpo.gov (visited November

1999).

—— (1998b), *Caribbean Basin: Worker Rights Progress Made, but Enforcement Issues Remain*: http://www.gpo.gov (visited November 1999).

Gathia, Joseph (1995), Cited in 'Part Five: Child Labour', in CEC, *Outright Rejection or Strategic Use? Perspectives from Various Sectors in India on the Linkage of Labour Standards, Environmental Standards and Human Rights Standards with International Trade*. New Delhi: CEC Report of the Proceedings of the National Consultation on Social Clause in Multilateral Trade Agreements, 20–22 March, pp. 12–13.

GATT (1986), *Communication from the US Delegation*, 25 June, prep.com(86)W/43. Geneva: GATT.

—— (1990), *Communication from the United States Concerning the Relationship of Internationally Recognized Labour Standards to International Trade*, 21 September, L/6729. Geneva: GATT.

GB (1994a), *Record of Decisions*, GB.260/205. Geneva: ILO.

—— (1994b), *The Social Dimensions of the Liberalization of World Trade*, November, GB.261/WP/SDL/1. Geneva: ILO.

—— (1994c), *Record of Proceedings*, November, GB.262/WP/SDL/RP. Geneva: ILO.

—— (1994d), *Minutes of the 260th Session*, June, GB.260/PV(Rev.). Geneva: ILO.

—— (1994e), *Record of Decisions*, June, GB.260/205. Geneva: ILO.

—— (1995a), *Fourteenth Item on the Agenda: Report of the Working Party on the Social Dimensions of the Liberalization of International Trade*, November, GB.264/14. Geneva: ILO.

—— (1995b), *Minutes of the 264th Session. Sixth Item on the Agenda: The Strengthening of the ILO's Supervisory System*, November, GB.264/PV(Rev.). Geneva: ILO.

—— (1995c), *Report of the Working Party on Policy Regarding the Revision of Standards*, November, GB.264/LILS/4. Geneva: ILO.

—— (1996a), *Continuation of Discussions Concerning the Programme of Work and Mandate of the Working Party*, November, GB.267/wp/sdl/1/4(Rev. 1). Geneva: ILO.

—— (1996b), *The Strengthening of the ILO's Supervisory System*, November, GB.267/LILS/5. Geneva: ILO.

—— (1996c), *Ninth Item on the Agenda. Reports of the Committee on Legal Issues and International Labour Standards (II, Standard-setting Policy: The Strengthening of the ILO's Supervisory System)*, November, GB.267/9/2. Geneva: ILO.

—— (1997a), *Sixth Item on the Agenda. Standard-setting Policy: The Strengthening of ILO Supervisory Procedures*, March, GB.268/LILS/6. Geneva: ILO.

—— (1997b), *Second Report: International Labour Standards and Human Rights. Report of the Working Party on Policy Regarding the Revision of Standards*, March, GB.268/8/2 268th Session. Geneva: ILO.

—— (1997c), *Third Item on the Agenda. Follow-up on the Discussion of the Report of the Director-General to the 85th Session (1997) of the International Labour Conference*, November, GB.270/3/1(Add.). Geneva: ILO.

—— (1997d), *First Item on the Agenda. Continuation of Discussions Concerning the Programme of Work and Mandate of the Working Party*, March, GB.268/wp/sdl/1/1. Geneva: ILO.

—— (1997e), *Third Item on the Agenda. Follow-up on the Discussion of the Report of the Director-General to the 85th Session (1997) of the International Labour Conference*, November, GB.270/3/2. Geneva: ILO.

Gephardt, Richard A. (1996), *Letter to US Ambassador Charlene Barshefsky*, 12 December. Washington, DC: USTR Archives.

Ghosh, Jayati (1995), 'Employment and Labour under Structural Adjustment', *Indian Journal of Labour Economics*, 38(4), 567–76.

Gilpin, Robert (1987), *The Political Economy of International Relations*. Princeton, NJ: Princeton University Press.

Global Policy Forum (1999), *Unemployment in Selected OECD Countries*: http://www.globalpolicy.org/socecon/tables/oecddemp1.htm

Goold, Bill (1994), *Letter to Mark Anderson et al.*, 31 July. Washington, DC: AFL-CIO Archives.

Gopeshwar (1988), *Letter to Dinesh Singhji on the Mid-term Review of the Uruguay Round*, 21 November. Brussels: ICFTU Archives.

—— (1990), *Letter to Arun Kumar Nehru on the Uruguay Round of Multilateral Trade Negations*, 26 October. Brussels: ICFTU Archives.

—— (1994), *Letter to Pranab Mukherjee on Workers' Rights and Trade: The GATT Uruguay Round Ministerial Meeting, Marrakesh (Morocco), 12–15 April*. Brussels: ICFTU Archives.

—— (1996), *Letter to Bill Jordan, General Secretary ICFTU*, 27 April. Brussels: ICFTU Archives.

Gordenker, Leon and Thomas G. Weiss (1995), 'Pluralising Global Governance. Analytical Approaches and Dimensions', *Third World Quarterly*, 16(3), 357–87.

Gothoskar, Sujata (1995), Cited in 'Part Four: The unorganised sector', in CEC, *Outright Rejection or Strategic Use? Perspectives from Various Sectors in India on the Linkage of Labour Standards, Environmental Standards and Human Rights Standards with International Trade*. New Delhi: CEC Report of the Proceedings of the National Consultation on Social Clause in Multilateral Trade Agreements, 20–22 March, pp. 10–11.

Government of India (1994), *Resolution 42011/70/94-E.I.*, 3 August. New Delhi: Ministry of Commerce.

—— (1998), *Summary Report of Meeting Taken by Secretary (Labour) on March 11 1998 to Discuss the Draft Possible Declaration of Principles Concerning Fundamental Rights and its Appropriate Follow-up.* New Delhi: Ministry of Labour.

—— (1999), http://w3.meadev.gov.in/economy/intl/fl-over.htm#fl (visited October 1999).

Greenwood, Justin, Jürgen R. Grote and Karsten Ronit (1992), 'Conclusions: Evolving Patterns of Organizing Interests in the European Community', in Justin Greenwood, Jürgen R. Grote and Karsten Ronit (eds), *Organized Interests in the European Community.* London: Sage, pp. 238–52.

Gumbrell-McCormick, Rebecca (2000), 'Facing New Challenges 1972–1990s', in Anthony Carew and Marcel van der Linden (eds), *The International Confederation of Free Trade Unions.* Bern: Peter Lang Books.

Gundersheim, Arthur (1990), *Letter to Shellyn McCaffrey, Deputy Under Secretary for International Affairs, US Department of Labor,* 17 October. Washington, DC: Department of Labor.

—— (1994), *Statement on the Uruguay Round GATT Agreement to the Subcommittee on Trade, House Ways and Means Committee,* 2 February. Washington, DC: US Government Printing Office.

Haggard, Stephan and Beth A. Simmons (1987), 'Theories of International Regimes', *International Organization*, 41(3), 491–517.

Hajer, Maarten (1995), *The Politics of Environmental Discourse. Ecological Modernization and the Policy Process.* Oxford: Clarendon Press.

Hansenne, Michel (1993), *Letter to Pursey (ICFTU)*, 22 February, reg. no. ICFTU 002770. Brussels: ICFTU Archives.

—— (1994), *Defending Values, Promoting Change. Social Justice in a Global Economy: An ILO Agenda.* Report of the Director-General. Geneva: International Labour Office.

—— (1996), *Trade and Labour Standards. Can Common Rules be Agreed?* Steyning, Address at the 464th Wilton Park Conference on Liberalising World Trade and Prospects for the Singapore Ministerial Meeting.

—— (1997), *The ILO, Standards Setting and Globalization.* Report of the Director-General. Geneva: International Labour Office.

Hansson, Goran (1981), *Social Clauses and International Trade. An Economic Analysis of Labour Standards in Trade Policy.* Sweden: Lund Economic Studies.

Harris, Nigel (1986), *The End of the Third World. Newly Industrializing Countries and the Decline of an Ideology.* London: Penguin.

Harvey, Pharis J. (1995), *US GSP Labor Rights Conditionality: 'Aggressive Unilateralism' or a Forerunner to a Multilateral Social Clause*. Washington, DC: International Labor Rights Fund.

Hecker, Steven (1993), 'US Unions, Trade and International Solidarity', *Economic and Industrial Economy*, 14, 355–67.

Heijden van der, Hein-Anton (1990), *Tussen Wetenschap en Politiek. Een verkenning van vertoogtheorie en politicologische paradigma's, en een vertoogtheoretisch-politicologische analyse van bestuurlijke reorganisatie en ruimtelijke planning in Nederland*. Kampen: Dissertatie-Uitgeverij Mondiss.

Helleiner, G. K. (1993), 'Protectionism and the Developing Countries', in Dominick Salvatore (ed.), *Protectionism and World Welfare*. Cambridge: Cambridge University Press, pp. 396–418.

Hensman, Rohini (1996), 'Minimum Labour Standards and Trade Agreements: An Overview of the Debate', *Economic and Political Weekly*, 20–27 April, 1030–4.

Herzenberg, Stephen A., Jorge F. Perez-Lopez and Stuart K. Tucker (1990), 'Labor Standards and Development in the Global Economy', in Stephen A. Herzenberg and Jorge F. Perez-Lopez (eds), *Labor Standards and Development in the Global Economy*. Washington, DC: US Department of Labor, pp. 1–16.

Hirst, Paul and Grahame Thompson (1996), *Globalization in Question*. Cambridge: Polity Press.

HMS (n.d.), *Uruguay Round of GATT. Social Clause and India*. New Delhi: HMS.

Hobsbawm, E. J. (1995), 'Guessing about Global Change', *International Labor and Working-class History*, 47 (Spring), 39–51.

Hoekman, Bernard M. and Micheal Kostecki (1995), *The Political Economy of the World Trading System. From GATT to WTO*. Oxford: Oxford University Press.

Hogenboom, Barbara (1998), *Mexico and the NAFTA Environmental Debate. The Transnational Politics of Economic Integration*. Utrecht: International Books.

Huberts, Leo W. (1988), *De Politieke Invloed van Protest en Pressie. Besluitvormingsprocessen over rijkswegen*. Leiden: DSWO Press.

Huberts, Leo W. and J. Kleinijenhuis (eds) (1994), *Methoden van Invloeds.onderzoek*. Meppel: Boom.

Hughes, Steve and Rorden Wilkinson (1998), 'International Labour Standards and World Trade: No Role for the World Trade Organization?', *New Political Economy*, 3(3), 375–89.

Human Rights Watch (1996), *The Small Hands of Slavery. Bonded Child Labor in India*. New York: Human Rights Watch.

ICDA (1994), 'Hectic Run-up to Marrakesh', *ICDA Update: The Uruguay Round and Trade Related Issues*, 15 (April–June), 1.

—— (1995), 'US Plans to Step Up Pressure', *ICDA Update: The Uruguay Round and Trade Related Issues*, 18 (March-May), p.12.

ICFTU (1985), *Agenda Item 6: Lomé Convention*. Meeting of the Economic and Social Committee, 16 December. (Appendix 88EB/12, ESC 6). Brussels: ICFTU Archives.

—— (1986), *Agenda Item 12: Report of the Economic and Social Committee*, 19–21 November. 90EB/12. Brussels: ICFTU Archives.

—— (1988), *Agenda Item 4: The Uruguay Round of Multilateral Trade Negotiations*. Meeting of the Economic and Social Committee, 12 December (Appendix 94EB/10, ESC 4). Brussels: ICFTU Archives.

—— (1989a), *Letter to Mr F. Blanchard*, 23 February 1989. Brussels: ICFTU Archives.

—— (1989b), *The Social Clause: Its Rationale and on its Operating Mechanisms*. Annex 1, Executive Board, 27 November. 96EB/8 ESC 3. Brussels: ICFTU Archives.

—— (1989c), *Agenda Item 3: Developments in Trade Policy. Appendix*, Executive Board, 27 November. 96EB/8 ESC 3. Brussels: ICFTU Archives.

—— (1990), *Letter of Laurijssen to Vanderveken*, 10 April. Brussels: ICFTU Archives.

—— (1994a), *Marrakesh: Further Progress in Union Campaign on Workers' Rights and Trade*, Com. 18/94. Brussels: ICFTU.

—— (1994b), *Agenda Item 17: Report of the Economic and Social Committee*, 105EB/17, 7–9 December. Brussels: ICFTU Archives.

—— (1994c), *Social Clauses in International Trade Policy*. Brussels: ICFTU.

—— (1994d), *Inter-office Memorandum*, 21 March. Brussels: ICFTU Archives.

—— (1994e), *Office Memorandum*, 23 November. Geneva: ICFTU Archives.

—— (1995a), *OECD Draft Paper on Trade and Labour Standards*, Correspondence between Guy Ryder and John Evans. Brussels: ICFTU Archives.

—— (1995b), *OECD Study on 'Trade and Labour Standards'*, Comments on Com/Deelsa/TD(95)5. Brussels: ICFTU Archives.

—— (1995c), *Agenda Item 3. Workers: Rights and International Trade in the Run-up to the First WTO Ministerial Meeting (Singapore, December 1996)*, 107EB/7, 27 November. Brussels: ICFTU Archives.

—— (1996a), *The Global Market: Trade Unionism's Greatest Challenge*, Sixteenth World Congress of the ICFTU, 25–29 June. Brussels: ICFTU.

—— (1996b), *Decision of the Congress*, Sixteenth World Congress of the ICFTU, 25–29 June. Brussels: ICFTU.

—— (1996c), *India and the Social Clause: The Recommendations of the Commission* on *Labour Standards*, ICFTU inter-office memorandum, 28 February. Brussels: ICFTU Archives.

—— (1996d), *International Labour Standards and Trade. Intensified Competition Threatens Basic Workers' Rights*, Sixteenth World Congress of the ICFTU, 25–29 June. Brussels: ICFTU Archives.

—— (1997a), *Letter of Bill Jordan to Hassan Sunmonu*, 20 January. Brussels: ICFTU Archives.

—— (1997b), *Note for Informal Consultations with the Employers' Group Members*, 10–11 February. Brussels: ICFTU Archives.

—— (1997c), *Internationally Recognised Core Labour Standards in Fiji*. Report for the WTO General Council Review of the Trade Policies of Fiji, 9–10 April: http://www.icftu.org (visited February 2000).

—— (1997d), *Geneva Office Memorandum*, 17 February. Brussels: ICFTU Archives.

—— (1998a), *Fighting for Workers' Human Rights in the Global Economy*. Brussels: ICFTU.

—— (1998b), *Internationally Recognized Core Labour Standards in India. Report for WTO General Council Review of the Trade Policies of India*, 16–17 April. Brussels: ICFTU.

—— (1998c), *Internationally Recognised Core Labour Standards in Nigeria*. Report for the WTO General Council Review of the Trade Policies of Nigeria: http://www.icftu.org (visited February 2000).

—— (1999), *Internationally Recognized Core Labour Standards in the United States*. Report for the WTO General Council Review of the Trade Policies of the United States, 12–14 July 1999. Brussels: ICFTU.

—— (2000), *ICFTU: What It Is, What It Does*: http://www.icftu.org/displaydocument.asp?DocType=Overview&Index=990916422 (visited November 2000).

—— (n.d.a), *International Workers' Rights and Trade: The Need for a Dialogue*. Brussels: ICFTU.

—— (n.d.b), *Discussion Document on International Workers' Rights and Trade: The Need for a Dialogue*. Brussels: ICFTU.

ICFTU/APRO (1995a), *ICFTU/APRO Round Table on New Strategies for Enforcement of Workers' Rights*, New Delhi, 16–18 January. Brussels: ICFTU Archives.

ICFTU/APRO (1995b), *Workers' Rights in the Global Market. Statement Adopted by ICFTU/APRO Round Table*, New Delhi, 16–18 January. Brussels: ICFTU Archives.

ILO (1993), *Complaints against the Governments of the United States Presented by the American Federation of Labor and Congress of Industrial Organizations (AFL-*

CIO) and the Public Services International (PSI). Geneva: ILO, Committee of Freedom of Association, Report no. 291, Case no. 1557.

—— (1994a), *Provisional Record 81st Session*. Geneva: ILO.

—— (1994b) *Resolutions Adopted by the International Labour Conference at Its 81st Session*. Geneva: ILO.

—— (1996a), *Export Processing Zones: The Social and Labour Issues*. ILO African Workshop on the Protection of Workers' Rights and Working Conditions in EPZs and the Promotion of the Tripartite Declaration of Principles Concerning Multinational Enterprises and Social Policy, Johannesburg, 15–18 July.

—— (1996b), *Working Party on the Social Dimensions of the Liberalization of International Trade*. Governing Body report to the 83th International Labour Conference. Geneva: ILO.

—— (1996c), *IPEC in India. 1992–95: Looking Back*. New Delhi: ILO.

—— (1996d), *ILO Comments on OECD Document Com/Deelsa/TD(96)8*. Geneva: ILO.

—— (1997a), *World Labour Report 1977–1998: Industrial Relations, Democracy and Social Stability*. Geneva: ILO.

—— (1997b), *Twelfth Asian Regional Meeting*. Report of the Director-General. Bangkok: ILO

—— (1997c), *Showing the Way. Trade Unions against Child Labour in India*. New Delhi: ILO.

—— (1998a), 'Export Processing Zones: The Cutting Edge of Globalization,' Paper presented at workshop, 9–10 March: http://www.ilo.org/public/english/bureau/inst/papers/confrnce/gps/heerden.htm (visited August 2000).

—— (1998b), *Overview of Global Developments and Office Activities Concerning Codes of Conduct, Social Labelling and Other Private Sector Initiatives Addressing Labour Issues*, GB.273/WP/SDL/1 (Rev. 1), November. Geneva: ILO.

—— (1998c), *ILO Declaration on Fundamental Principles and Rights at Work*. International Labour Conference, 86th Session, June: http://www.ilo.or/public/english/standards/relm/ilc86/com-dtxt.htm (visited August 2000).

—— (1998d), *Consideration of a Possible Declaration of Principles of the International Labour Organization Concerning Fundamental Rights and Its Appropriate Follow-up Mechanism*. Report VII, 86th Session ILC, Geneva, June: http://www.ilo.or/public/english/standards/relm/ilc86/rep-vii.htm (visited August 2000).

—— (1998e), *Committee on the Application of Standards, 86th session of the ILC*. Geneva: ILO.

—— (1998f), *Report of the Committee on the Declaration of Principles: Discussion in Plenary*, June. Geneva: ILO.

—— (1999), *Structure*: http://www.ilo.org/public/english/depts/fact.htm (visited August 1999).

—— (2000a), *Characteristics of International Labour Standards*: http://www.ilo.org/public/english/standards/norm/whatare/charact/index.htm (visited October 2000).

—— (2000b), *Fundamental ILO Conventions*: http://www.ilo.org/public/english/standards/norm/whatare/fundam/index.htm (visited October 2000).

ILRF (1996), *Rugmark after One Year*. Washington, DC: International Labor Rights Fund: http://www.laborrights.org/library/rugmark96.html (visited August 2000).

Immergut, Ellen M. (1998), 'The Theoretical Core of the New Institutionalism', *Politics and Society*, 26(1), 5–34.

INTUC (1994a), *Letter of Ramanujam (President INTUC) to Martin Ferguson (President ACTU)*, 20 June. Brussels: ICFTU Archives.

—— (1994b), *Child Labour*. INTUC: New Delhi.

IUF (1999), *International Agreement Signals Fight against Child Labour in Agriculture*: http://www.iuf.tob/6%2D10.htm (visited June and October 1999).

Jain, Sunil (1997), 'Not Out of the Woods Yet', *India Today*, 12 January, 102–3.

Johnson (1999), *How Our Laws Are Made*: http://Thomas.loc.gov/home/lawsmade.toc.html (visited November 1999).

Jönsson, Christer (1993), 'Cognitive Factors in Explaining Regime Dynamics', in Volker Rittberger (ed.), *Regime Theory and International Relations*. Oxford: Clarendon Press, pp. 202–22.

Jordan, Bill (1998), *Letter to INTUC/Letter to HMS*. Brussels: ICFTU Archives.

—— (1996), *International Labour Standards and Trade*. Address by Bill Jordan to special ICFTU Conference Singapore, December. Brussels: ICFTU Archives.

Joshi, Vijay and I. M. D. Little (1996), *India's Economic Reform*. New Delhi: Oxford University Press.

Kannan, K. P. (1999), 'Changing the Economic Structure and Labour Institutions in India: Some Reflections on Emerging Perspectives on Organising the Unorganised', *Indian Journal of Labour Economics*, 42(4), 753–68.

Kantor, Michael (1994), *Letter to Peter Sutherland (GATT)*, 25 March 1994. Washington, DC: AFL-CIO Archives.

Kapstein, Ethan B. (1996), 'Workers and the World Economy', *Foreign Affairs*, 75(3), 16–37.
Katz, Lawrence and Kevin Murphy (1992), *Changes in Relative Wages, 1963–1987. Supply and Demand Factors*. Cambridge: NBER Working Paper No. 3927.
Keck, Margaret and Kathryn Sikkink (1995), 'Transnational Issue Networks in International Politics', Paper presented at the XIX International Congress of the Latin America Studies Association, Washington, DC, 28–30 September.
Keohane, Robert O. (1993), 'The Analysis of International Regimes', in Volker Rittberger (ed.), *Regime Theory and International Relations*. Oxford: Clarendon Press, pp. 23–45.
Khan, Rehman (1997), *Speech of Shri Rehman Khan, Labour Minister, Government of Tamil Nadu (India) and Deputy Leader of the Delegation for the Plenary of the 85th Session of the International Labour Conference*. Geneva: ILO.
Khor, Martin (1997), *The WTO and the Battle over Labor Standards*. Third World Network Features, 13 January.
Kirkland, Lane (1987), *Testimony before the Senate Finance Committee on the Goals of US Trade Policy*, 20 January. Washington, DC: AFL-CIO Archives.
Knoke, David, Franz Urban Pappi, Jeffrey Broadbent and Yutaka Tsujinaka (1996), *Comparing Policy Networks. Labour Politics in the US, Germany, and Japan*. Cambridge: Cambridge University Press.
Kocherty, Thomas (1995), Cited in 'Part Four: The Unorganised Sector', in CEC, *Outright Rejection or Strategic Use? Perspectives from Various Sectors in India on the Linkage of Labour Standards, Environmental Standards and Human Rights Standards with International Trade*. New Delhi: CEC Report of the Proceedings of the National Consultation on Social Clause in Multilateral Trade Agreements, 20–22 March, pp. 9–10.
Kohli, Atul (1995), *Democracy and Discontent. India's Growing Crisis of Governability*. New Delhi: Foundation Books.
Krasner, Stephen D. (ed.) (1983), *International Regimes*. Ithaca, NY: Cornell University Press.
Krasner, Stephen D. (1985), *Structural Conflict. The Third World against Global Liberalism*. Berkeley: University of California Press.
Kriesi, Hanspeter, Philip van Praag, Ruud Koopmans and Jan Willem Duyvendak (1995), *New Social Movements in Western Europe. A Comparable Analysis*. Minneapolis: University of Minnesota Press.
Krugman, Paul (1996), 'Workers and Economics. The Global Economy Has Left Keynes in Its Train', *Foreign Affairs*, 75(4), 164–70.
Kumar, Arun (1997), 'The Informal Sector in India: Trade Union Initiatives',

in Ruddar Datt (ed.), *Organising the Unorganised Workers*. New Delhi: Vikas Publishing House, pp. 283–302.

Kumar, T. Krishna (1996), 'Management of Development in the Newly Emerging Global Economic Environment,' *Economic and Political Weekly*, 31(25), 1598–605.

LAC (1988), *Report of the Labor Advisory Committee for Trade Negotiations and Trade Policy on The Uruguay Round of Multilateral Trade Negotiations. Submitted to the United States Trade Representative*, 8 September. Washington, DC: USTR Archives.

—— (1989), *Labor Advisory Committee for Trade Negotiations and Trade Policy Advice on Uruguay Round Negotiating Issues*, 12 September. Washington, DC: USTR Archives.

—— (1994), *Statement of the Labor Advisory Committee for Trade Negotiations and Trade Policy on the Uruguay Round of Multilateral Trade Negotiations. Submitted to the United States Trade Representative*, 11 January. Washington, DC: USTR Archives.

Langille, Brian A. (1994), 'Labour Standards in the Globalized Economy and the Free Trade/Fair Trade Debate', in Werner Sengenberger and Duncan Campbell (eds), *International Labour Standards and Economic Interdependence. Essays in Commemoration of the 75th Anniversary of the International Labour Organization and the 50th Anniversary of the Declaration of Philadelphia*. Geneva: International Institute for Labour Studies, pp. 329–38.

—— (1997), *Eight Ways to Think about Labour Standards and Globalization*. Geneva: The Graduate Institute of International Studies, PSIO.

Laumann, Edward O. and David Knoke (1989), 'Policy Networks of the Organizational State: Collective Action in the National Energy and Health Domains', in Robert Perrucci and Harry R. Potter (eds), *Networks of Power: Organizational Actors and the National, Corporate, and Community Levels*. New York: Aldine de Gruyter, pp. 17–55.

Lawrence, Robert Z. (1996), 'Resist the Binge', *Foreign Affairs*, 75(4), 171–3.

Lawyers Committee for Human Rights (1988), *Workers Rights under the US Trade Laws*. Washington, DC: Lawyers Committee for Human Rights, 1988 Project Series on Human Rights and US Foreign Policy, No. 2.

Lehman Schlozman, Kay and John T. Tierney (1986), *Organized Interests and American Democracy*. New York: Harper & Row.

Lim, Linda Y. C. (1990), 'Singapore', in Stephen A. Herzenberg and Jorge F. Perez-Lopez (eds), *Labor Standards and Development in the Global Economy*. Washington, DC: US Department of Labor, pp. 73–95.

Locke, Richard, Thomas Kochan and Michael Piore (1996), 'Reconceptualizing Comparative Industrial Relations: Lessons from International

Research', *International Labour Review*, 134(2), 138–61.
Lok Sabha (1996), *Discussion under Rule 193*. New Delhi: Lok Sabha Secretariat.
Low, Patrick (1993), *Trading Free. The GATT and US Trade Policy*. New York: The Twentieth Century Fund Press.
McCormick, John (1999), *Understanding the European Union: A Concise Introduction*. New York: St Martin's Press.
McDowell, Stephen D. (1997), *Globalization, Liberalization and Policy Change. A Political Economy of India's Communications Sector*. New York: St Martin's Press.
McKinnon, Malcolm and Marie Niven (1996), *Trade and Labour Standards*. UK Comments to OECD, 16 February, unpublished.
Malhotra, Vinay Kumar (1997), 'Emerging Scenario for Indo-US Economic Relations', in V. S. Mahajan (ed.), *Political Economy of Reforms and Liberalisation*. New Delhi: Deep and Deep Publishers, pp. 431–40.
Mandel, Harlan (1989), 'In Pursuit of the Missing Link: International Workers' Rights and International Trade?', *Columbia Journal of Transnational Law*, 27(2), pp.179–94.
Masilamani, Samuel (1995), *Economic Reforms and Trade Unions in India*. New Delhi: Friedrich Ebert Stiftung.
Meijnen, Joop (1994), 'Moeizame Kruistocht van de ILO voor Sociale Consensus', *NRC*, 7 July.
—— (1996–7), *Annual Report 1996–97*. New Delhi: Government of India.
Ministry of External Affairs (n.d.a), *Meet Jalil Ahmed Ansari. Successful Owner of a Carpet Manufacturing Unit. And Former 'child Labourer'*. New Delhi: Ministry of External Affairs.
—— (n.d.b), *Think Twice*. New Delhi: Ministry of External Affairs.
Ministry of Labour (n.d.), *Annual Report 1994–95*. New Delhi: Government of India.
Moore, Mike (1999), 'Labour Issue Is "False Debate", Obscures Underlying Consensus, WTO Chief Mike Moore Tells Unions', Press release, 28 November.
Mumme, Stephen and Dimitris Stevis (n.d.), 'NAFTA and International Social Policy', Revised version of a paper presented at the 36th Annual International Studies Association Convention, 21–25 February.
Myrdal, Hans-Goran (1994), 'The ILO in the Cross-Fire: Would It Survive the Social Clause?', in Werner Sengenberger and Duncan Campbell (eds), *International Labour Standards and Economic Interdependence. Essays in Commemoration of the 75th Anniversary of the International Labour Organization and the 50th Anniversary of the Declaration of Philadelphia*. Geneva:

International Institute for Labour Studies, pp. 339–56.

NAM (1995a), *Effects of International Trade and Labour Standards on Employment, Working Conditions and Development in Non-aligned and other Developing Countries. Agenda Item Six.* New Delhi: Fifth Conference of Labour Ministers of Non-aligned and other Developing Countries, 19–23 January, NAC/LM/CONF.5/DOC.5.

—— (1995b), *Draft Programme of Action.* New Delhi: Fifth Conference of Labour Ministers of Non-aligned and other Developing Countries, 19–23 January, NAC/LM/CONF.5/DOC.7/Rev.1.

—— (1995c), *Draft Delhi Declaration.* New Delhi: Fifth Conference of Labour Ministers of Non-aligned and other Developing Countries, 19–23 January, NAC/LM/CONF.5/DOC.6/Rev.1.

—— (1999), *Introduction*: http://www.nonaligned.org/intro.html (visited November 1999).

NATLEX (1999), http://ILO.org (visited July 1999).

NCL (n.d.a), *Campaign Fact Sheet.* National Consumers League: http://www.ncl.net/child%20labor/fields.htm (visited November 1999).

—— (n.d.b), *Child Labor Abuses Remain a Problem in the US. The Child Labor Coalition's Response to the State of the Union Address*: http://www.ncl.net/child%20labor/childpr122.htm (visited November 1999).

OATUU (1997), *The Singapore Ministerial Conference of the World Trade Organization (WTO) and the Issue of the 'Social Clause'.* Press release, 16 January.

ODI (1995), *Developing Countries in the WTO.* London: Overseas Development Institute.

OECD (1994), *Outline of 'Trade and Labour Standards' Project*, COM/TD/DEELSA(94)79, org. Eng., 5 September. Paris: OECD.

—— (1995a), *Trade and Labour Standards*, COM/DEELSA/TD(95)4, January. Paris: OECD.

—— (1995b), *Trade and Labour Standards*, COM/DEELSA/TD(95)5, March. Paris: OECD.

—— (1995c), *Report on Trade and Labour Standards*, (Second Draft COM/DEELSA/TD(95)5), October. Paris: OECD.

—— (1996a), *Trade and Labour Standards*, COM/DEELSA/TD(96)8/REV1, March. Paris: OECD.

—— (1996b), *Trade, Employment and Labour Standards. A Study of Core Workers' Rights and International Trade.* Paris: OECD.

—— (1996c), *Trade and Labour Standards*, COM/DEELSA/TD(96)8, January. Paris: OECD.

—— (1996d), *Meeting of the Council at Ministerial Level*, Paris, 21–22 May.

OECD News release, http://www.oecd.org/news_and_events (visited September 1999).
—— (1996e), *Workshop on Trade, Employment, and Labour Standards*, 3–4 October. Paris: OECD.
—— (2000), http://www.oecd.org
Okogwu, G. Chike (1994), 'Labour Standards across Countries with Different Levels of Development', in Werner Sengenberger and Duncan Campbell (eds), *International Labour Standards and Economic Interdependence. Essays in Commemoration of the 75th Anniversary of the International Labour Organization and the 50th Anniversary of the Declaration of Philadelphia*. Geneva: International Institute for Labour Studies, pp. 145–58.
O'Shea, Timothy J. C. (1993), 'The Domestic Political Setting of US Trade Policy', in Robert Stephen Walters (ed.), *Talking Trade: US Policy in International Perspective*. Boulder, CO: Westview Press, pp. 33–47.
Oxley, Alan (1990), *The Challenge of Free Trade*. New York: Harvester Wheatsheaf.
Passey, S. L. (1996), *Addendum to the Final Draft Report of the Commission on Labour Standards*, Faridabad, 18 April. New Delhi: INTUC Archives.
Patnaik, Jagadish Kumar (ed.) (1997), *India and the GATT. Origin, Growth and Development*. New Delhi: APH Publishing Corporation.
Patra, M. K. (1993), 'New Industrial Policy and Labour: A Critique', in Purnima Rao and S. T. Sawant (eds), *New Economic Policy: Problems and Alternatives*. New Delhi: Friedrich Ebert Stiftung, pp. 41–53.
Pease, Donald J. (1986), *Beware of Misinformation on the Trade Bill and Its Worker Rights Provisions*, 12 May. Washington, DC: AFL-CIO Archives.
—— (1994), 'Policy Perspectives and Future Directions: A view from a Former Congressman', in US Department of Labor, *International Labor Standards and Global Economic Integration: Proceedings of a Symposium (July 1994)*. Washington DC: US Department of Labor, Bureau of International Labour Affairs, pp. 51–3.
Perez-Lopez, Jorge F. (1993), 'Promoting International Respect for Worker Rights through Business Codes of Conduct', *Fordham International Law Journal*, 17(1), 1–47.
Peter D. Hart Research Associates (1993), *AFL-CIO Communications Survey*, study no. 3843B. Washington, DC: AFL-CIO Archives.
Piore, Michael J. (1990), 'Labour Standards and Business Strategies', in Stephen A. Herzenberg and Jorge F. Perez-Lopez (eds), *Labor Standards and Development in the Global Economy*. Washington, DC: US Department of Labor, pp. 35–49.
—— (1994), 'International Labor Standards and Business Strategies', in US

Bibliography

Department of Labour, *International Labor Standards and Global Economic Integration: Proceedings of a Symposium (July 1994)*. Washington, DC: US Department of Labor, Bureau of International Labour Affairs, pp. 21–5.

Portes, Alejandro (1994), 'By-passing the Rules: The Dialectics of Labour Standards and Informalization in Less Developed Countries', in Werner Sengenberger and Duncan Campbell (eds), *International Labour Standards and Economic Interdependence. Essays in Commemoration of the 75th Anniversary of the International Labour Organization and the 50th Anniversary of the Declaration of Philadelphia.* Geneva: International Institute for Labour Studies, pp. 159–76.

Prasad, Sunil (1999), *Indian Trade Unions: A Vision 2010.* Brussels: ICFTU.

Pursey, Stephen (1994), *Social Clauses in International Trade Policy.* Brussels: ICFTU.

Raghavan, Chakravarthi (1994), 'Whoever Won or Lost, It Wasn't the Workers or the People', *Third World Economics* (Trends and Analysis), 16 April, 2–4.

Ramaswamy, E. A. (1988), *Worker Consciousness and Trade Union Response.* Delhi: Oxford University Press.

—— (1992), *Six Essays for Trade Unionists.* New Delhi: Friedrich Ebert Stiftung.

—— (1997), *A Question of Balance. Labour, Management and Society.* Delhi: Oxford University Press.

Ramaswamy, E. A. and Uma Ramaswamy (1988), *Industry and Labour: An Introduction.* Delhi: Oxford University Press.

Reddy, G. Sanjeeva (1998), *Letter to Bill Jordan on ICFTU Draft Report on Respect for Core Labour Standards in India*, 25 March. Brussels: ICFTU Archives.

Reich, Robert (1994a), *Testimony Prepared for United States Secretary of Labor Robert B. Reich for the Committee on Banking, Finance, and Urban Affairs, Subcommittee on International Development, Finance, Trade, and Monetary Policy,* 28 June. Washington, DC: US Congress.

—— (1994b), *Keynote Address of the Labor Secretary Robert B. Reich to Symposium on International Labor Standards and Global Economic Integration,* 25 April.

—— (1994c), *Address Published in Provisional Record 81st Session.* Geneva: ILC.

Reinalda, Bob (1994), *Labour Relations and Intergovernmental Decision Making.* Nijmegen: Nijmegen University Political Science Report, no. 32.

—— (1997), 'Private in Form and Public in Purpose. (I)NGOs as Political Actors in World Politics', Paper presented at the ECPR 25th joint session of workshops, Bern, 27 February to 4 March.

—— (1998), 'Organization Theory and the Autonomy of the International Labour Organization. Two Classic Studies Still Going Strong', in Bob

Reinalda and Bertjan Verbeek (eds), *Autonomous Policy Making by International Organizations*. London: Routledge, pp. 42–61.

—— (1999), *Handboek Internationale Organisaties en Arbeidsverhoudingen. Een politicologische visie op international sociaal-economisch beleid*. Nijmegen: School voor Beleidswetenschappen.

Reisen, Miriam van (1999), *EU 'Global Player'. The North–South Policy of the European Union*. Utrecht: International Books.

Riedel, Eibe and Martin Will (1999), 'Human Rights Clauses in External Agreements of the EC', in Philip Alston, Mara Bustelo and James Heenan (eds), *The EU and Human Rights*. Oxford: Oxford University Press, pp. 724–54.

Risse-Kappen, Thomas (ed.) (1995), *Bringing Transnational Relations Back In. Non-state Actors, Domestic Structures and International Institutions*. Cambridge: Cambridge University Press.

Ruigrok, Winfried and Rob van Tulder (1993), 'The Ideology of Interdependence', Phd thesis, University of Amsterdam.

—— (1995), *The Logic of International Restructuring*. London: Routledge.

SACCS (n.d.), *Carpet Consumer Campaign and SACCS's Response to the Tom Harkin Bill*. New Delhi: SACCS.

Salter, W. (1998), 'International OSH Programme on the Informal Sector', Paper presented in the Philippines, 12 November: http://www.ilo.org/public/english/region/asro/mdtmanila/speeches/osh/htm (visited September 2000).

Salvatore, Dominick (1993), 'Trade Protectionism and Welfare in the United States', in Dominick Salvatore (ed.), *Protectionism and World Welfare*. Cambridge: Cambridge University Press, pp. 311–35.

Satyarthi, Kailash (1995), Cited in 'Part Five: Child Labour', in CEC, *Outright Rejection or Strategic Use? Perspectives from Various Sectors in India on the Linkage of Labour Standards, Environmental Standards and Human Rights Standards with International Trade*. New Delhi: CEC Report of the Proceedings of the National Consultation on Social Clause in Multilateral Trade Agreements, 20–22 March 1995, pp. 12–13.

Sawant, S. T. and Purnima Rao (1993), 'Background Note', in Purnima Rao and S. T. Sawant (eds), *New Economic Policy: Problems and Alternatives*. New Delhi: Friedrich Ebert Stiftung, pp. 1–8.

Sengenberger, Werner (1994a), 'Labour Standards: An Institutional Framework for Restructuring and Development', in Werner Sengenberger and Duncan Campbell (eds), *Creating Economic Opportunities: The Role of Labour Standards in Industrial Restructuring*. Geneva: Institute for International Labour Studies, pp. 3–41.

—— (1994b), 'Restructuring at the Global Level: The Role of International Labour Standards', in Werner Sengenberger and Duncan Campbell (eds), *Creating Economic Opportunities: The Role of Labour Standards in Industrial Restructuring.* Geneva: Institute for International Labour Studies, pp. 394–418.

—— (1994c), 'International Labour Standards in a Globalized Economy', in Werner Sengenberger and Duncan Campbell (eds), *International Labour Standards and Economic Interdependence. Essays in Commemoration of the 75th Anniversary of the International Labour Organization and the 50th Anniversary of the Declaration of Philadelphia.* Geneva: International Institute for Labour Studies, pp. 3–14.

Servais, J. M. (1989), 'The Social Clause in Trade Agreements. Wishful Thinking or an Instrument of Social Progress?' *International Labour Review,* 128(4), 423–32.

Sharma, Alakh N. (1996), *Structural Adjustment and Labour.* Delhi: V.V. Giti National Labour Institute (draft version).

Simma, Bruno, Jo Beatrix Aschenbrenne and Constanze Schulte (1999), 'Human Rights Considerations in the Development Co-operation Activities of the EC', in Philip Alston, Mara Bustelo and James Heenan (eds), *The EU and Human Rights.* Oxford: Oxford University Press, pp. 571–626.

Sinha, Pravin (1994), 'Indian Trade Unionism at Cross Road', *Indian Journal of Labour Economics,* 37(4), 771–9.

SLC (1994), *Item 5. Labour Standards and International Trade,* Standing Labour Committee, 27 October. New Delhi: Ministry of Labour Archives.

Smith, Martin J. (1993), *Pressure, Power and Policy. State Autonomy and Policy Networks in Britain and the United States.* New York: Harvester/Wheatsheaf.

Smith, Michael B. (1987), *Testimony of the Deputy United States Trade Representative Before the Committee on Finance, United States Senate,* 18 March. Washington, DC: US Government Printing Office.

South Asian Consultation on Social Clause/Labour Rights in Multilateral Trade Agreements (1996), *Draft South Asia Labour Rights Charter and UN Labour Rights Convention for Discussion and Approval.* Kathmandu, 20–23 May.

Spyropoulus, Georges (1987), 'The Role of Trade Unions in a Changing World', in Georges Spyropoulus (ed.), *Trade Unions in a Changing Europe.* Maastricht: Presses Interuniversitaires Europeennes, pp. 35–53.

Srinivasan, T.N. (1990), 'Comments on Fields and Piore', in Stephen A. Herzenberg and Jorge F. Perez-Lopez (eds), *Labor Standards and Development in the Global Economy.* Washington, DC: US Department of Labor, pp. 63–70.

—— (1994), 'International Labor Standards Once Again!', in US Department of Labour, *International Labor Standards and Global Economic Integration: Proceedings of a symposium (July 1994)*. Washington, DC: US Department of Labor, Bureau of International Labour Affairs, pp. 34–9.

Stensland, Julie (1995), 'Internationalizing the North American Agreement on Labor Cooperation', *Minnesota Journal of Global Trade*, 4, 141–64.

Stone, Milan (1985), *Statement before the Subcommittee on Trade on Trade Adjustment Assistance*. Committee on Ways and Means, House of Representatives, 99th Congress, 6 April. Washington, DC: US Government Printing Office.

Strange, Susan (1996), *The Retreat of the State. The Diffusion of Power in the World Economy*. Cambridge: Cambridge University Press.

Streeck, Wolfgang (1992), *Social Institutions and Economic Performance. Studies of Industrial Relations in Advanced Capitalist Economies*. London: Sage.

Sutherland, Peter (1994), *Consolidating Economic Globalization*. Address by Peter D. Sutherland to the Canadian Club (Toronto), 21 March. Geneva: Media Relations Division of GATT.

Swaminathan, Sreelatha (1995), Cited in 'Part Four: The Unorganised Sector', in CEC, *Outright Rejection or Strategic Use? Perspectives from Various Sectors in India on the Linkage of Labour Standards, Environmental Standards and Human Rights Standards with International Trade*. New Delhi: CEC Report of the Proceedings of the National Consultation on Social Clause in Multilateral Trade Agreements, 20–22 March, p. 11.

Tarrow, Sidney (1995), *Power in Movement. Social Movements, Collective Action and Politics*. Cambridge: Cambridge University Press.

TechLaw (2000), 'WTO Upholds Section 301 of the Trade Act', *TechLaw Journal*: http://techlawjournal.com/trade/20000129.html (visited July 2000).

Thomas (n.d.) *US Congress on Internet*: http//thomas.loc.gov (visited February 2000).

Tiwana, S. S. (1994), 'Trade Union Movement in India: Emerging Trends', *Indian Journal of Labour Economics*, 37(4), 741–7.

TPRB (1997a), *Implementation and Single Market Completion Lead to Greater Liberalization. The European Union*: http://www.wto.org/wto/reviews/tprb65.htm (visited July 1999).

—— (1997b), *Trade Policy Review of Fiji. Minutes of Meeting*. Geneva: Trade Policy Review Body, 9–10 April. Doc. WT/TPR/M/24: http://www.wto.org/wto/ddf/ep/public/html (visited June 1999).

—— (1998a), *Trade Policy Review of Nigeria. Minutes of Meeting*. Geneva: Trade Policy Review Body, 23–24 June. Doc. WT/TPR/M/39: http://

BIBLIOGRAPHY

www.wto.org/wto/ddf/ep/public/html (visited June 1999).

—— (1998b), *Overview of Developments in the International Trading Environment*. Geneva: WTO, Annual Report by the Director-General, 30 November.

—— (1999), *The United States' Strong Economic Performance Due to Liberalization of Trade and Investment*: http://www.wto.org/wto/reviews/tprb108.htm (visited July 1999).

—— (2000), *European Union: July 2000*. Press release 4 July: http://www.wto.org/english/tratop_e/tpr_e/tp137_e.htm (visited August 2000).

TUAC (1994), *Labour Standards and the Multilateral Trade and Investment System*. TUAC discussion paper for consultations with the OECD Liasons Committee, Paris, 2 December. Paris: TUAC Archives.

—— (1995a), *TUAC Comments on the OECD Report on Trade and Labour Standards* (second draft COM/DEELSA/TD(95)5). Paris: TUAC Archives.

—— (1995b), *TUAC Preliminary Comments on the OECD Report on Trade and Labour Standards* (third draft COM/DEELSA/TD(95)7). Paris: TUAC Archives.

—— (1996), *TUAC Comments on the OECD Report on Trade and Labour Standards* (second draft COM/DEELSA/TD(96)8). Paris: TUAC Archives.

—— (1995c), *Foreign Direct Investments and Labour Standards*. TUAC discussion paper for consultations with the OECD Committee on International Investment and Multinational Enterprises, 13 December. Paris: TUAC Archives.

—— (2000), http://www.tuac.org (visited February 2000).

—— (n.d.), *Brief Descriptive Note*. Paris: TUAC.

UN High Commissioner for Human Rights (1996), *Question of Fundamental Trade Union and Workers' Rights*. Geneva: Commission on Human Rights resolution 1996/60: http://www.unhcr.ch/html/menu4/chrres/1996.res/660.1 (visited September 1999).

United Nations (1995), *Preliminary Report of the World Summit for Social Development*, Copenhagen, 6–12 March (A/Conf.166/9, 19 April). Geneva: UN.

Uruguay Round Agreements Act (1994), *Public Law 103–465*, December 1994. Washington, DC: US government.

US DOC (1999), *US Total Trade Balances with Individual Countries* (HL98t08): http://www.ita.doc.gov (visited October 1999).

US DOL (1989a), *Memorandum for Steering Subcommittee Members*, 12 September. Washington, DC: US Department of Labour.

—— (1989b), *Worker Rights and the Uruguay Round*, 3 November. Washington, DC: US Department of Labour.

—— (1996), *Comments of the United States*. OECD, 15 February.

US Equal Employment Opportunity Commission (1998a), *Federal Laws Prohibiting Job Discrimination: Questions and Answers*: http://www.eeoc.gov/facts/qanda.html (visited November 1999).
—— (1998b), *Charge Statistics FY 1992 through FY 1998*: http://www.eeoc.gov/stats/chargesa.html (visited November 1999).
US Government (1994), *International Labor Standards and the GATT/WTO*. Washington, DC: US Administration Discussion Paper.
Van Beers, Cees (1996), 'Het Effect van Arbeidsnormen', *ESB*, 4 December, 1999.
Van Liemt, Gijsbert (1989), 'Minimum Labour Standards and International Trade: Would a Social Clause Work?', *International Labour Review*, 128(4), 433–48.
—— (1992), 'Economic Globalization: Labour Options and Business Strategies in High Labour Cost Countries', *International Labour Review*, 131(4/5), 453–69.
van Roozendaal, Gerda (2001), 'Social Challenges to Trade: Trade Unions and the Debate on International Labour Standards', PhD thesis, University of Amsterdam.
Van Wezel Stone, Katherine (1995), 'Labor and the Global Economy: Four Approaches to Transnational Labor Regulation', *Michigan Journal of International Law*, 16 (Summer), 988–1028.
Venkata Ratnam, C. S. (1996), 'Tripartism and Structural Changes: The Case of India', *Indian Journal of Industrial Relations*, 31(3), 346–77.
Venture Dias, Vivianne (1995), 'Open Regionalism, Nation-states and the Learning Process of Integrating into a Global Trading System', Paper presented at the seminar 'Challenges to the New World Trade Organization. Regionalism, Labour Standards and Environmental standards', Clingendael Institute, The Hague.
Venugopal, M. (1997), *Speech Delivered by the Indian Workers' Delegate at the 85th Session of the International Labour Organisation*. Geneva: ILO.
Visclosky, Peter J. and George Brown (1994), *Letter to Bill Clinton*, 11 March. Washington, DC: AFL-CIO Archives.
—— (1994), *Letter to Thomas Donahue (AFL-CIO)*, 22 April. Washington, DC: AFL-CIO Archives.
Visser, Jelle (1992), 'The Strength of Union Movements in Advanced Capital Democracies: Social and Organizational Variations', in Marino Regini (ed.), *The Future of Labour Movements*. London: Sage, pp. 17–52.
Vogel, David (1995), *Trading Up. Consumer and Environmental Regulation in a Global Economy*. Cambridge, MA: Harvard University Press.
Waer, Paul (1996), 'Social Clauses in International Trade. The Debate in the

European Union', *Journal of World Trade*, 30(4), 25–42.
Wallach, Lori (1994), *Statement on Behalf of Public Citizens before the Committee on Commerce, Science, and Transport of the United States Senate*, 17 October. Washington, DC: US Government Printing Office.
Weiner, Myron (1996), 'Child Labour in India. Putting Compulsory Primary Education on the Political Agenda', *Economic and Political Weekly*, 21(45/46), 3007–14.
Western, Bruce (1995), 'A Comparative Study of Working-class Disorganization: Union Decline in Eighteen Advanced Capitalist Countries', *American Sociological Review*, 60 (April), 179–201.
White, Ben (1999), *Defining the Intolerable. Child Work, Global Standards and Cultural Relativism*. London: Sage.
Wilkinson, Rorden (1998), 'Labour Standards and Trade-related Regulation: Beyond the Trade- and Labour Standards Debate?', Paper presented at the British International Studies Association, 14–16 December.
—— (1999a), *Labour, International Organisation and Global Economic Governance*. Manchester: University of Manchester, Department of Government, Manchester Paper No. 2/99.
—— (1999b), 'Labour and Trade-related Regulation: Beyond the Trade–Labour Standards Debate?', *British Journal of Politics and International Relations*, 1(2), 165–91.
Willetts, Peter (ed.) (1982), *Pressure Groups in the Global System. The Transnational Relations of Issue-oriented Non-governmental Organizations*. London: Frances Pinter Publishers.
Wood, Adrian (1994), *North–South Trade, Employment and Inequality. Changing Fortunes in a Skill-driven World*. Oxford: Clarendon Press.
Worker Rights News (1988), 'Worker Rights Update', *Newsletter of the International Labor Rights Education and Research Fund*, 1(1).
World Bank (1995), *Workers in an Integrated World*, World Development Report 1995. Washington, DC: World Bank.
World of Work (1998), 'Forced Labour in Myanmar. Report of ILO Commission of Inquiry Reveals Widespread and Systematic Use of Forced Labour in Myanmar', *World of Work*, 26 (September/October): http://www.ilo.org/public/english/235press/magazine/26/news.htm (visited June 1999).
WTO (1996a), *Singapore Ministerial Declaration*, adopted on 13 December 1996. Geneva: WTO.
—— (1996b), *Singapore Draft Declaration*, 13 December 1996. Geneva: WTO.
—— (1996c), *Statement by HE Mr GJ Campbell, Minister of International Economic Relations*: http://www.wto.org/english/thewto_e/minist_e/min96_e/

st4.htm (visited October 2000).
—— (1996d), *Statement by Mr Donald J. Johnston*: http://www.wto.org/english/thewto_e/minist_e/min96_e/st32.htm (visited October 2000).
—— (1999a), *Principles of the Trading System*: http://www.wto.org/about/facts2.htm (visited June 1999).
—— (1999b), *The Organization*: http://www.wto.org/wto/inbrief/inbr02.htm (visited June 1999).
—— (1999c), *The Trade Policy Review Mechanism*: http://www.wto.org/wto/reviews/tprm.htm (visited June 1999).
—— (1999d), http://www.wto.org.eol/e/wto06/wto6_37.htm#note3 (visited October 1999).
Yankelovich Partners Inc (1994), *GATT Survey Results*, 28 November. Washington, DC: AFL-CIO Archives.
Yeutter, Clayton (1986), *Letter to Thomas Donahue*, 30 July 1986. Washington, DC: AFL-CIO Archives.
You, Jong-il (1990), 'South Korea', in Stephen A. Herzenberg and Jorge F. Perez-Lopez (eds), *Labor Standards and Development in the Global Economy*. Washington, DC: US Department of Labor, pp. 97–121.
Zolberg, Aristide R. (1995), 'Response: Working-class Dissolution', *International Labor and Working-class History*, 47 (Spring), 28–37.

Index

Page numbers in italics indicate tables.

Advisory Committee for Trade Policy and Negotiations (ACTPN) 85–6, 96, 104, *104*, 105
Africa: informal sector employment 8
Age Discrimination in Employment Act (1967) 73
Agnivesh (of Bandhua Mukti Mocha) 139
Agreement on Trade-related Investment Measures (TRIMS) 16
aid agencies 12
All Indian Trade Union Congress (AITUC) 122
Alliance for Responsible Trade 84
American Federation of Labor and Congress of Industrial Organizations (AFL-CIO)
 alliance with governments supporting a social clause 205
 criticizes the OPIC 59
 and definition of fundamental labour standards 94–5
 Dunkel's warning 17
 and fast-track 99–100
 fights GSP renewal 106, 108, 206, 217
 government consults 31
 and the ICFTU 95, 216
 inclusion of labour standards in GSP 80–3
 inclusion of labour standards in trade laws 71, 77, 93, 218
 influence 103, 107, 213–14
 interests of 101, 102, 107
 lobbying 105, 148
 membership 78
 and the Multi-Fibre Arrangement 100
 and the NAFTA 82, 83, 84, 88, 206
 and the OECD report 167–8
 protectionism 109
 supports trade liberalization 75, 85
 and the Trade Act 92
 and the trade deficit 89
American Institute for Free Labor Development (AIFLD) 84
Americans with Disabilities Act (1990) 73
anti-dumping regulations 58, 59, 74
Asia
 an emerging market for imports 4
 informal sector employment 8
Asia and Pacific Regional Organization (APRO) 137
Asia-Pacific Group 187, 190, 191, 196

Australian Council of Trade Unions (ACTU) 23
automobile industry (US) 76, 210

Bandhua Mukti Mocha (Bonded Labour Liberation Front) 139
Bangladesh, and EPZs 8
Berlin Wall, fall of 167, 178
Berne Convention (1905) 13
Bhagwati, Jagdish 46, 118
Bharatiya Janata Party (BJP) 113
Bharatiya Mazdoor Sangh (BMS) 122, 126, 134
Bonded Labour System (Abolition) Rules (1976) 121
Bretton Woods institutions 174, 175
Brock, Secretary of Labor 91
Brown, Congressman 99, 105
Bush, President George 83, 86, 87, 92
Business and Industry Advisory Committee to the OECD (BIAC) 148–51, 155
Business Round Table 98

Canada 76, 110, 139
Caribbean Basin Initiative (CBI) 14, 79, 101, 102, 109, 142
central trade union organizations (CTOs) 123–5, 129, 131–2, 137, 138
Centre for Education and Communication (CEC) 138
Centre of Concern for Child Labour 139
Centre of Indian Trade Unions (CITU) 122
child labour 2, 72–3, 88, 91, 94, 95, 98, 100, 121, 122, 126, 127, 129, 130, 132, 137–41, 160, *169*, 185, 202, 204, 226
Child Labour Deterrence Act (Harkin) 100, 139–40
Child Labour (Prohibition and Regulation) Rules (1986) 121
China
 foreign investment in 162
 human rights record 97
 US trade with 124
Citizen Trade Watch Campaign, The 85
Civil Rights Act (1964) 73
Civil Service Reform Act 73
claims, defined 69n
Clinton, President Bill 72–3, 75, 79, 82, 83, 86–7, 96–9, 102, 109, 110, 118–19, 207

codes of conduct 11
Cold War 77
collective action, characteristics of 36
collective bargaining 1–2, 73, 74, 81, 91, 94, 120, 121, *169*, 204, 224
Collins, Phil 141
Colombia 3, 53
Commission on International Labour Standards and Trade 141
Committee of Experts 189
Committee on International Investment and Multinational Enterprises (CIME) 158
Communist Party of India 113
competition 75, 95
 see also global competition
Congress Party (India) 113, 123
Conseil National du Patronat Français 148
consumer labels 12
Convention on Freedom of Association (CFA) 21
Copenhagen Social Summit Declaration 203
core labour standards 1, 20, 46, 67, 72–4, 155–6, 159–60, 183, 186, 203–4, 208, 214
credit conditionality 11

Danfort, Senator 92
Decision on the Establishment of the Preparatory Committee for the World Trade Organization (1994) 18
Declaration of Fundamental Principles and Rights at Work (ILO Workers' Group, 1996) 189, 208
Declaration of Philadelphia 174, 189
demands and effects
 relationship 31–6
 contextual approach 33–5
 explaining success and failure 35–6
 the role of discourses in the policy process 32–3
Democratic Party (US) 78–9, 97–8, 109, 210, 215
Development GAP (Development Group for Alternative Policies) 84
discursive closure 32
Dominican Republic 82
Donahue, Thomas R. 88
donor support 12
Dunkel, Arthur 17, 94, 95

256

INDEX

Economic and Social Commission of Asia and the Pacific (ESCAP) 135
economic globalization/internationalization 2, 3, 9, 16
employment
  discrimination in 2, 73, 81, 204, 225
  free choice of 42
  hours of work 81
  increase in temporary workers, part-timers and home workers 7
  informal sector 5, 7, 8
  minimum age 2, 81, 160, 204, 225–6
  occupational health and safety 81, 88, 91, 94
  right to work 42
EPZs *see* export processing zones
Equal Opportunity Commission 73
Equal Pay Act (1963) 73
equal remuneration 2, 42, 204, 224
Equal Remuneration Act (1976) (India) 121
ethnic minorities, US labour market 73
Europe, unemployment 5
European Commission 119, 147
European Parliament 17
European Trade Union Confederation (ETUC) 148
European Union (EU) 176, 195, 196
  labour directives 13–14
  and the WTO 95
export processing zones (EPZs) 5, 7–8, 21, 121, 149, 157, 158, 162, *163*, 164, 166

Fair Labor Standards Act (1938) 72
Fair Trade Campaign, The 85
Fair Trade Caucus 99
Federal Labor Relations Act 73
Federation CTM 83–4
Fédération des Entreprises de Belgiques 148
Fiji, labour standards 20, 21
financial deregulation (1980s) 9
First World War 173
forced labour 2, 3, 73, 81, 91, 94, 126, 128, 220, 223
  abolition of 2, 72, 204, 225
Foreign Affairs 6
foreign direct investment (FDI) 4, 9, 49, 50, 54, 135–6, 155, 158, *169*, 170, 186, 203
Frank, Congressman 105
Free Trade Area of the Americas (proposed) 97
freedom of association 1, 2, 73, 81, 91, 94, 120, 121, 166, *169*, 204, 223
freedom of peaceful assembly and association 42
Friends of the Earth 84

G-7 10, 135, 171n, 175
G-15 135
Gandhi, Indira 132
Ganesan, A. V. 129
Gathia, Joseph 139
GATT NOW 96
General Agreement on Tariffs and Trade (GATT)
  break-up of the Southern front 115
  Council 94, 95
  and developing countries 114
  established 15
  and goods produced by prison labour 15, 64, 136, 150
  and GSP renewal 80
  and the ILO 195
  interests and impacts *103*
  and the ITO 15
  labour standards issue 107
  negotiating rounds 57, 109
    Tokyo Round 15, 58, 63, 204
    Uruguay Round 1, 16, 17, 19, 63, 72, 85, 88, 93, 95, 96, 97, 107, 110, 113, 117, 119, 120, 123, 129, 175, 178, 204, 206, 207, 209, 211
  and the 'new issues' 135
  TPRM of 20
  trade/'non-trade' issues 65
  transition to the WTO 18, 173
  and the US 93–7
General Agreement on Trade in Services (GATS) 16, 63
Generalized System of Preferences (GSP) 14, 34, 72, 80–2, 92, 95, 101–2, *101*, 102, 107, 108, 109, 114, 206, 209, 217
Gephardt, Congressman Richard 80, 99, 105, 210
Gephardt Amendment 90
Germany, manufacturing output 3
global competition
  increasing 3
  possible consequences of 4–10
    decreasing membership 6–7
    decreasing state authority 9–10
    EPZs 7–8
    informalization of the formal sector 8
    unemployment and wage inequality 5–6
global restructuring 5
GNP, world 4
Gopeshwar, INTUC General Secretary 123
Government Accounting Office report (1998) 82
Greenpeace 84
Group of 77 (G-77) 114, 176
Group of Fifteen 18
Group of Five 4, 117
GSP Renewal Act 92

Hajer, Maarten 32–3
Hansenne, Michel 18, 178–80, 183, 188, 189, 212
Hansson, Goran 61
Harkin, Senator Tom 139–40
Heritage Foundation 100
Hills, Ambassador Carla 20
Hind Mazdoor Sabha (HMS) 122, 123, 125, 142, 144n
House Ways and Means Committee 90, 99, *104*, 105, 213
HR 3 bill 90, 91

IMEC group (Industrial Market Economy Countries) 176, 184, 187, 196
immigrants, US labour market 73
India 113–45, 211–12
  bonded labour 121–2, 132
  and the CFA procedure 190
  child labour 121, 122, 126, 127, 129, 130, 132, 137–41, 202
  Commerce Ministry 129, 130
  Constitution 120, 121
  core labour rights 120–2
  emergence of a broad national coalition 122–35
    central trade union organizations 123–6
    development at the national level 128–31
    discursive similarities 131–5
    Indian government: discursive consistency 126–8
    and the ILO 121, 131, 185, 190, 192, 198
    independence (1947) 114
    international coalition formation 135–7
    Labour Ministry 129, 130
    Ministry of External Affairs 141, 143
    New Economic Policy (NEP) 116, 119
    origins of distrust: counter-hegemony and liberalization 114–20
    social clause *see under* social clause
    Special/Additional Customs Duty 119
    Standing Committee on Labour and Welfare 122
    Structural Adjustment Programme (SAP) 116
Indian National Trade Union Congress (INTUC) 23, 122–5, 132, 144n
Indian trade unions
  distrust of foreign intention 113, 114, 207
  lack of interest in unprotected labourers 114
  and a social clause 110–11, 113, 207, 217, 220
  weak domestic political position 113, 207
Industrial Disputes Act (1947) (India) 120
inflation 9
informal sector
  defined 26n
  increasing employment 5, 7, 8
  in India 121
intellectual property rights (IPRs) 64, 65, 67, 93, 116–17, 119, 128
interest group, characteristics of 35
International Bill of Rights 69n
International Confederation of Free Trade Unions (ICFTU)
  and the AFL-CIO 95, 216
  annual surveys 3
  child labour in India 122
  conflict with INTUC 144n
  the discourse of the 65–7
  dominates TUAC 205
  Economic and Social Committee 23
  and economic internationalization 2, 9
  factors hampering effectiveness 2
  on global competition 5
  and illegally fired workers 74
  and the ILO 176, 183, 194, 198, 205
  Indian distrust of 125
  and INTUC 123
  national trade union federations in 39
  and the OECD 148, 157, 158, 170

257

INDEX

International Confederation of Free Trade Unions (ICFTU)—*continued*
and regulation of core labour standards 203, 204
and the Singapore Declaration 196
Sixteenth World Congress (1996) 9, 10–11
and a social clause 19–20, 23, 29, 110, 123–4, 204, 217, 219, 220
and the Swamy Commission 130–1
a tertiary organization 29
International Covenant on Civil and Political Rights 42, 44
International Covenant on Economic, Social and Cultural Rights 42, 44–5
International Labor Rights Fund 84
International Labour Conferences (of the ILO) 91, 174, 176, 191, 195, 212
international labour courts of appeal 13
International Labour Organization (ILO) 10, 13, 173–201, 203, 211
assessment of influence 193–8
defining impacts 193, *194*
explanation: impacts, successes and failures 194–8, *195*
Commission of Inquiry 21
Committee on Employment and Social Policy 185
Committee on Freedom of Association 73–4, 177
Committee on Legal Issues and International Labour Standards (LILS) 185
Conference Committees 177
Constitution 174, 199
Convention No. 29 (on forced labour) 2, 3, 120, 149, 159, 160, 183, 200n, 204, 223
Convention No. 87 (on freedom of association and protection of the right to organize) 1, 120, 149, 155, 156, 159, 160, 179, 183, 200n, 204, 223
Convention No. 98 (on the right to organize and collective bargaining) 1–2, 20, 120, 149, 155, 156, 159, 160, 183, 200n, 224
Convention No. 100 (on equal remuneration) 2, 120, 149, 159, 162, *163*, 183, 200n, 204, 207, 224
Convention No. 105 (on the abolition of forced labour) 2, 72, 73, 120, 149, 159, 160, 183, 200n, 204, 225
Convention No. 111 (on discrimination in employment and occupation) 2, 120, 149, 159, 160, 162, 166, 183, 200n, 207, 225
Convention No. 138 (on minimum age) 2, 120, 149, 159, 160, *163*, 182, 183, 200n, 204, 225–6
Convention No. 182 (on the abolition of the worst forms of child labour) 2, 72, 204, 226
Convention ratification 175–6, 182
decision-making 28–9, 31
Declaration on Fundamental Principles and Rights at Work (1998) 43–4, 45–6, 63, 191–3,
196, 198, 199, 213
Director-General (DG) 177, 178, 188, 193, 195, 197, 198
discursive strongholds, change and outside effects 198–9
Employers' Group 176, 180, 182, 187, 189, 190, 195, 196, 214
and EPZs 7, 8
Governing Body (GB) 174, 177, 183, 195, 196
historical developments and present position 173–6
and human rights 167
and the ICFTU 176, 183, 194, 198
and India 121, 131, 185, 190, 192, 198
International Labour Office 177
and IPEC 141
and the ITO 174–5
labour rights regime 34
and labour standards 19, 165
and NAM 137
and the OECD 147, 155, 171
organization and function of the ILO 176–7
phase 1: discursive clashes 178–84
containing conflict within the ILO 183–4
discursive conflicts 180–2, *180*
phase 2: strengthening the ILO 184–93
alternative mechanisms 188–91
applying the CFA procedure 186–8, *186*
Declaration (1998) 191–3
Recommendations 177
Resolution (November 2000) 3
Resolutions 177
Secretariat 1
and the social clause 28, 39, 125, 150, 151, 178, 179, 204, 205
standard-setting activities 11
strengthened or weakened 62–3
and trade sanctions 127
Tripartite Declaration of Principles Concerning Multinational Enterprises and Social Policy 11
weakness of 175
Workers' Group 23, 29, 173, 176, 180, 181, 183, 185–9, 191–9, 205, 208, 214
Working Party on the Social Dimensions of the Liberalization of International Trade (SDL) 177, 178, 184, 185, 193, 194, *194*
World Labour Report 9
and the WTO 179, 181, 193, *194*, 199
International Monetary Fund (IMF) 11, 21, 117, 130, 147, 174
International Organization of Employers (IOE) 176
International Programme on the Elimination of Child Labour (IPEC) 141, 143
International Tobacco Growers' Association 11
International Trade Organization (ITO) 15, 26n, 174–5
'Havana Charter' 174–5
International Union of Food, Agricultural, Hotel, Restaurant, Catering, Tobacco and Allied Workers' Associations (IUF) 11

International Union of Service Employees 77
interventionism 67
investment
and increasing investment 3
labour standards and 158
IPEC *see* International Programme on the Elimination of Child Labour

Jamaica 53
Japan
manufacturing exports 4
manufacturing output 3
Jordan, Bill 137

Kaleen label 141
Kantor, Micky 95, 97, 100, 107
Kirkland, Lane 75

Labor Advisory Committee (LAC) 94, 96–7, 104, *104*, 105
labour market decentralization 7
labour standards
the discourse of the ICFTU 65–7
effectiveness and ineffectiveness claims 56–63, 67
decreasing or increasing protectionist policies 57–60
social clause as an expression of solidarity 60–2
a strengthened or weakened ILO 62–3
interventionist claim 65, 67
regulating across borders 10–14
socio-economic claims 47–56, *47*, 67
challenges to neo-classical theory 54–6
effect of labour market policies on economic development 50–4
flow of capital and low labour costs 49–50
Northern slowdown and Southern low labour costs 48–9
sovereignty claim 65, 68
spillover and exclusion claims 63–5
universality and relativity claims 41–6
Latin America
and the ILO 191
informal sector employment 8
tariff barriers 59
trade union movement 84
League of Nations 13, 174
legitimacy, defined 36

Maastricht Protocol on Social Policy 13
MacBride Principles 11
Malaysia 19
manufacturing
decline of manufacturing sectors 6
growth in exports 3–4
output 3
Maquiladora Standards of Conduct 11
Marrakech (GATT ministerial meeting, 1994) 17, 18, 97, 98, 99, 139, 143
Marshall Plan 147, 148
Mexico 76, 83–5, 102, 104, 106, 109, 110, 139
Moore, Mike 220–1

INDEX

most favoured nation (MFN) rule   15, 16, 34
most favoured nation tariffs   58
Multi-Fibre Arrangement (MFA)   58, 100, 114
multinational enterprises (MNEs)   158
Myanmar   3

NAM *see* Non-Aligned Movement
nation states   10
National Authority for the Elimination of Child Labour   141
National Farmers Union   84
neo-classical perspective   50–2, 53, 55–6, 64, 68
neo-institutional perspective   51–2
New Protectionism   57
newly industrialized countries (NICs)
 economic growth   51, 54, 56, 115
 labour costs   50
 manufacturing   3, 4
 repression of trade unions   53
Nigeria   3, 21
Non-Aligned Movement (NAM)   114
 Fifth Conference (Delhi, 1995)   135–7
non-governmental organizations (NGOs)   10, 12, 22, 24, 84, 85, 96, 143, 216
non-tariff barriers   57, 58
North American Free Trade Agreement (NAFTA)   14, 72, 83–8, 93, 96, 97, 98, 101, 102, *102*, 104, 106–10, 139, 206, 209, 213
Northern Ireland: MacBride Principles   11

occupation, discrimination in   2, 204, 225
Old Protectionism   57
Omnibus Trade and Competitiveness Act (1988)   14, 89, 92, 118, 119
Organization for Economic Co-operation and Development (OECD)   114, 214
 Employment, Labour and Social Affairs Committee (ELSA)   146, 155
 Guidelines for Multinational Enterprises   11
 and labour standards   203
 Secretariat   147
 and the social clause   28, 186, 204
 Trade Committee (TC)   146, 155
 and unemployment   5
Organization for Economic Co-operation and Development Report on Trade, Employment and Labour Standards (1996)   39, 43, 67, 146–72, 197, 207–8, 212
 competing views   *169*
 opposing trade unions' and employers' discourses   148–51
 organizational features of the OECD   147–8
 trade, employment and labour standards: the OECD Report   151–5
 labour standards and economic efficiency   152–3
 labour standards and investment   154–5
 labour standards and trade   153–4, 205
 trade, employment and wages   154
 trade unions' interventions and impacts   160–8
 explanation of trade unions' influence   166–8
 trade unions' interests and effects   160, 162, *163*, 164–6
 TUAC's interests and the evolution of draft texts   155–60
 core labour standards   159–60, *161*
 labour standards and economic efficiency   155–6
 labour standards and investment   158
 labour standards and trade   156–7
 trade, employment and wages   157–8
Organization of African Trade Union Unity (OATUU)   23
Overseas Private Investment Corporation (OPIC)   59

Pakistan, and EPZs   8
Paris Peace Conference   173
Passey, S. L.   129
Pease, Congressmember Donald   80–1, 90, 105, 210, 214
Petersen, Senator David   87
Political Action Committees (PAC)   78, 79
political process, characteristics of   35
population growth   5
protectionism   57–60, 89, 112n, 182, 210, 219
Public Citizens   84

Quakers conference (1994)   195, 196

Reagan, President Ronald   79, 81, 89–90, 109
recessions   5, 16
credibility, defined   36
regional attempts to regulate labour   13–14
regulatory competition   3
Rehabilitation Act (1973)   73
Reich, Robert   87
Republican Party (US), and fast-track   97–8
rest and leisure rights   42
Richardson, Congressman Bill   99
right to organize   1, 81, 94, 120, 204, 223, 224
Rostenkowski, Congressmember   91
Ruggiero, Renato   195, 196
Rugmark label   139, 140

Sanders, Congressman   105
Satyarthi, Kailash   139, 140
Second World War   174
service sector, growth of trade in   4, 7
Sierra Club   84
Singapore   53, 54
Singapore Declaration (World Trade Organization) (1996)   1, 17, 19, 20, 43, *194*, 196
slavery   42
social accommodation   32
social clause   36
 and competition   66
 a controversial issue   2, 18–19
 defined   1
 as an expression of solidarity   60–2
 and global competition   5
 and the ICFTU   19–20, 23, 110
 ILO and   28
 Indian opposition   110–11, 113, 123–32, 135, 137, 142, 205, 211
 and a neo-classical discourse   68
 OECD and   28
 and protectionism   58
 trade unions and the social clause debate   19–22
 and the WTO   16, 17, 146, 168, 170
Social Summit (World Summit for Social Development)   197, 198, 199
socially responsible investment (SRI)   12–13
South Africa
 investment in   12
 Sullivan Principles   11
South Korea   53–4, 166
Soviet exports, sanction on   91
spillover claim   63, 65, 67
Standing Labour Committee (SLC) (India)   129
Sullivan Principles   11
Sutherland, Peter   17–18, 97
Swamy, Subramanian   129, 140–1
Swamy Commission   129–31

technological development, acceleration of   5–6
Times of India   130
Trade Act (1974)   88–9, 90, 91
Trade Act (1988)   92, 94, *103*, 107, 206, 209
Trade Adjustment Assistance Act   87
trade adjustment assistance (TAA)   89
Trade and Omnibus Act (1988)   72, 101, 109
Trade Policy Review Body (TPRB)   21
trade policy review mechanism (TPRM)   20, 21
Trade Policy Reviews   20
Trade Union Advisory Committee   21–2
Trade Union Advisory Committee to the OECD (TUAC)   148–9, 151, 155, 156, 158–60, 164, 166, 167, 205, 207–8
Trade Union Advisory Council   29
trade unions   202–21
 the compatibility between demands and outcomes   208–9
 conclusions   218–19
 constraints   22–4
 and the Democratic Party (US)   78–9
 explaining the relationship
  the accessibility assumption   213–14
  the compatibility assumption   209–12
  double pressure assumption   217–18
  the internal unity assumption   216–17
  the moderation assumption   212–13
 globalization of   9
 influence   30, *30*, 36–7
 interests   38

259

INDEX

trade unions—*continued*
    and the debate on international labour standards 205–8
    and negative effects of economic globalization 3
    oppression of their members 3
    resistance to their activities 3
    right to form and join 42
    the selection of the trade union studies 28–9
    shared interests and political action 29–31
    and the social clause debate 19–22
    and success 37, *37*
Trade Unions Act (1926) (India) 120
Trade-related Aspects of Intellectual Property Rights (TRIPs) 16, 21, 63
Trade-related International Labour Standards (TRILS) 21
Trade-related Investment Measures (TRIMs) 63, 64, 117
transnational corporations (TNCs) 5, 8, 9, 21, 25n, 66, 117, 130, 158, 162, *163*, 164

underemployment 5–6
unemployment 5–6, 22, 42, 48, 49, 66, 68, *169*, 204
Union of Needletraders, Industrial and Textile Employees (UNITE!) 75, 76, 77, 80, 89, 95, 104, 105
United Automobile, Aerospace and Agricultural Implement Workers of America (UAW) 75, 77, 80, 106, 109, 111n
United Front (India) 113
United Nations Conference on Trade and Development (UNCTAD) 114, 115, 116–17
United Nations (UN) 34, 135, 174
    General Assembly 42
    World Summit for Social Development (1995) 43
United States 71–112
    the 1984 GSP renewal 79–82
    the inclusion of labour standards in GSP 80–82
    resistance to the GSP renewal: 1984 79–80
    assessment of influence 100–7
    defining impacts, successes and failures 101–3
    modes of collective action 103–6
    time lag and decision-making authority 106–7
Congress Committee on Appropriations 140
core labour standards 72–4
Department of Labor (DOL) 91, 140
domestic battles: slowing down fast-track 97–100
explaining impacts, successes and failures 107–11
and forced labour 128
GATT moves 93–100
and the Group of Five 117
House Foreign Affairs Subcommittee 92
India's largest single investor 118
and labour standards 17, 18, 202–3
labour's failure in NAFTA 82–8
    Clinton's victory and labour's loss 86–8
    fast-tracking NAFTA 85–6
    resisting NAFTA 83–5
manufacturing output 3
and the OECD 156
Senate 91
    Finance Committee 99, *104*, 105
    Labor and Human Resources Committee 88
Trade Mission 148, 214
Trade Office 195
trade remedy 89–93
trade unions and the emergence of the fair trade discourse 74–9
    the interest of trade unions in 'fair' trade 74–7
    trade unions and the Democratic Party 78–9
trade with China 124
and the Uruguay Round 88
wage inequality 5
United States Trade Representative (USTR) 80, 96, 104, 106
Universal Declaration on Human Rights 19, 42, 44
Uruguay Round Implementation Bill/Agreements Act 72, 99, 100, 101, *103*, 108, 209

Vienna Convention on the Law of Treaties 188
Visclosky, US Representative 99, 105

voluntary export restraints (VERs) 57, 58

wages
    and EPZs 7–8
    inequality 5–6, 48, 49, 68, *169*
    minimum wage 61, 81, 88, 91, 94, 128
Wood's study (1994) 149, 158, *161*, 162, 164
World Bank 3, 11, 21, 117, 130, 147, 174
World Development Report (1995) 3
World Intellectual Property Organization (WIPO) 116–17
World Labour Report (1997) 9, 25n
World Trade Organization (WTO)
    anti-dumping regulations 59
    CTOs reject 131–2
    decision-making 28
    Dispute Settlement Body 119
    establishment of 15–16, 99, 175, 198
    and the ILO 179, 181, 193, *194*, 199
    Indian distrust of 124–5
    main function 16
    mandate of 63, 117
    Ministerial Conference (Geneva, 1998) 19
    Ministerial Conference (Seattle, 1999) 19, 27n, 221
    Ministerial Conference (Singapore, 1996) 18, 23, 146, 165, 187, 188, 217
    most favoured nation principle 34
    and the OECD 147, 160, 164–8, 170
    powers 98
    Preparatory Committee 17, 18
    Secretariat 1
    Singapore Declaration (1996) 1, 17, 19, 20, 43
    and a social clause 16, 17, 146, 168, 170, 204, 205
    succeeds GATT 18, 173
    trade policy review mechanism (TPRM) 1
    and trade sanctions 151
    and VERs 58

Yeutter, US Trade Representative 90, 93